THE ART OF WEBASSEMBLY

D1568451

THE ART OF WEBASSEMBLY

BUILD SECURE, PORTABLE, HIGH-PERFORMANCE APPLICATIONS

no starch press

San Francisco

Printed in the United States of America

First printing

25 24 23 22 21   1 2 3 4 5 6 7 8 9

ISBN-13: 978-1-7185-0144-7 (print)
ISBN-13: 978-1-7185-0145-4 (ebook)

Publisher: William Pollock
Executive Editor: Barbara Yien
Production Editor: Katrina Taylor
Developmental Editor: Liz Chadwick
Cover Design: Josh Ellingson
Interior Design: Octopod Studios
Technical Reviewer: Conrad Watt
Copyeditor: Anne Marie Walker
Compositor: Maureen Forys, Happenstance Type-O-Rama
Proofreader: James Fraleigh

For information on book distributors or translations, please contact No Starch Press, Inc. directly:
No Starch Press, Inc.
245 8th Street, San Francisco, CA 94103
phone: 1-415-863-9900; info@nostarch.com
www.nostarch.com

Library of Congress Control Number: 2021930212

In loving memory of my grandmother,
Sue Battagline. I miss you dearly.

About the Author

Rick Battagline is a game developer and author of *Hands-On Game Development with WebAssembly* (Packt Publishing, 2019). He has been working with browser-based technologies since 1994, and in 2006 founded BattleLine Games LLC., an independent game studio focused on web games. His game Epoch Star was nominated for an award at the Slamdance Guerilla Games Competition. Since then, he has written hundreds of games developed in various web technologies including WebAssembly, HTML5, WebGL, JavaScript, TypeScript, ActionScript, and PHP.

About the Tech Reviewer

Conrad Watt is a Research Fellow at Peterhouse, University of Cambridge. Prior to his PhD in computer science at the University of Cambridge, he completed an undergraduate degree at Imperial College London. His research is primarily focused on the formal semantics and security characteristics of WebAssembly. He developed and maintains WasmCert-Isabelle, the first mechanization, in Isabelle/HOL, of the WebAssembly language's semantics.

Conrad is an active participant in the WebAssembly Community Group and continues to contribute to the specification of new language features, with a particular focus on threads and concurrency. His research into the relaxed memory characteristics of JavaScript and WebAssembly is a key component of WebAssembly's threads specification. Outside of his professional life, his two greatest interests would ordinarily be choral singing and foreign travel, both of which are inadvisable at the time of this writing.

BRIEF CONTENTS

CONTENTS IN DETAIL

6
LINEAR MEMORY
115

7
WEB APPLICATIONS
139

8
WORKING WITH THE CANVAS
157

FOREWORD

With every other language compiling to JavaScript nowadays, WebAssembly is the next step in an evolution to break free from these pre-existing boundaries. WebAssembly enables everyone's favorite language to run on the web performantly, while bringing with it the potential to redefine how you can bundle up reusable software components that run not only on the web but on any platform, from blockchain to edge computing to IoT.

While the technology is still young and requires some time to mature, its sheer potential has inspired many people from all backgrounds to explore where we can take this journey. One example is AssemblyScript, a project Rick and I are working on, that looks at WebAssembly less from a systems language perspective, and more exploring the potential of fusing the best of JavaScript and the web platform with WebAssembly. AssemblyScript makes it possible to compile a variant of JavaScript that resembles TypeScript to WebAssembly, yielding super small and efficient modules, while enabling everyone with a JavaScript background to take advantage of what WebAssembly has to offer today.

There are many exciting facets to WebAssembly and its feature set, especially to those who like to explore and help shape the future of the technology. *The Art of WebAssembly* lays out a solid foundation to dive deeper into what may well become the future of computing, and in particular on the web.

—DANIEL WIRTZ
Creator of AssemblyScript

ACKNOWLEDGMENTS

Thank you, Liz Chadwick. She spent a tremendous amount of time working on the first several drafts of this book. Her tireless efforts transformed my vague ideas and stream-of-consciousness writing into a coherent, well-polished draft. If you enjoy reading this book, you can attribute that to Liz's effort throughout its development.

I want to thank Conrad Watts (Invited Expert in the W3C WebAssembly Working Group), who generously provided the book's technical review. His brilliance humbles me. I cannot overstate his technical expertise in this field. Any technical errors in this book were almost certainly introduced after his thorough and deeply technical review.

Thanks to Katrina Taylor and Anne Marie Walker (copyeditor). I truly appreciate the work you did to make the book ready for printing. Thank you to my friends Vineet Kapur, Steve Tack, and Terri Cohen, who took the time to read my first draft of the book and give me feedback. All of you helped me make this a better book.

Finally, thanks to Bill Pollock. Your input at critical moments helped me move forward and complete this book.

INTRODUCTION

Welcome to *The Art of WebAssembly*. This book teaches you how to read, write, and understand WebAssembly at the virtual machine level. It will help you learn how WebAssembly interacts with JavaScript, the web browser, and the embedding environment. By the end, you'll comprehend what WebAssembly is, its ideal use cases, and how to write WebAssembly that performs at near-native speeds.

Who Should Read This Book

This book is for web developers interested in understanding when and why to use WebAssembly. If you truly want to grasp WebAssembly, you need to learn it in detail. Several books have been written on various WebAssembly toolchains. This book is not specific to writing C/C++ or Rust, or any other language for WebAssembly; instead, it explores WebAssembly's mechanisms and capabilities.

This book is for users who want to understand what WebAssembly is, what it can do, and how to use it best. WebAssembly can perform better and create smaller downloads and memory footprints than JavaScript. But developing high-performing WebAssembly applications requires more than simply writing an app in a language like C++/Rust or AssemblyScript and compiling it in WebAssembly. To build an application that executes two or three times as fast as its JavaScript equivalent, you'll need to know how WebAssembly works at a deeper level.

Readers should have a basic familiarity with web technologies, such as JavaScript, HTML, and CSS, but don't need to be experts in any of them. In its current incarnation, it isn't easy to use WebAssembly without understanding the web and how it works. I don't explain the basics of a web page, but I also don't assume readers have much knowledge of how the web works either.

Why Users Are Interested in WebAssembly

At the first WebAssembly summit, Ashley Williams (@ag_dubs) presented the result of her Twitter polls asking WebAssembly users why they were interested in the technology. Here are the results:

- Multi-language, 40.1 percent
- Smaller faster code, 36.8 percent
- Sandboxed (security), 17.3 percent

She then asked users who were interested in WebAssembly for its support of multiple languages why that was so:

- JavaScript doesn't meet my needs, 43.5 percent
- Reuse of existing libraries, 40.8 percent
- Preexisting app distro (distribution), 8.1 percent

Of those users who thought JavaScript didn't meet their needs, she asked why:

- Performance is bad or inconsistent, 42 percent
- The ecosystem doesn't meet my needs, 17.4 percent
- I don't like or understand it, 31.3 percent

You can watch her talk, "Why the #wasmsummit Website Isn't Written in Wasm," on YouTube at *https://www.youtube.com/watch?v=J5Rs9oG3FdI*.

Although these polls weren't scientific, they're still rather illuminating. For one, if you combine the first and third poll users interested in using WebAssembly to improve an app's performance, the total is more than 55 percent. Improving your code's performance with WebAssembly is unquestionably possible. But to really utilize WebAssembly isn't magic; you just need to know what you're doing. By the end of this book, you'll know enough about WebAssembly to drastically improve the performance of your web apps.

Why the World Needs WebAssembly

I've been developing web applications since the mid-1990s. Initially, web pages were no more than documents with images. That changed with the emergence of Java and JavaScript. At the time, JavaScript was a toy language that could add rollover effects to buttons on your web pages. Java was the real deal, and the Java virtual machine (JVM) was an exciting technology. But Java never reached its full potential on the web platform. Java requires a plug-in, and the plug-in technology eventually fell out of fashion when it became a security and malware nightmare.

Unfortunately, Java is a proprietary technology, which prevented its direct integration into the web browser. However, WebAssembly is different in that it wasn't created unilaterally by a single technology company. WebAssembly began its life as a collaboration between many hardware and software vendors, such as Google, Mozilla, Microsoft, and Apple. It's available without a plug-in in every modern web browser. You can use it to write hardware-independent software using Node.js. Because it's not proprietary, any hardware or software platform can use it without royalty or permission. It fulfills the 1990s-era dream of *one binary to rule them all.*

What's in This Book

In this book, we will walk you through how WebAssembly works at a low level by introducing you to WebAssembly Text format. We will cover many low-level topics and take some time to show you how WebAssembly works with JavaScript in Node.js and web-based applications. The book is intended to be read in order, with concepts building on each other. There are also references throughout the book to code examples that can be found at *https://wasmbook.com.*

Chapter 1: An Introduction to WebAssembly

We go into detail about what WebAssembly is, what it isn't, and when best to use it. You're introduced to WebAssembly Text (WAT), which allows you to understand how WebAssembly works at the lowest level. We also set up the environment you'll use to follow along with the examples in the book.

Chapter 2: WebAssembly Text Basics

We cover the basics of WAT and how it relates to high-level languages that deploy to WebAssembly. You'll write your first WAT program, and we'll discuss fundamentals like variable use and control flow.

Chapter 3: Functions and Tables

We discuss creating functions in WebAssembly modules and calling them from JavaScript. You'll build a program to check for prime numbers to illustrate these concepts. We investigate calling functions from tables and performance implications.

Chapter 4: Low-Level Bit Manipulation

You learn about the low-level concepts you can use to improve your WebAssembly modules' performance, such as number systems, bit masking, and 2s complement.

Chapter 5: Strings in WebAssembly

WebAssembly doesn't have a built-in string data type, so in this chapter you will learn how strings are represented in WebAssembly, and how to manipulate them.

Chapter 6: Linear Memory

You're introduced to linear memory and how WebAssembly modules use it to share large data sets with JavaScript or an alternative embedding environment. We start creating an object collision program that sets objects moving randomly and checks for object collisions, which we then use throughout the book.

Chapter 7: Web Applications

You learn how to create a simple web application using HTML, CSS, JavaScript, and WebAssembly.

Chapter 8: Working with the Canvas

We discuss how to use the HTML canvas with WebAssembly to create lightning-fast web animations. We use the canvas to improve our object collision application.

Chapter 9: Optimizing Performance

You learn how WebAssembly works well for computationally intensive tasks, such as collision detection. You spend some time using Chrome and Firefox profilers and other optimization tools to improve our applications' performance.

Chapter 10: Debugging WebAssembly

We will cover debugging basics such as logging to the console using alerts and stack traces. You will also learn how to use the debuggers in Chrome and Firefox to step through our WebAssembly code.

Chapter 11: AssemblyScript

We discuss using WAT to understand high-level languages by using it to evaluate AssemblyScript, a high-level language designed to deploy to WebAssembly in an efficient way.

1

AN INTRODUCTION TO WEBASSEMBLY

In this chapter, you'll acquire background knowledge of WebAssembly and explore the tools you'll need to start working with WebAssembly and its textual representation, WebAssembly Text (WAT). We'll discuss the benefits of WebAssembly, including improved performance, legacy library integration, portability, security, and its use as an alternative to JavaScript. We'll consider JavaScript's relationship with WebAssembly and what WebAssembly is and isn't. You'll learn the WAT inline and S-expression syntax. We'll introduce the concepts of the embedding environment and discuss embedding WebAssembly in web browsers, Node.js, and the WebAssembly System Interface (WASI).

Then we'll discuss the benefits of using Visual Studio Code as a development environment for WAT. You'll learn the basics of Node.js and how to use it as an embedding environment for WebAssembly. We'll show you how to use npm to install the wat-wasm tool, which provides you with everything you need to build WebAssembly applications from WAT. In addition, we'll write our first WebAssembly app and execute it with Node.js as the embedding environment.

What Is WebAssembly?

WebAssembly is a technology that will massively improve the performance of web applications over the next several years. Because WebAssembly is new and requires some explanation, many people misunderstand it and how to use it. This book teaches you what WebAssembly is and how to use it to make high-performing web applications.

WebAssembly is a virtual *Instruction Set Architecture (ISA)* for a stack machine. Generally, an ISA is a binary format designed to execute on a specific machine. However, WebAssembly is designed to run on a *virtual* machine, meaning it's not designed for physical hardware. The virtual machine allows WebAssembly to run on a variety of computer hardware and digital devices. The WebAssembly ISA was designed to be compact, portable, and secure, with small binary files to reduce download times when deployed as part of a web application. It's easy to port the bytecode to a variety of computer hardware, and it has a secure platform for deploying code over the web.

All major browser vendors have adopted WebAssembly. According to the Mozilla Foundation, WebAssembly code runs between 10 percent and 800 percent faster than the equivalent JavaScript code. One eBay WebAssembly project executed 50 times faster than the original JavaScript version. Later in the book we'll build a collision detection program that we can use to measure performance. When we ran it, our performance benchmarking found that our WebAssembly collision detection code ran more than four times faster than JavaScript in Chrome and more than two times faster than JavaScript in Firefox.

WebAssembly offers the most significant performance improvement the web has seen since the introduction of the just-in-time (JIT) JavaScript compilers. Modern browser JavaScript engines can parse and download the WebAssembly binary format an order of magnitude faster than JavaScript. The fact that WebAssembly is a binary target, not a programming language like JavaScript, allows the developer to choose the programming language that best suits their application's needs. The saying "JavaScript is the assembly language of the web" might have become fashionable recently, but the JavaScript format is a terrible compilation target. Not only is JavaScript less efficient than a binary format like WebAssembly, but any JavaScript target code also has to handle the specifics of the JavaScript language.

WebAssembly offers tremendous web application performance improvements in two areas. One is startup speed. Currently, the most compact Java-Script format is minified JavaScript, which improves application download sizes but must parse, interpret, JIT compile, and optimize the JavaScript code. These steps are unnecessary with a WebAssembly binary, which is also more compact. WebAssembly still needs to be parsed, but it's faster because it's a bytecode format rather than text. Web engines still do optimization passes on WebAssembly, but it's much faster because the language is more cleanly designed.

The other significant performance improvement WebAssembly offers is in throughput. WebAssembly makes it easier for the browser engine to optimize. JavaScript is a highly dynamic and flexible programming language, which is helpful to a JavaScript developer, but creates a code optimization nightmare. WebAssembly doesn't make any web-specific assumptions (despite its name) and can be used beyond the browser.

Eventually, WebAssembly might be able to do everything JavaScript can. Unfortunately, the current version, its MVP (Minimum Viable Product) release version 1.0, cannot. In the MVP release, WebAssembly can do certain tasks very well. It's not intended to be a drop-in replacement for JavaScript or a framework, such as Angular, React, or Vue. If you want to work with WebAssembly right now, you should have a specific computationally intensive project that requires very high performance. Online games, WebVR, 3D math, and crypto are effective ways people currently use WebAssembly.

Reasons to Use WebAssembly

Before we take a closer look at WebAssembly, let's consider a few reasons you might be interested in using it. These explanations should also give you an idea of what WebAssembly is and why and how to use it.

Better Performance

JavaScript requires software engineers to make choices that will affect how they design the JavaScript engine. For example, you can optimize a JavaScript engine for peak performance using a JIT optimizing compiler, which can execute code faster but requires more startup time. Alternatively, you can use an interpreter, which starts running code right away but won't reach the peak performance of a JIT optimizing compiler. The solution most JavaScript engine designers use in their web browsers is to implement both, but that requires a much larger memory footprint. Every decision you make is a trade-off.

WebAssembly allows for a faster startup time and higher peak performance without all of the memory bloat. Unfortunately, you can't just rewrite your JavaScript in AssemblyScript, Rust, or C++ and expect this to happen without a little extra work. WebAssembly isn't magic, and merely porting JavaScript to another language and compiling it without understanding what WebAssembly is doing at a lower level can lead to some disappointing results. Writing C++ code and compiling it to WebAssembly using optimization flags will usually be a bit faster than JavaScript. Occasionally, programmers will complain that they've spent all day rewriting their app in C++ and it only runs 10 percent faster. If that's the case, it's likely that these apps wouldn't benefit from converting to WebAssembly, and their C++ gets compiled into mostly JavaScript. Take the time to learn WebAssembly, not C++, and make your web applications run lightning fast.

Integrating Legacy Libraries

Two popular libraries for porting existing libraries to WebAssembly are *wasm-pack* for Rust and *Emscripten* for C/C++. Using WebAssembly is ideal for when you have existing code written in C/C++ or Rust that you want to make available to web applications, or want to port entire existing desktop applications to make them available on the web. The Emscripten toolchain is particularly efficient at porting existing C++ desktop applications to the web using WebAssembly. If this is your path, you'll likely want your app to perform as closely as possible to the native speed of your existing application, which should be feasible as long as the application isn't a resource hog. However, you might also have an app that needs performance tuning to make it run as it does on the desktop. By the end of this book, you'll be able to evaluate the WebAssembly module your toolchain generates from your existing code.

Portability and Security

We combined the portability and security features into one section because they frequently go together. WebAssembly started as a technology to run in the browser but is quickly expanding to become a sandboxed environment to run anywhere. From server-side WASI code to WebAssembly for embedded systems and the internet of things (IoT), the WebAssembly working group is creating a highly secure runtime that prevents bad actors from compromising your code. I recommend listening to Lin Clark's excellent talk about WebAssembly security and package reuse at the first WebAssembly Summit (*https://www.youtube.com/watch?v=IBZFJzGnBoU/*).

Even though the WebAssembly working group focuses on security, no system is entirely secure. Learning to understand WebAssembly at a low level will prepare you for any future security risks.

JavaScript Skeptics

Some people simply dislike JavaScript and would rather that JavaScript not be the dominant web programming language. Unfortunately, WebAssembly isn't in a position to dethrone JavaScript. Today, JavaScript and WebAssembly must coexist and play well together, as shown in Figure 1-1.

But there is good news for the JavaScript skeptics in the world: WebAssembly toolchains offer many options for writing web applications without having to write JavaScript. For example, Emscripten allows you to write web applications in C/C++ with very little, if any, JavaScript. You can also write entire web applications using Rust and wasm-pack. Not only do these toolchains generate WebAssembly, but they also create copious JavaScript glue code for your application. The reason is that currently, there are limits to WebAssembly's capabilities, and the toolchains fill these gaps with JavaScript code. The beauty of mature toolchains like Emscripten is that they do this for you. If you're developing with one of these toolchains, it's helpful to understand when your code will turn into WebAssembly and when it will be JavaScript. This book helps you know when this will happen.

Figure 1-1: JavaScript and WebAssembly can coexist in harmony.

WebAssembly's Relationship with JavaScript

It's important to clarify how WebAssembly is used with and compares to JavaScript. WebAssembly isn't a direct replacement for JavaScript; rather, WebAssembly:

- Is faster to download, compile, and execute
- Allows you to write applications for the web in languages other than JavaScript
- Can provide near-native speed for your application when used properly
- Works *with* JavaScript to improve the performance of your web applications when appropriately used
- Isn't an assembly language, although there is a pseudo assembly language associated with it (WAT)
- Isn't only for the web but can execute from non-browser JavasScript engines, such as Node.js, or can execute using runtimes that implement the WASI
- Isn't yet a one-size-fits-all solution for creating web applications

WebAssembly is the result of all major browser vendors collaborating to create a new platform for distributing applications over the internet. The JavaScript language evolved from the needs of web browsers in the late 1990s to the mature scripting language it is today. Although JavaScript has become a reasonably fast language, web developers have noticed that it sometimes performs inconsistently. WebAssembly is a solution to many of the performance problems associated with JavaScript.

Even though WebAssembly can't do everything JavaScript can, it can execute certain operations much faster than JavaScript while consuming less memory. Throughout this book, we compare JavaScript code with the corresponding WebAssembly. We'll repeatedly benchmark and profile the code for comparison. By the end of this book, you'll be able to judge when you should use WebAssembly and when it makes sense to continue using JavaScript.

Why Learn WAT?

Many WebAssembly books and tutorials focus on specific toolchains, such as the aforementioned wasm-pack for Rust or Emscripten for C/C++. Toolchains for other languages like AssemblyScript (a subset of TypeScript) and Go are currently in development. These toolchains are a major reason programmers turn to WebAssembly, and more WebAssembly language toolchains are continually becoming available. In the future, web developers will be able to choose the language they use to develop based on project needs rather than language availability.

One factor that is useful across any of these languages is understanding what WebAssembly does at its lowest level. A deep understanding of WAT tells you why the code might not run as fast as you thought it would. It can help you comprehend how WebAssembly interacts with its embedding environment. Writing a module in WAT is the best way to work as close to the metal (low-level) as possible in a web browser. Knowledge of WAT can help you make the highest-performing web applications possible and allows you to disassemble and evaluate any web application written for the WebAssembly platform. It helps you assess any potential future security risks. In addition, it enables you to write code that is as close to native speed as possible without writing native code.

So what is WAT? WAT is like an assembly language for the WebAssembly virtual machine. Let's look at what this means in a practical sense. Writing WebAssembly programs in a language like Rust or C++ uses a toolchain, which, as mentioned earlier, compiles a WebAssembly binary file as well as JavaScript glue code and HTML that embeds the WebAssembly module. A WebAssembly file is very similar to machine code because it includes sections, opcodes, and data all stored as a series of binary numbers. When you have an executable file in machine code, you can disassemble that file into that machine's *assembly language,* the lowest level of programming languages. Assembly replaces the numeric opcodes in the binary with mnemonic codes that are intended to be readable by a human being. WAT acts as the assembly language for WebAssembly.

WAT Coding Styles

There are two primary styles of WAT coding to choose from. One style is the *linear instruction list* style. This coding style requires the developer to mentally keep track of items on the stack. Most WAT instructions push items onto a stack, pop them off a stack, or both. If you choose to write in the linear instruction style, there is an implicit stack where the parameters of your instructions must be placed before the instruction is called. The other coding style is called *S-Expressions*. S-Expressions are a tree-like coding structure where parameters are passed into the tree in a way that looks a bit more like function calls in JavaScript. If you have trouble visualizing the stack and the items being pushed onto and off of it, the S-Expression syntax might be more your style. You can also mix the two styles depending on the implicit stack for less complicated instructions and use an S-Expression when the number of parameters become challenging to keep track of.

Example Using Linear Instruction List Style

Consider the simple addition function in Listing 1-1, which is in JavaScript.

```
function main() {
    let a_val = 1;
    let b_val = 2;
    let c_val = a_val + b_val;
}
```

Listing 1-1: JavaScript code adding a_val and b_val variables

After executing these lines, the value in the c_val variable is now 3, which is the result of adding a_val and b_val. To do the same task in WAT, you would need quite a few lines of code. Listing 1-2 shows the same program using WAT.

```
(module
❶  (global $a_val (mut i32) (i32.const 1))
❷  (global $b_val (mut i32) (i32.const 2))
   (global $c_val (mut i32) (i32.const 0))
   (func $main (export "main")
       global.get $a_val
       global.get $b_val

       i32.add
       global.set $c_val
   )
)
```

Listing 1-2: WebAssembly adding $a_val to $b_val

Listing 1-2 contains more lines of code because WAT must be more explicit than JavaScript. JavaScript has no idea whether the types in the previous two examples are floating-point data, integers, strings, or a mix until the code runs. The WebAssembly is compiled into a bytecode ahead of time and must be made aware of the types it's using when it's compiled. The JavaScript must be parsed and tokenized before the JIT compiler can turn it into bytecode. Once the optimizing compiler begins working on that bytecode, the compiler must watch to see whether the variables are consistently integers. If they are, the JIT can create a bytecode that makes that assumption.

However, JavaScript is never quite sure whether it will end up with string data or floating-point data when it expected integers; so at any time, it must be ready to throw out its optimized code and start over again. The WAT code might be harder to write and to understand, but it's much easier for the web browser to run. WebAssembly moves a lot of work from the browser to the toolchain compiler or the developer. Not having to do as much work makes for happy browsers and faster applications.

Stack Machines

As mentioned earlier, WebAssembly is a virtual stack machine. Let's explore what this means. Think of a stack as a stack of dishes. Each dish in this metaphor is a piece of data. When you add a dish to the stack, you place it on top of the dishes already there. When you take a dish off the stack, you don't take it from the bottom, you take it off the top. For this reason, the last dish you put on the stack is the first dish you remove. In computer science, this is called *last-in, first-out* (*LIFO*). Adding data to a stack is called a *push*, and taking data off a stack is called a *pop*. When you use a stack machine, almost all commands perform some interaction with the stack, either adding more data to the top of the stack with a push or removing data from the top with a pop. Figure 1-2 shows a depiction of stack interaction.

Figure 1-2: A stack machine pops values off and pushes values onto the stack.

As you saw earlier, the first two lines of the $main function in Listing 1-2 push $a_val on the top of the stack ❶ and then push $b_val on top of that ❷. The result is a stack with two values on it. The bottom of the stack has the value in $a_val because we added it first, and the top has the value in $b_val because it was added last.

It's important to make the distinction between an ISA for a stack machine, like WebAssembly, and an ISA for a register machine, such as x86, ARM, MIPS, PowerPC, or any other popular hardware architecture of the past 30 years. Register machines must move data from memory into CPU registers to perform mathematical operations on them. WebAssembly is a virtual stack machine that must run on register machines. As we write WAT formatted code, you'll see this interaction up close.

Stack machines push data onto and off of a stack to perform calculations. Hardware stack machines are a rare breed of computer. Virtual stack machines like WebAssembly are more common; examples include Java's JVM, Adobe Flash player's AVM2, Ethereum's EVM, and the CPython bytecode interpreter. The advantage of virtual stack machines is that they create smaller bytecode sizes, which is handy for any bytecode intended to be downloaded or streamed over the internet.

Stack machines make no assumptions about the number of general-purpose registers available to the embedding environment. That allows the hardware to choose which registers to use and when. The WAT code can be a little confusing if you're not aware of how a stack machine works, so let's take another look at the first two lines of the function $main with the stack in mind (Listing 1-3).

```
global.get $a_val ;; push $a_val onto the stack
global.get $b_val ;; push $b_val onto the stack
```

Listing 1-3: Retrieving $a_val and $b_val, and then pushing them on the stack

The first line gets the value of $a_val, which we define as a global value, and the second line gets the global variable $b_val. Both items end up on the stack waiting to be processed.

The function i32.add takes two 32-bit integer variables off the stack, adds them together, and then pushes the result back onto the top of the stack. Once the two values are on the stack, we can call i32.add. If you run a function that pops more values off the stack than were available, the tools you use to convert your WAT into a WebAssembly binary won't allow this and will throw a compiler error. We use the final line in the $main function to set the $c_val variable to the value on the stack. That value is the result of the i32.add function call.

Example Using S-Expressions

S-Expressions are a nested tree structure coding style used in programming languages, such as Lisp. In Listing 1-3, we used the linear instruction list style for writing WAT. The linear instruction style implicitly uses the stack for each call statement and expression called. For those with some assembly language experience, this method might feel comfortable for you. But if you come to WebAssembly from a high-level language, like JavaScript, the S-Expression syntax for WAT is likely to feel more familiar. S-Expressions organize your calls to WAT statements and expressions in a nested structure. The linear style requires you to mentally push items onto the stack and pop them off as you write your code. The S-Expressions look more like JavaScript function calls than the linear style.

In Listing 1-2, we set c_val to a_val + b_val using the stack. The code in Listing 1-4 is the fragment of code in Listing 1-2 where we added those values together:

```
❶ global.get $a_val ;; push $a_val onto the stack
  global.get $b_val ;; push $b_val onto the stack

❷ i32.add            ;; pop two values, add and place result on stack
  global.set $c_val ;; pop a value off the stack and set $c_val
```

Listing 1-4: Adding and setting $c_val in WebAssembly

We push two 32-bit integer variables onto the stack that we retrieved from global variables using global.get ❶. We then popped those two values off the stack with a call to i32.add. After adding those two values together, the i32.add ❷ function pushed the resulting value back onto the stack. That's how the stack machine works. Each instruction either pushes a value onto the stack, pops a value off, or both.

Listing 1-5 shows the same function using the alternative S-Expression syntax.

```
(module
  (global $a_val (mut i32) (i32.const 1))
  (global $b_val (mut i32) (i32.const 2))
  (global $c_val (mut i32) (i32.const 0))
  (func $main (export "main")
❶  (global.set $c_val
      (i32.add (global.get $a_val) (global.get $b_val))
    )
  )
)
```

Listing 1-5: WebAssembly module to add two values

Don't let the parentheses confuse you: they work the same way as the {} characters do in many languages to create code blocks. When writing a WAT function, we enclose the function in parentheses. When you bring a matching parenthesis below the opening parenthesis with the same indentation, it looks similar to the way you would indent the { and } characters in a language like JavaScript. For instance, look at the indentation of the (before the global.set ❶ call and match it up by eye with the closing) below it.

This code looks more like a conventional programming language than Listing 1-2, because it appears to pass parameters into a function instead of pushing and popping values with a stack. To be clear, this code compiles into the same binary. If you write your code in an S-Expressions style, you're still pushing items on and off the stack. This style of writing WAT is just *syntactic sugar* (syntax to make code easier to read). When you're comfortable disassembling WebAssembly files into WAT, you'll find that the S-Expression syntax isn't provided by disassemblers, such as *wasm2wat*.

The Embedding Environment

As mentioned earlier, WebAssembly doesn't run directly on hardware. You must embed the WebAssembly binary in a host environment that controls the loading and initializing of a WebAssembly module. In this book, we work with JavaScript engines, such as Node.js, and web browsers as embedding environments. Other environments include WASI, such as wasmtime (defined shortly). But even though we discuss WASI, we won't use it in this book because it's still very new and under development. It's up to the embedding environment to implement the stack machine. Because modern hardware is typically a register machine, the embedding environment manages the stack using the hardware registers.

The Browser

There's a good chance that you're interested in WebAssembly because you want it to improve the performance of your web applications. All modern browser JavaScript engines implement WebAssembly. Currently, Chrome and Firefox have the best tools for debugging WebAssembly, so we suggest choosing one of those browsers for development. Your WAT applications should also run just fine in Microsoft Edge, but Internet Explorer is no longer adding features. Unfortunately, Internet Explorer doesn't support WebAssembly and never will.

When you're writing WAT for a web browser, it's crucial to understand which parts of an application you can write in WAT and which you must write in JavaScript. There might also be cases where the performance improvement you gain with WebAssembly might not be worth the additional development time. If you understand WAT and WebAssembly, you'll be able to make these decisions. When you're working with WebAssembly, you must frequently trade performance for development time, or sacrifice CPU cycles for memory, or vice versa. Performance optimization is about choices.

WASI

WASI is a runtime specification for WebAssembly applications and is a standard for WebAssembly interaction with the operating system. It allows WebAssembly to use the filesystem, make system calls, and handle input and output. The Mozilla Foundation has created a WebAssembly runtime called *wasmtime* that implements the WASI standard. With WASI, WebAssembly can do everything that a native application can do but in a secure and platform-independent way. It does it all with performance similar to native apps.

Node.js can also run a WASI experimental preview using the `--experi` `mental-wasi-unstable-preview1` flag. You can use it to run WebAssembly applications that interact with the operating system outside of a web browser. Windows, macOS, Linux, or any other operating system can implement a WASI runtime, because it's designed to make WebAssembly portable, secure, and eventually universal.

Visual Studio Code

Visual Studio Code (VS Code) is an open source integrated development environment (IDE), and the one I used to write the examples in this book. VS Code is available for Windows, macOS, and Linux at *https://code.visualstudio.com/download*. We use VS Code with the WebAssembly extension written by Dmitriy Tsvettsikh, which is available at *https://marketplace.visualstudio.com/items?itemName=dtsvet.vscode-wasm*. The extension provides code coloring for the WAT format, as well as several other useful menu items. For example, if you have a WebAssembly file, you can disassemble it into WAT by right-clicking the file and choosing the **Show WebAssembly** menu option. This is very useful if you want to look at WebAssembly code you didn't write or code that was compiled using a toolchain. The extension can also compile your WAT files into a WebAssembly binary. You can right-click the *.wat* file and choose **Save as WebAssembly binary file**. A save file prompt appears, allowing you to specify the filename where you want to save the WebAssembly file.

Figure 1-3 shows a screenshot of the extension.

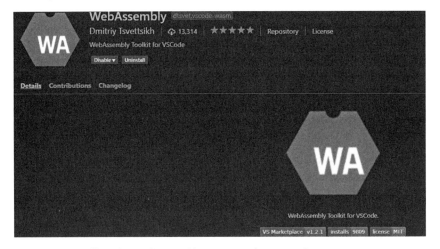

Figure 1-3: Installing the WebAssembly extension for VS Code

Node.js

Node.js is an excellent tool for testing the performance of WebAssembly modules against existing JavaScript modules and is the JavaScript runtime environment we use in much of this book. Node.js comes with *npm (Node Package Manager)*, which you can use to easily install packages of code. WebAssembly is a great alternative to writing a native module in Node.js, which locks you into using specific hardware. If you want to create an npm module for general use, writing for WebAssembly can give you the performance of a native module with the portability and security of a JavaScript module. We'll execute many of the applications we write in this book using Node.js.

Node.js is our preferred development tool for executing WebAssembly, whether it be from JavaScript or through a web server. We'll begin by using Node.js to execute WebAssembly modules from JavaScript, and in Chapter 7, we'll write a simple web server to serve WebAssembly web applications.

Node.js comes with the npm, which makes it easy to install some tools you can use to develop WebAssembly. In this section, we'll show you how to use npm to install the *wat-wasm* module, a tool for compiling, optimizing, and disassembling WebAssembly. We'll also show you how to use Node.js to write a simple WebAssembly application. Many readers might already be familiar with Node.js, but if not, there is a mountain of Node.js documentation available if you want to learn more than the short introduction and setup we discuss here.

Installing Node.js

You must have Node.js installed to complete the code examples in this book. Fortunately, the installation isn't complicated. If you're using Windows or macOS, installers are available for both operating systems at *https://nodejs.org/en/download/*.

For Ubuntu Linux, you can install Node using the following apt command:

```
sudo apt install nodejs
```

Once you have Node installed, run the following command from a command prompt (on any platform) to make sure everything installed as intended:

```
node -v
```

If everything is installed, you should see the version of Node.js installed as output. When we run the command node -v on our Windows machine, it produces the following output:

```
v12.14.0
```

This means that we're running version 12.14.0.

NOTE   *If you're having problems executing the code in this book, you might want to install this specific version of Node.js from the "Previous Releases" page at* https://nodejs.org/ en/download/releases/.

Installing wat-wasm

Many tools are available for converting WAT code to a WebAssembly binary. In fact, while writing this book, I used many of these tools. In the end, I wrote *wat-wasm* on top of *WABT.js* and *Binaryen.js* to reduce the number of packages needed for the features I wanted to demonstrate. To install wat-wasm, execute the following npm command:

```
npm install -g wat-wasm
```

The -g flag installs wat-wasm globally. Throughout this book we'll use command line tools like wat2wasm in the terminal window. To use the tools for more than just the current project, you need to install it globally. Once you have wat-wasm installed, make sure you can run it by running the wat2wasm command from the command line:

```
wat2wasm
```

You should then see the wat-wasm usage logged to your console. This will show you a variety of flags that you'll learn about later in this book.

You can test wat2wasm by creating the simplest possible WAT module, as shown in Listing 1-6. Create a new file called *file.wat* and enter the following code into that file:

```
(module)
```

Listing 1-6: The simplest possible WebAssembly module

With wat-wasm installed, you can use the command in Listing 1-7 to compile *file.wat* file to *file.wasm*, which is the WebAssembly binary file:

```
wat2wasm file.wat
```

Listing 1-7: Assembling the file.wat file with wat2wasm

We'll use Node.js throughout this book to run WebAssembly command line apps and serve WebAssembly web apps to open in a browser. In the next section, we'll write the first WebAssembly app that we'll execute using Node.js.

Our First Node.js WebAssembly App

We'll begin the book by using Node.js as the embedding environment instead of the web browser so as to remove the need for HTML and CSS in the code examples and keep them simple. Later, once you have the basics, we'll explore using the browser as the embedding environment.

The WAT code in our Node.js apps will work the same as they do in the browser. The WebAssembly engine inside Node.js is the same as the one inside Chrome, and the WebAssembly part of the app is completely unaware of the environment it's running in.

Let's begin by creating a simple WAT file and compiling it using wat2wasm. Create a file called *AddInt.wat* and add the WAT code in Listing 1-8 to it.

AddInt.wat
```
(module
    (func (export "AddInt")
    (param $value_1 i32) (param $value_2 i32)
    (result i32)
```

```
        local.get $value_1
        local.get $value_2
        i32.add
    )
)
```

Listing 1-8: WebAssembly module with a function that adds two integers

By now, you should be able to understand this code. Take some time to look it over until you're comfortable with the logic. This is a straightforward WebAssembly module with a single function `AddInt` that we export to the embedding environment. Now compile *AddInt.wat* into *AddInt.wasm* using `wat2wasm`, as shown in Listing 1-9.

```
wat2wasm AddInt.wat
```

Listing 1-9: Compiling AddInt.wat into AddInt.wasm

Now we're ready to write the JavaScript portion of our first Node.js app.

Calling the WebAssembly Module from Node.js

We can call the WebAssembly module from Node.js using JavaScript. Create a file called *AddInt.js* and add the JavaScript code in Listing 1-10.

```
AddInt.js  ❶ const fs = require ('fs');
             const bytes = fs.readFileSync (__dirname + '/AddInt.wasm');
           ❷ const value_1 = parseInt (process.argv[2]);
             const value_2 = parseInt (process.argv[3]);

           ❸ (async () => {
             ❹ const obj = await WebAssembly.instantiate (
                                         new Uint8Array (bytes));
             ❺ let add_value = obj.instance.exports.AddInt( value_1, value_2 );
             ❻ console.log(`${value_1} + ${value_2} = ${add_value}`);
             })();
```

Listing 1-10: Calling the `AddInt` WebAssembly function from an asynchronous IIFE

Node.js can read the WebAssembly file directly from the hard drive where the application is running using the built-in module called `fs` ❶ that reads files from local storage. We load this module using Node.js's `require` function. We use the `fs` module to read in the *AddInt.wasm* file using the `readFileSync` function. We also take in two arguments from the command line using the `process.argv` ❷ array. The `argv` array has all the arguments passed in from the command line to Node.js. We'll run the function from the command line; `process.argv[0]` will contain the command `node` and `process.argv[1]` will contain the name of the JavaScript file *AddInt.js*. When we run the program, we pass in two numbers on the command line, which will set `process.argv[2]` and `process.argv[3]`.

We use an asynchronous *immediately invoked function expression (IIFE)* to instantiate the WebAssembly module, call the WebAssembly function, and output the results to the console. For those unfamiliar with the

IIFE syntax, it's a means by which JavaScript is able to wait for a promise before executing the rest of the code. When you do tasks like instantiate a WebAssembly module, it takes time, and you don't want to tie up the browser or node while waiting for that process to finish. The (async () => {})(); ❸ syntax tells the JavaScript engine that there is a promise object coming, so go do something else while waiting for the result. Inside the IIFE, we call WebAssembly.instantiate ❹ passing the bytes we retrieved from the WebAssembly file earlier with the call to readFileSync. After instantiating the module, we call the AddInt ❺ function exported from the WAT code. We then call a console.log ❻ statement to output the values we're adding and the result.

Now that we have the WebAssembly module and the JavaScript file, we can run the app from the command line using the call to Node.js, as shown in Listing 1-11.

```
node AddInt.js 7 9
```

Listing 1-11: Running AddInt.js *using Node.js*

Running that command results in the following output:

```
7 + 9 = 16
```

The addition of the two integers happens in WebAssembly. Before we move on, we'll quickly show you how to use the .then syntax as an alternative to the asynchronous IIFE.

The .then Syntax

The other widely used syntax to wait for the return of promises is the .then syntax. We prefer to use the IIFE syntax in Listing 1-10, but either syntax is perfectly acceptable.

Create a file called *AddIntThen.js* and add the code in Listing 1-12 to replace the asynchronous IIFE syntax in Listing 1-10 with the .then code.

AddIntThen.js
```
const fs = require ('fs');
const bytes = fs.readFileSync (__dirname + '/AddInt.wasm');
const value_1 = parseInt (process.argv[2]);
const value_2 = parseInt (process.argv[3]);

❶ WebAssembly.instantiate (new Uint8Array (bytes))
❷ .then (obj => {
    let add_value = obj.instance.exports.AddInt(value_1, value_2);
    console.log(`${value_1} + ${value_2} = ${add_value}`);
  });
```

Listing 1-12: Using the .then *syntax to call a WebAssembly function*

The primary difference here lies in the WebAssembly.instantiate ❶ function, followed by .then ❷, and containing an arrow function callback that passes in an object obj.

The Time Is Now

Now is a great time to learn WAT. At the time of writing this, the current release of WebAssembly 1.0 has a relatively small instruction set with a total of 172 different opcodes in the WebAssembly binary, although you don't need to remember all of them. WebAssembly supports four different data types: i32, i64, f32, and f64, and many of the opcodes are duplicate commands for each type (for example, i32.add and i64.add). If you eliminate the duplicate opcodes, you only need to know about 50 different mnemonics to know the entire language. The number of opcodes supported by WebAssembly will increase over time. Starting WebAssembly now in its early days gives you a leg up. In the future, remembering every opcode will become difficult or impossible.

As mentioned earlier, writing your modules in WAT is the best way to work as close to the metal as possible within a web browser. The way JavaScript is implemented in the browser today can create performance inconsistencies depending on a wide variety of factors. WebAssembly can eliminate these inconsistencies, and WAT can help you streamline your code to make it as fast as possible.

You can use a toolchain like Emscripten with only a minimal understanding of the WebAssembly platform. However, using the toolchains this way might result in minimal performance improvements in your application and mislead you to conclude that WebAssembly isn't worth the effort. You would be wrong. If you want to get the highest possible performance from your web application, you must learn as much as you can about WebAssembly. You need to know what it can and cannot do. You must understand what it's good at and what you should do in JavaScript. The best way to gain this knowledge is to write WAT code. In the end, you might not write your application in WAT, but knowing the language helps you comprehend WebAssembly and the web browser.

2

WEBASSEMBLY TEXT BASICS

In this chapter, we'll dive into the basics of WAT code. We'll write most of the code in this book in WAT, the lowest level of programming you can write for deployment to WebAssembly (although for experienced assembly coders, it might seem rather high level).

This chapter covers a lot of ground. We'll begin by showing you the two comment styles in WebAssembly. Next, we'll write the traditional hello world application. We don't start with hello world because working with strings from within WAT is more challenging than you might expect.

Then we'll discuss how to import data from JavaScript into our WebAssembly module using an import object. We'll look at named and unnamed global and local variables, as well as the data types that WebAssembly supports. We'll discuss the S-Expression syntax and how the `wat2wasm` compiler unpacks those S-Expressions when it compiles your code. You'll delve into conditional logic, including `if`/`else` statements and branch tables, and you'll learn how to use loops and blocks in conjunction with conditional logic.

By the end of this chapter, you should be able to write simple WebAssembly apps that you can execute from the command line using Node.js.

Writing the Simplest Module

Every WAT application must be a module, so we'll first look at the module syntax. We declare a module in a block, like the one in Listing 2-1.

```
(module
  ;; This is where the module code goes.
)
```

Listing 2-1: Single line WAT comment

We declare a module with the module keyword, and anything inside the surrounding parentheses is part of the module. To add a comment, we use two semicolons ;; , and everything on the line that follows is a comment. WAT also has block comment syntax; you open the block comment with (; and close it with ;) , as shown in Listing 2-2.

```
(module
  (;
  This is a module with a block comment.
  Like the /* and */ comments in JavaScript
  you can have as many lines as you like inside
  between the opening and closing parenthesis
  ;)
)
```

Listing 2-2: Multi-line WAT comment

Because this module doesn't do anything, we won't bother to compile it. Instead, we'll move on to writing our hello world application.

Hello World in WebAssembly

WAT doesn't have any native string support, so working with strings requires you to work directly with memory as an array of character data. That memory data then must be converted into a string in JavaScript code, because manipulating strings from within JavaScript is much simpler.

When working with strings in WAT, you need to declare an array of character data that is stored within WebAssembly linear memory. Linear memory is a topic we'll discuss in detail in Chapter 6, but for now know that linear memory is similar to a memory heap in native applications, or a giant typed array in JavaScript.

You'll also need to call an imported JavaScript function from Web-Assembly to handle I/O operations. Unlike in a native application where the operating system usually handles I/O, in a WebAssembly module, I/O must be handled by the embedding environment, whether that environment is a web browser, an operating system, or runtime.

Creating Our WAT Module

In this section, we'll create a simple WebAssembly module that creates a hello world! string in linear memory and calls JavaScript to write that string to the console. Create a new WAT file and name it *helloworld.wat*. Open that file and add the WAT code in Listing 2-3.

helloworld.wat
```
(module
  (import "env" "print_string" (func $print_string( param i32 )))
)
```

Listing 2-3: Importing a function

This code tells WebAssembly to expect the import object env from our embedding environment, and that within that object we're expecting the function print_string. When we write our JavaScript code later, we'll create this env object with the print_string function, which will be passed to our WebAssembly module when we instantiate it.

We also set up the signature as requiring a single i32 parameter representing the length of our string. We name this function $print_string so we can access it from our WAT code.

Next, we'll add an import for our memory buffer. Add the line in bold in Listing 2-4.

helloworld.wat
```
(module
  (import "env" "print_string" (func $print_string( param i32 )))
  (import "env" "buffer" (memory 1))
)
```

Listing 2-4: Importing a function and memory buffer

This new import tells our WebAssembly module that we'll be importing a memory buffer from the object env and the buffer will be called buffer. The (memory 1) statement indicates that the buffer will be a single page of linear memory: a *page* is the smallest chunk of memory you can allocate at one time to linear memory. In WebAssembly, a page is 64KB, which is more than we need for this module, so we need just one page. Next, in Listing 2-5, we add a few global variables to *helloworld.wat*.

helloworld.wat
```
(module
  (import "env" "print_string" (func $print_string( param i32 )))
  (import "env" "buffer" (memory 1))
❶ (global $start_string (import "env" "start_string") i32)
❷ (global $string_len i32 (i32.const 12))
)
```

Listing 2-5: Adding global variables

The first global ❶ variable is a number imported from our JavaScript import object; it maps to a variable with the name env in JavaScript (which we've yet to create). That value will be the starting memory location of our string and can be any location in our linear memory page up to the maximum 65,535. Of course, you wouldn't want to choose a value close to the end of linear memory because it would limit the length of the string you could store. If the value passed in is 0, you can use the entire 64KB for your string. If you passed in the value 65,532, you would only be able to use the last four bytes to store character data. If you try to write to a memory location that is greater than what was allocated, you'll get a memory error in your JavaScript console. The second global variable, $string_len ❷, is a constant that represents the length of the string we'll define, and we set it to 12.

In Listing 2-6, we define our string in linear memory using a data expression.

helloworld.wat
```
(module
  (import "env" "print_string" (func $print_string( param i32 )))
  (import "env" "buffer" (memory 1))
  (global $start_string (import "env" "start_string") i32)
  (global $string_len i32 (i32.const 12))
  (data (global.get $start_string) "hello world!")
)
```

Listing 2-6: Adding a data string

We first pass the location in memory where the module will write data. The data is stored in the $start_string global variable that the module will import from JavaScript. The second parameter is the data string, which we define as the string "hello world!".

Now we can define our "helloworld" function and add it to the module, as shown in Listing 2-7.

helloworld.wat
```
(module
  (import "env" "print_string" (func $print_string (param i32)))
  (import "env" "buffer" (memory 1))
  (global $start_string (import "env" "start_string") i32)
  (global $string_len i32 (i32.const 12))
  (data (global.get $start_string) "hello world!")
❶ (func (export "helloworld")
  ❷ (call $print_string (global.get $string_len))
  )
)
```

Listing 2-7: Adding a "helloworld" function to the WebAssembly module

We define and export our function as "helloworld" for use in JavaScript ❶. The only thing this function does is call the imported $print_string ❷ function, passing it the length of the string we defined as a global. We can now compile our WebAssembly module, like so:

```
wat2wasm helloworld.wat
```

Running wat2wasm generates a *helloworld.wasm* module. To execute the WebAssembly module, we'll need to create a JavaScript file that executes it.

Creating the JavaScript File

Now we'll create *helloworld.js* to run our WebAssembly module. Create and open the JavaScript file in your text editor, and add the Node.js file constants as well as three variables, as shown in Listing 2-8.

helloworld.js

```
const fs = require('fs');
const bytes = fs.readFileSync(__dirname + '/helloworld.wasm');

❶ let hello_world = null; // function will be set later
❷ let start_string_index = 100; // linear memory location of string
❸ let memory = new WebAssembly.Memory ({ initial: 1 }); // linear memory
  ...
```

Listing 2-8: Declaring the JavaScript variables

NOTE   *Notice the ... in the last line of code in Listing 2-8. In this book, we'll use ... to indicate that there is more code to be added to this file in the next few sections. If the ... appears at the beginning of a block of code, it indicates that this is a continuation from code in a previous section that ended with the ... syntax.*

The `hello_world` ❶ variable will eventually point to the `helloworld` function exported by our WebAssembly module, so we set it to `null` for the time being. The `start_string_index` ❷ variable is the starting location of our string in the linear memory array. We set it to `100` here, so as not to be close to the 64KB limit. We chose the address 100 arbitrarily. You can choose any address as long as none of the memory you're using extends past the 64KB limit.

The last variable holds the `WebAssembly.Memory` ❸ object. The number passed represents the number of pages you want to allocate. We initialize it with a size of one page by passing in `{initial: 1}` as the only parameter. You can allocate up to two gigabytes this way, but setting this value too high can result in an error if the browser is unable to find enough contiguous memory to fulfill the request.

Listing 2-9 shows the next variable we need to declare, `importObject`, which will be passed into our WebAssembly module when we instantiate it.

helloworld.js

```
  ...
  let importObject = {
❶  env: {
❷    buffer: memory,
❸    start_string: start_string_index,
❹    print_string: function (str_len) {
       const bytes = new Uint8Array (memory.buffer,
         start_string_index, str_len);
       const log_string = new TextDecoder('utf8').decode(bytes);
       console.log (log_string);
     }
```

```
    }
};
...
```

Listing 2-9: Declaring the `importObject` in JavaScript

Inside our `importObject`, we add an object named `env` ❶, an abbreviation of *environment*, although you can call this object anything you like as long as it matches the name inside the WebAssembly import declaration. These are the values that will be passed into the WebAssembly module when it's instantiated. If there is any function or value from the embedding environment you want to make available to the WebAssembly module, pass them in here. The `env` object contains the memory buffer ❷ and the starting location ❸ of our string within `buffer`. The third property in `env` ❹ contains our JavaScript function, `print_string`, which our WebAssembly module will call as we instructed in Listing 2-9. This function retrieves the length of the string in our memory buffer and uses it in combination with our starting string index to create a string object. The app then displays the string object on the command line.

Additionally, we add the IIFE that asynchronously loads our Web-Assembly module and then calls the `helloworld` function, as shown in Listing 2-10.

helloworld.js
```
...
( async () => {
  let obj = await
❶ WebAssembly.instantiate(new Uint8Array (bytes), importObject);
❷ ({helloworld: hello_world} = obj.instance.exports);
❸ hello_world();
})();
```

Listing 2-10: Instantiating the WebAssembly module in an asynchronous IIFE

The first line of the async module awaits the `WebAssembly.instantiate` ❶ function call, but unlike the simple addition example from Listing 1-1, we're passing that function the `importObject` we declared earlier. We then pull the `helloworld` function out of `obj.instance.exports` using the destructuring syntax to set the `hello_world` variable to the `obj.instance.exports` function ❷.

The last line of our IIFE calls the `hello_world` ❸ function. We enclose our arrow function in parentheses, and then add the function call parentheses to the end of our function declaration, which causes this function to execute immediately.

NOTE   *We declare asynchronous code using the IIFE async/await syntax in an async function; alternatively, you can create a named async function that you call immediately after the function's declaration.*

Once you have the JavaScript and WebAssembly files, run the following call to node from the command line:

```
node helloworld.js
```

You should see the following output on the command line:

```
hello world!
```

We've built the ubiquitous hello world application! Now that you have the hello world application under your belt, we'll explore variables and how they work in WAT.

WAT Variables

WAT treats variables a little differently than other programming languages, so it's worth providing you with some details here. However, the browser manages local or global WAT variables in the same way it manages JavaScript variables.

WAT has four global and local variable types: i32 (32-bit integer), i64 (64-bit integer), f32 (32-bit floating-point), and f64 (64-bit floating-point). Strings and other more sophisticated data structures need to be managed directly in linear memory. We'll cover linear memory and the use of more complicated data structures in WAT in Chapter 6. For now, let's look at each variable type.

Global Variables and Type Conversion

As you might expect, you can access globals in WAT from any function, and we generally use globals as constants. *Mutable globals* can be modified after they're set and are usually frowned upon because they can introduce side effects in functions that use them. You can import global variables from JavaScript, allowing the JavaScript portion of your application to set constant values inside your module.

When importing global variables, keep in mind that, at the time of this writing, standard JavaScript number variables don't support 64-bit integer values. Numbers in JavaScript are 64-bit floating-point variables. A 64-bit floating-point variable can represent every value in a 32-bit integer, so JavaScript has no trouble making this conversion. However, you cannot represent all possible 64-bit integer values with a 64-bit floating-point value. Unfortunately, this means that you can work with 64-bit integers in WebAssembly, but if you want to send 64-bit values to JavaScript, it requires additional effort, which is beyond the scope of this book.

NOTE *The BigInt WebAssembly proposal will make support for JavaScript BigInt types available in WebAssembly. That will make it easier for JavaScript to exchange 64-bit integers with a WebAssembly module. At the writing of this book the BigInt proposal is in the final stages of development by the WebAssembly Working Group.*

Another detail you must know about data types in WebAssembly and JavaScript is that JavaScript treats all numbers as 64-bit floating-point numbers. When you call a JavaScript function from WebAssembly, the JavaScript engine will perform an implicit conversion to a 64-bit float, no matter what data type you pass. However, WebAssembly will define the imported function as having a specific data type requirement. Even if you pass the same function into the WebAssembly module three times, you'll need to specify a type that the parameter passed from WebAssembly.

Let's create a module named *globals.wat* that imports three numbers from JavaScript. The WAT file in Listing 2-11 declares global variables for a 32-bit integer, a 32-bit floating-point, and a 64-bit floating-point numeric value.

globals.wat
```
(module
❶ (global $import_integer_32  (import "env" "import_i32") i32)
  (global $import_float_32    (import "env" "import_f32") f32)
  (global $import_float_64    (import "env" "import_f64") f64)

❷ (import "js" "log_i32" (func $log_i32 (param i32)))
  (import "js" "log_f32" (func $log_f32 (param f32)))
  (import "js" "log_f64" (func $log_f64 (param f64)))

  (func (export "globaltest")
❸ (call $log_i32 (global.get $import_integer_32))
❹ (call $log_f32 (global.get $import_float_32))
❺ (call $log_f64 (global.get $import_float_64))
  )
)
```

Listing 2-11: Importing alternative versions of the JavaScript function

We first declare the globals, including their types and import location ❶. We're also importing a log function from JavaScript. WebAssembly requires us to specify data types, so we import three functions, each with different types for the parameter: a 32-bit integer, a 32-bit float, and a 64-bit float ❷.

The variable passed into $log_f64 is (global.get $import_float_64), which tells WebAssembly that the variable we're pushing onto the stack is global. If you wanted to push a local variable called $x onto the stack, you would need to execute the expression (local.get $x). We'll cover local variables later in this chapter.

In JavaScript, all of these functions take a dynamic variable. The JavaScript functions will be almost identical. In the function globaltest, we call the 32-bit integer version of the log function ($log_i32) ❸, followed by the 32-bit float ($log_f32) ❹ and the 64-bit float (log_f64) ❺. These functions will log three different messages to demonstrate the perils of moving between the native 64-bit floating-point values in JavaScript and the data types supported by WebAssembly. Before we look at the output, we need to create a JavaScript file to run our WebAssembly module. We'll start by declaring a global_test variable followed by a log_message function that will be called for each of our data types, as shown in Listing 2-12.

```
globals.js    const fs = require('fs');
              const bytes = fs.readFileSync('./globals.wasm');
              let global_test = null;

              let importObject = {
                js: {
                  log_i32: (value) => { console.log ("i32: ", value) },
                  log_f32: (value) => { console.log ("f32: ", value) },
                  log_f64: (value) => { console.log ("f64: ", value) },
                },
                env: {
                  import_i32: 5_000_000_000, // _ is ignored in numbers in JS and WAT
                  import_f32: 123.0123456789,
                  import_f64: 123.0123456789,
                }
              };
              ...
```

Listing 2-12: Setting `importObject` functions and values

In Listing 2-12, there are three different JavaScript functions passed to the WebAssembly module using importObject: log_i32, log_f32, and log_f64. Each of these functions is a wrapper around the console.log function. The functions pass a string as a prefix to the value from the WebAssembly module. These functions take in only a single parameter called value. JavaScript doesn't assign a type to the parameter in the same way WebAssembly does, so the same function could have been used three times. The only reason we didn't use the same function three times is because we wanted to change the string that prefixed the values to keep the output clear.

We chose the values in Listing 2-12 to demonstrate the limitations of each data type. We set the global variable import_int32 to a value of 5,000,000,000, which we pass into WebAssembly as a 32-bit integer. That value is larger than can be held by a 32-bit integer. We set the global variable import_f32 to 123.0123456789, which has a higher level of precision than is supported by the 32-bit floating-point variable set in our WebAssembly module. The final global variable set in the importObject is import_f64, which, unlike the previous two variables, is large enough to hold the value passed into it.

The code in Listing 2-13 instantiates our WebAssembly module and executes the globaltest function.

```
globals.js    ...
              ( async () => {
                let obj = await WebAssembly.instantiate(new Uint8Array (bytes),
                                                        importObject);
                ({globaltest: global_test} = obj.instance.exports);

                global_test();
              })();
```

Listing 2-13: Instantiating the WebAssembly module in the asynchronous IIFE

Now that we have all our code in the JavaScript and WAT files, we can compile the WAT file into *globals.wasm* using the following `wat2wasm` call:

```
wat2wasm globals.wat
```

After compiling *globals.wasm*, we run our application using the following `node` command:

```
node globals.js
```

When you run this JavaScript file using `node`, you should see the output in Listing 2-14 logged to the console.

```
i32: 705032704
f32: 123.01234436035156
f64: 123.0123456789
```

Listing 2-14: Output logged to the console from globals.js

We passed in a value of `5,000,000,000` using our `importObject`, but our output shows a value of `705,032,704`. The reason is that a 32-bit unsigned integer has a maximum value of 4,294,967,295. If you add 1 to that number, the 32-bit integer wraps back around to a value of 0. So if you take the 5,000,000,000 number we passed in and subtract 4,294,967,296, the result is 705,032,704. The lesson is, if you're dealing with numbers larger than a few billion, you might not be able to work with 32-bit integers. Unfortunately, as mentioned earlier, you can't pass 64-bit integers to JavaScript from WebAssembly. If you want to pass 64-bit integers to JavaScript from WebAssembly, you'll need to convert them to 64-bit floats or pass them as two 32-bit integers.

We passed a value of `123.0123456789` to our WebAssembly module, but because the 32-bit floating-point number has such limited precision, the best it can do is approximate that number, and it doesn't do a great job of it. A 32-bit floating-point number in JavaScript and WebAssembly uses 23 bits to represent the number and multiplies it by two raised to an 8-bit exponent value. All floating-point numbers are approximations, but 64-bit floating-point numbers do a much better job of those approximations. The performance differences you'll see using 32-bit versus 64-bit floating-point numbers vary with your hardware. If you want to use 32-bit floating-point numbers to improve the performance of your application, it's a good idea to know the target hardware. Some mobile devices might see a larger performance boost using 32-bit floating-point numbers.

The final message shows the 64-bit floating-point value returned to JavaScript as `f64: 123.0123456789`.

As you can see, this is the first number that remains unmodified from what we passed into the WebAssembly module. That by no means indicates that you should always use 64-bit floating-point numbers. Addition, subtraction, and multiplication typically perform three to five times faster with integers. Dividing by powers of two is also several times faster. However, division by anything but a power of two can be faster with floating-point numbers.

We'll explore these data types in more detail in Chapter 4. Now that you have a better understanding of globals and types, let's examine local variables.

Local Variables

In WebAssembly, the values stored in local variables and parameters are pushed onto the stack with the `local.get` expression. In Chapter 1, we wrote a small function that performed the addition of two parameters passed into the function that looked like Listing 2-15.

AddInt.wat
```
(module
    (func (export "AddInt")
    (param $value_1 i32) (param $value_2 i32)
    (result i32)
        local.get $value_1
        local.get $value_2
        i32.add
    )
)
```

Listing 2-15: WebAssembly module with a 32-bit integer add

Let's make a few modifications to the code. To demonstrate how we can use local variables, we'll square the value of the sum that `AddInt` returned. Create a new file named *SumSquared.wat* and add the code in Listing 2-16. The changes are called out with numbers.

SumSquared.wat
```
(module
    (func (export ❶"SumSquared")
    (param $value_1 i32) (param $value_2 i32)
    (result i32)
  ❷ (local $sum i32)

  ❸ (i32.add (local.get $value_1) (local.get $value_2))
  ❹ local.set $sum

    ❺ (i32.mul (❻local.get $sum) (local.get $sum))
    )
)
```

Listing 2-16: Bit integer parameter and local variable definition

First, we change the name in the export to `SumSquared` ❶. We add a local variable called `$sum` ❷ that we'll use to store the result of the call to `i32.add` ❸. We change `i32.add` to use the S-Expression syntax. Immediately after that, we call `local.set $sum` to pop the value off the stack and set the new local variable `$sum` ❹. Then we call `i32.mul` ❺ using the S-Expression syntax, passing in the value of `$sum` for both parameters. This is done through a call to `local.get` ❻.

To test this function, create a new JavaScript file named *SumSquared.js* and add the code in Listing 2-17.

<table>
<tr><td>SumSquared.js</td><td>

```
const fs = require('fs');
const bytes = fs.readFileSync(__dirname + '/SumSquared.wasm');
const val1 = parseInt(process.argv[2]);
const val2 = parseInt(process.argv[3]);

(async () => {
  const obj =
    await WebAssembly.instantiate(new Uint8Array (bytes));
  let sum_sq =
    obj.instance.exports.SumSquared(val1, val2);
    console.log (
      `(${val1} + ${val2}) * (${val1} + ${val2}) = ${sum_sq}`
    );
})();
```

</td></tr>
</table>

Listing 2-17: JavaScript that executes the SumSquared.js *WebAssembly module*

Once you've created your *SumSquared.js* function, you can run it the same way you ran the *AddInt.js* file earlier, making sure to pass in two extra parameters that represent the values you want to sum and then square. The following command will add 2 and 3, and then square the result:

```
node SumSquared.js 2 3
```

The output of that run looks like this:

```
(2 + 3) * (2 + 3) = 25
```

You should now understand how to set a local variable from a value on the stack and how to add a value to the stack from a global variable. Next, let's explore how to unpack the S-Expression syntax.

Unpacking S-Expressions

So far we've been mixing the use of S-Expressions with the linear WAT syntax. However, the browser debugger doesn't keep your S-Expressions intact when you're debugging; instead, it unpacks them. Because you'll want to use your knowledge of WAT to decompile and debug WebAssembly, you'll need to understand the unpacking process. We'll walk through the process the wat2wasm compiler uses to unpack a short piece of WAT code. The unpacking process evaluates the expressions inside out first and then in order. It initially dives into each S-Expression looking for subexpressions. If subexpressions exist, it evaluates the subexpressions first. If two expressions are at the same depth, it evaluates them in order. Let's look at Listing 2-18.

```
❶ (i32.mul          ;; executes 7th (last)
❷ (i32.add          ;; executes 3rd
  ❸ (i32.const 3) ;; executes 1st
  ❹ (i32.const 2) ;; executes 2nd
  )
```

```
❺ (i32.sub        ;; executes 6th
  ❻ (i32.const 9) ;; executes 4th
  ❼ (i32.const 7) ;; executes 5th
  )
)
```

Listing 2-18: Using the S-Expression syntax

First, we need to go inside our i32.mul expression ❶ to see if any subexpressions exist. We find two subexpressions, an i32.add expression ❷ and an i32.sub expression ❺. We look at the first of these two expressions and go inside i32.add ❷, evaluating (i32.const 3) ❸, which pushes a 32-bit integer 3 onto our stack. Because nothing is left to evaluate inside that statement, we move on to evaluate (i32.const 2) ❹, which pushes a 32-bit integer 2 onto the stack. Then the S-Expression executes i32.add ❷. The first three lines executed in the S-Expression are shown in Listing 2-19.

```
i32.const 3
i32.const 2
i32.add
```

Listing 2-19: Code from i32.add after it's unpacked

Now that i32.add is executed, the next piece to get unpacked is i32.sub. Similarly, the code first goes inside the S-Expression and executes the (i32.const 9) expression ❻ followed by the (i32.const 7) expression ❼. Once those two constants are pushed onto the stack, the code executes i32.sub. The unpacked subexpression looks like Listing 2-20.

```
i32.const 9
i32.const 7
i32.sub
```

Listing 2-20: Code from i32.sub after the S-Expression is unpacked

After the i32.add and i32.sub S-Expressions have been executed, the unpacked version executes the i32.mul command.

The fully unpacked version of the S-Expression is shown in Listing 2-21.

```
i32.const 3  ;; Stack = [3]
i32.const 2  ;; Stack = [2, 3]
i32.add      ;; 2 & 3 popped from stack, added sum of 5 pushed onto stack [5]

i32.const 9  ;; Stack = [9,5]
i32.const 7  ;; Stack = [7,9,5]
i32.sub      ;; 7 & 9 popped off stack . 9-7=2 pushed on stack [2,5]

i32.mul      ;; 2,5 popped off stack, 2x5=10 is pushed on the stack [10]
```

Listing 2-21: Example of using the WAT stack

How the stack machine works might seem a little daunting at first, but it will feel more natural once you get accustomed to it. We recommend using S-Expressions until you're comfortable with the stack machine. The S-Expression syntax is an excellent way to ease your way into WAT if you're only familiar with higher-level languages.

Indexed Variables

WAT doesn't require you to name your variables and functions. Instead, you can use index numbers to reference functions and variables that you haven't yet named. From time to time, you might see WAT code that uses these indexed variables and functions. Sometimes this code comes from disassembly, although we've also seen people write code that looks like this occasionally.

Code that calls local.get followed by a number is retrieving a local variable based on the order it appears in the WebAssembly code. For example, we could have written our *AddInt.wat* file in Listing 2-21 like the code in Listing 2-22.

```
(module
    (func (export "AddInt")
❶ (param i32 i32)
    (result i32)
      ❷ local.get 0
      ❸ local.get 1
        i32.add
    )
)
```

Listing 2-22: Using variables

As you can see, we don't name the parameters in the param ❶ expression. A convenient part of this code style is that you can declare multiple parameters in a single expression by adding more types. When we call local.get, we need to pass in a zero indexed number to retrieve the proper parameter. The first call to local.get ❷ retrieves the first parameter by passing in 0. The second call to local.get ❸ retrieves the second parameter by passing in 1. You can also use this syntax for functions and global variables. I find this syntax difficult to read, so I won't use it in this book. However, I felt it was necessary to introduce because some debuggers use it.

Converting Between Types

JavaScript developers don't need to deal with converting between different numeric types. All numbers in JavaScript are 64-bit floating-point numbers. That simplifies coding for developers but comes at a performance cost. When you're working with WebAssembly, you need to be more familiar with your numeric data. If you need to perform numeric operations between two variables with different data types, you'll need to do some conversion. Table 2-1 provides the conversion functions you can use in WAT to convert between the different numeric data types.

Table 2-1: Numeric Type Conversion Functions

Function	Action
i32.trunc_s/f64 i32.trunc_u/f64	Convert a 64-bit float to a 32-bit integer
i32.trunc_s/f32 i32.trunc_u/f32 i32.reinterpret/f32	Convert a 32-bit float to a 32-bit integer
i32.wrap/i64	Convert a 64-bit integer to a 32-bit integer
i64.trunc_s/f64 i64.trunc_u/f64 i64.reinterpret/f64	Convert a 64-bit float to a 64-bit integer
i64.extend_s/i32 i64.extend_u/i32	Convert a 32-bit integer to a 64-bit integer
i64.trunc_s/f32 i64.trunc_u/f32	Convert a 32-bit float to a 64-bit integer
f32.demote/f64	Convert a 64-bit float to a 32-bit float
f32.convert_s/i32 f32.convert_u/i32 f32.reinterpret/i32	Convert a 32-bit integer to a 32-bit float
f32.convert_s/i64 f32.convert_u/i64	Convert a 64-bit integer to a 32-bit float
f64.promote/f32	Convert a 32-bit float to a 64-bit float
f64.convert_s/i32 f64.convert_u/i32	Convert a 32-bit integer to a 64-bit float
f64.convert_s/i64 f64.convert_u/i64 f64.reinterpret/i64	Convert a 64-bit integer to a 64-bit float

I omitted quite a bit of information from this table to stay focused. The _u and _s suffixes on expressions, such as convert, trunc, and extend, let WebAssembly know whether the integers you're working with are unsigned (cannot be negative) or signed (can be negative), respectively. A trunc expression truncates the fractional portion of a floating-point number when it converts it to an integer. Floating-point numbers can be promoted from an f32 to an f64 or demoted from an f64 to an f32. Integers are simply converted to floating-point numbers. The wrap command puts the lower 32 bits of a 64-bit integer into an i32. The reinterpret command keeps the bits of an integer or floating-point value the same when it reinterprets them as a different data type.

if/else Conditional Logic

One way that WAT differs from an assembly language is that it contains some higher-level control flow statements, such as if and else. WebAssembly doesn't have a boolean type; instead, it uses i32 values to represent booleans. An if statement requires an i32 to be on the top of the stack to evaluate control flow. The if statement evaluates any non-zero value as true and zero as false. The syntax for an if/else statement using S-Expressions looks like Listing 2-23.

```
;; This code is for demonstration and not part of a larger app
(if (local.get $bool_i32)
  (then
    ;; do something if $bool_i32 is not 0
    ;; nop is a "no operation" opcode.
    nop ;; I use it to stand in for code that would actually do something.
  )
  (else
    ;; do something if $bool_i32 is 0
    nop
  )
)
```

Listing 2-23: The `if/else` syntax using S-Expressions

Let's also look at what the unpacked version of the if/else statements look like. Unpacking an if/else statement might look a little different than you would expect. There is no (then) expression in the unpacked version. Listing 2-24 shows how the code in Listing 2-23 would look after it's unpacked.

```
;; This code is for demonstration and not part of a larger app
local.get $bool_i32

if
  ;; do something if $bool_i32 is not 0
  nop
else
  ;; do something if $bool_i32 is 0
  nop
end
```

Listing 2-24: The `if/else` statement using the linear syntax

The then S-Expression is pure syntactic sugar and doesn't exist in the unpacked version of our code. The unpacked version requires an end statement that doesn't exist in the S-Expression syntax.

When you're writing high-level programs, you use boolean logic with your if/else statements. In JavaScript, you might have an if statement that looks something like this:

```
if( x > y && y < 6 )
```

To replicate this in WebAssembly, you would need to use expressions that conditionally return 32-bit integer values. Listing 2-25 shows how we would do the logic from the JavaScript if example with x and y as 32-bit integers.

```
;; This code is for demonstration and not part of a larger app
(if
  (i32.and
    (i32.gt_s (local.get $x) (local.get $y) ) ;; signed greater than
    (i32.lt_s  (local.get $y) (i32.const 6) ) ;; signed less than
  )
  (then
    ;; x is greater than y and y is less than 6
    nop
  )
)
```

Listing 2-25: An if expression with an i32.and using S-Expression syntax

It looks a bit complicated in comparison. The i32.and expression performs a bitwise AND operation on 32-bit integers. It ends up working out because i32.gt_s and i32.lt_s both return 1 if true and 0 if false. In WebAssembly, you must keep in mind that you're using bitwise AND/OR operations; if you use an i32.and on a value of 2 and a value of 1, it will result in 0 because of the way the binary AND works. You might want a logical AND instead of a binary AND, but i32.and is a binary AND. If you're unfamiliar with binary AND/OR operations, we discuss them in more detail in Chapter 4. In some ways, complicated if expressions look better when they're unpacked. Listing 2-26 shows the code in Listing 2-25 without the sugar.

```
;; This code is for demonstration and not part of a larger app
local.get $x
local.get $y
i32.gt_s        ;; pushes 1 on the stack if $x > $y

local.get $y
i32.const 6
i32.lt_s        ;; pushes 1 on the stack if $y < 6

i32.and         ;; do a bitwise and on the last two values on the stack

if
  ;; x is greater than y and y is less than 6
  nop
end
```

Listing 2-26: An if statement with i32.and using stack syntax

Listing 2-27 shows there are similar expressions you can use if $x and $y are 64-bit or 32-bit floating-point numbers.

```
;; This code is for demonstration and not part of a larger app
(if
```

```
      (i32.and
❶ (f32.gt (local.get $x) (local.get $y) )
  ❷ (f32.lt  (local.get $y) (f32.const 6) )
  )
  (then
    ;; x is greater than y and y is less than 6
    nop
  )
)
```

Listing 2-27: Using f32 comparisons but i32.and results

Notice that we changed i32.gt_s and i32.lt_s to f32.gt ❶ and f32.lt ❷, respectively. Many integer operations must specify whether they support negative numbers using the _s suffix. You don't have to do that for floating-point numbers, because all floating-point numbers are signed and have a dedicated sign bit.

There are a total of 40 comparison expressions in WebAssembly. Table 2-2 shows expressions that are useful in conjunction with the if/else expressions. Unless otherwise stated, these functions pop two values off the stack, compare them, and push 1 on the stack if true and 0 on the stack if false.

Table 2-2: Functions to Use with if/else

Function	Action
i32.eq i64.eq f32.eq f64.eq	Test for equality
i32.ne i64.ne f32.ne f64.ne	Not equal
i32.lt_s i32.lt_u i64.lt_s i64.lt_u f32.lt f64.lt	Less than test. The _s suffix indicates signed comparison; _u indicates unsigned.
i32.le_s i32.le_u i64.le_s i64.le_u f32.le f64.le	Less than or equal test. The _s suffix indicates signed comparison; _u indicates unsigned.

Function	Action
i32.gt_s i32.gt_u f32.gt f64.gt i64.gt_s i64.gt_u	Greater than test. The _s suffix indicates signed comparison; _u indicates unsigned.
i32.ge_s i32.ge_u i64.ge_s i64.ge_u f32.ge f64.ge	Greater than or equal test. The _s suffix indicates signed comparison; _u indicates unsigned.
i32.and i64.and	Bitwise AND
i32.or i64.or	Bitwise OR
i32.xor i64.xor	Bitwise exclusive OR
i32.eqz i64.eqz	Test a floating-point number to see if it has a zero value

Loops and Blocks

The branching expressions in WAT are different than branching statements you might find in an assembly language. The differences prevent the spaghetti code that comes about as the result of jumps to arbitrary locations. If you want your code to jump backward, you must put your code inside a loop. If you want your code to jump forward, you must put it inside a block. For the kind of functionality you would see in a high-level programming language, you must use the loop and block statements together. Let's explore these structures with some throwaway code examples that won't be a part of a larger app.

The block Statement

First, we'll look at the block expression. The block and loop statements in WAT work a bit like goto statements in assembly or some low-level programming languages. However, the code can only jump to the end of a block if it's inside that block. That prevents the code from arbitrarily branching to a block label from anywhere within your program. If the code jumps to the end of a block, the code that performs that jump must exist inside that block. Listing 2-28 shows an example.

```
;; This code is for demonstration and not part of a larger app
❶ (block $jump_to_end
  ❷ br $jump_to_end

    ;; code below the branch does not execute. br jumps to the end of the block
  ❸ nop
  )

  ;; This is where the br statement jumps to
❹ nop
```

Listing 2-28: Declaring a block in WAT

The br ❷ statement is a branch statement that instructs the program to jump to a different location in the code. You might expect br to jump back to the beginning of the block where the label is defined ❶. But that isn't what happens. If you use a br statement within a block to jump to the block's label, it exits that block and begins to execute the code immediately outside the block ❹. That means that the code directly below the br statement ❸ never executes. As mentioned earlier, this code isn't meant to be used, we only wanted to demonstrate how the block and br statements work.

The way we use the br statement here isn't useful. Because the br statement always branches to the end of the labeled block, you want it to branch conditionally.

The br_if conditional branch in Listing 2-29 is used to branch given a condition, unlike the code in Listing 2-28.

```
;; This code is for demonstration and not part of a larger app
(block $jump_to_end
❶ local.get $should_I_branch
❷ br_if $jump_to_end

  ;; code below the branch will execute if $should_I_branch is 0
❸ nop
)

❹ nop
```

Listing 2-29: Branching to the end of the block with br_if

The new version of the code pushes a 32-bit integer value $should_I_branch onto the stack ❶. The br_if statement pops the top value off the stack ❷, and if that value isn't 0, branches to the end of the $jump_to_end block ❹. If $should_I_branch is 0, the code in the block below the br_if statement ❸ executes.

The loop Expression

The block expression always jumps to the end of the block on a branch. If you need to jump to the beginning of a block of code, use the loop statement. Listing 2-30 shows how a WAT `loop` statement works. You would be mistaken if you think this code executes in an infinite loop.

```
;; This code is for demonstration and not part of a larger app
(loop $not_gonna_loop
  ;; this code will only execute once
❶ nop
)

;; because there is no branch in our loop, it exits the loop block at the end
❷ nop
```

Listing 2-30: A loop expression that doesn't loop

In fact, a `loop` expression in WAT doesn't loop on its own; it needs a branch statement located inside the loop to branch back to the beginning of the `loop` expression. A `loop` block will execute the code inside it ❶ just like a `block` expression and, without a branch, exits at the end of the block ❷.

If for any reason you want to create an infinite loop, you need to execute a `br` statement at the end of your `loop`, as shown in Listing 2-31.

```
;; This code is for demonstration and not part of a larger app
  (loop $infinite_loop
    ;; this code will execute in an infinite loop
    nop

❶ br $infinite_loop
  )

  ;; this code will never execute because the loop above is infinite
❷ nop
```

Listing 2-31: Branching in an infinite loop

The `br` statement ❶ always branches back to the top of the `$infinite _loop` block with every iteration. The code below the loop ❷ never executes.

NOTE   *When you write WAT to execute in the browser, you never want to use an infinite loop because WebAssembly doesn't do your browser rendering; so you need to relinquish control back to the browser, or the browser hangs.*

Using block and loop Together

To make your loop able to break and continue, you need to use the `loop` and the `block` expressions together. Let's put together a little WebAssembly module and JavaScript app that finds factorials. The program will run a loop until we have the factorial value of the number passed into the function. That will allow us to test the `continue` and `break` functionality of our `loop` expression. Our simple loop will calculate the factorial value for each number up to some parameter value n that we'll pass in from JavaScript. Then the value of n factorial will be returned to JavaScript.

Create a new file named *loop.wat* and add the code in Listing 2-32.

loop.wat

```
(module
❶ (import "env" "log" (func $log (param i32 i32)))

  (func $loop_test (export "loop_test") (param $n i32)
    (result i32)

    (local $i         i32)
    (local $factorial i32)

    (local.set $factorial (i32.const 1))

❷ (loop $continue (block $break ;; $continue loop and $break block
❸ (local.set $i                 ;; $i++
     (i32.add (local.get $i) (i32.const 1))
   )

❹ ;; value of $i factorial
   (local.set $factorial ;; $factorial = $i * $factorial
     (i32.mul (local.get $i) (local.get $factorial))
   )

   ;; call $log passing parameters $i, $factorial
❺ (call $log (local.get $i) (local.get $factorial))

❻ (br_if $break
     (i32.eq (local.get $i) (local.get $n)));;if $i==$n break from loop
❼ br $continue         ;; branch to top of loop
   ))

❽ local.get $factorial  ;; return $factorial to calling JavaScript
   )
)
```

Listing 2-32: Branching forward and backward with a `loop` and a `block`

The first expression in this module is an import of the $log function ❶. In a moment, we'll write this function in JavaScript and call it on every pass through our loop to log the value of $i factorial for each pass. We labeled the loop $continue ❷ and the block $break ❷ because branching to $continue will continue to execute the loop and branching to $break will break out of the loop. We could have done this without using the $break block, but we want to demonstrate how the loop can work in conjunction with a block. This allows your code to work like a break and a continue statement in a high-level programming language.

The loop increments $i ❸ and then calculates a new $factorial value by multiplying $i by the old $factorial value ❹. It then makes a call to log with $i and $factorial ❺. We use a br_if to break out of the loop if $i == $n ❻. If we don't break out of loop, we branch back to the top of loop ❼. When the loop exits, we push the value of $factorial onto the stack ❽ so we can return that value to the calling JavaScript.

Once you have your WAT file, compile it into a WebAssembly file using the following command:

```
wat2wasm loop.wat
```

Now we'll create a JavaScript file to execute the WebAssembly. Create a *loop.js* file and enter the code in Listing 2-33.

loop.js
```
const fs = require('fs');
const bytes = fs.readFileSync(__dirname + '/loop.wasm');
❶ const n = parseInt(process.argv[2] || "1"); // we will loop n times
let loop_test = null;

let importObject = {
  env: {
❷   log: function(n, factorial) { // log n factorial to output tag
      console.log(`${n}! = ${factorial}`);
    }
  }
};


( async() => {
❸ let obj = await WebAssembly.instantiate( new Uint8Array(bytes),
                                          importObject );

❹ loop_test = obj.instance.exports.loop_test;

❺ const factorial = loop_test(n); // call our loop test
❻ console.log(`result ${n}! = ${factorial}`);
❼ if (n > 12) {
    console.log(`
    ==========================================================
    Factorials greater than 12 are too large for a 32-bit integer.
    ==========================================================
    `)
  }
})();
```

Listing 2-33: Calling the loop_test *from JavaScript*

The log ❷ function, which our WAT code will call, logs a string to the console with the values of n ❶ and n factorial passed from the WAT loop. When we instantiate the module ❸, we pass a value of n to the loop_test ❹ function. The loop_test function finds the factorial as a result ❺. We then use a console.log ❻ call to display the value of n and n factorial. We have a check at the end to make sure the number we enter isn't greater than a value of 12 ❼, because signed 32-bit integers only support numbers up to about 2 billion. Run *loop.js* using node by executing the following on the command line:

```
node loop.js 10
```

Listing 2-34 shows the output you should see on the command line.

```
1! = 1
2! = 2
3! = 6
4! = 24
5! = 120
6! = 720
7! = 5040
8! = 40320
9! = 362880
10! = 3628800
result 10! = 3628800
```

Listing 2-34: Output from loop.js

Now that you know how loops work in WAT, let's look at branch tables.

Branching with br_table

Another way to use the block expression in WAT is in conjunction with a
br_table expression, which allows you to implement a kind of switch statement. It's meant to provide the kind of jump table performance you get
with a switch statement when there are a large number of branches. The
br_table expression takes a list of blocks and an index into that list of blocks.
It then breaks out of whichever block your index points to. The awkward
thing about using a branch table is that the code can only break out of a
block it's inside. That means you must declare all of your blocks ahead of
time. Listing 2-35 shows what the WAT code looks like to build a br_table.

```
;; This code is for demonstration and not part of a larger app
❶ (block $block_0
  (block $block_1
  (block $block_2
  (block $block_3
  (block $block_4
  (block $block_5
❷ (br_table $block_0 $block_1 $block_2 $block_3 $block_4 $block_5
    (local.get $val)
  )
❸ ) ;; block 5
i32.const 55
return

)   ;; block 4
i32.const 44
return

)   ;; block 3
i32.const 33
return

)   ;; block 2
i32.const 22
```

```
return

)    ;; block 1
i32.const 11
return

)    ;; block 0
i32.const 0
return
```

Listing 2-35: Using the br_table syntax from within WAT

We define all the `block` expressions before the `br_table` expression ❶. So when the `br_table` expression is called ❷, it's not always completely clear where in the code it will jump. This is why we added the comments ❸ in the code indicating which `block` was ending.

The `br_table` provides some performance improvement over the use of `if` expressions when you have a large number of branches. In our testing, using the `br_table` expression wasn't worthwhile until there were about a dozen branches. Of course this will depend on the embedding environment and hardware it runs on. Even at this number of branches, the `br_table` was still slower on Chrome than `if` statements. Firefox with about a dozen branches was noticeably faster with the `br_table` expression.

Summary

In this chapter, we covered many of the WAT programming basics. After learning to create and execute a WebAssembly module in Chapter 1, you moved on to creating the traditional hello world application in this chapter. Creating a hello world application is a bit more advanced in WAT than in most programming languages.

After completing a few initial programs, we began looking at some of the basic features of WAT and how they differ from a traditionally high-level language like JavaScript. We explored variables and constants and how they can be pushed onto the stack using WAT commands. We discussed the S-Expression syntax and how to unpack it. We also briefly mentioned indexed local variables and functions, and introduced you to that syntax. You learned the basic branching and looping structures, and how to use them within the WAT syntax. In the next chapter, we'll explore functions and function tables in WAT, and how they interact with JavaScript and other WAT modules.

3

FUNCTIONS AND TABLES

In this chapter, we explore functions in WebAssembly: how and when we should import functions from JavaScript or a different WebAssembly module and how to export WebAssembly functions to the embedding environment and call those functions from JavaScript. You'll learn about tables in WebAssembly and how to call functions defined in tables. We also examine the performance implications of calling functions that we define inside and outside of the WebAssembly module.

A WebAssembly module interacts with the embedding environment using imported and exported functions. We must import functions from the embedding environment for WebAssembly to use and export functions for a web page to call. We can also write functions from within the WebAssembly module to export to the embedding environment using an export statement. Otherwise, functions are by default contained for use only within the module.

Function calls will always result in some lost computing cycles. But it's necessary to know that a WebAssembly module will lose *more* cycles when calling an imported JavaScript function than when calling a function defined inside your WebAssembly module.

When to Call Functions from WAT

Every function we've defined up to this point includes the (export) expression to export the function so JavaScript can call it. However, not every function should use export. Every call to a WebAssembly function from JavaScript incurs an overhead cost, so you generally wouldn't export WAT functions that do only small tasks. Small functions that don't use many computing cycles might be better kept in the JavaScript to reduce overhead. Make sure your WAT code does as much as possible before returning to JavaScript; smaller functions shouldn't use export.

The WAT functions most suited for exporting are those that loop over and process a lot of data. We recommend using many WAT functions in the early versions of your code to aid in the debugging process. Stepping through your WAT code in a debugger is easier to follow when your code is broken into many small functions. Chapter 10 covers debugging WebAssembly code in detail. As you tune your code for performance, you might decide to remove some of these functions by placing their code inline wherever the function had been called. Any internal function that's called thousands of times from your exported WebAssembly function is a good candidate for moving inline. Chapter 9 covers performance tuning in detail.

Writing an is_prime Function

We've already seen examples of exporting functions to JavaScript in previous chapters, but those functions were terrible candidates for WebAssembly performance improvement because they didn't do a whole lot. Here we'll write an intentionally slow algorithm to determine whether an input is a prime number. This function is a good candidate for creation in WebAssembly and improved performance over JavaScript because it involves a significant number of calculations. Create an *is_prime.js* file and an *is_prime.wat* file to start creating this app.

Passing Parameters

Let's start with the basics. First, we create a module, and then create a function inside that module that can be exported as is_prime. This function takes a single 32-bit integer parameter and returns a 32-bit integer that is 1 if the number passed in is prime and 0 if it's not. Place the code in Listing 3-1 in the *is_prime.wat* file.

```
(module
  (func (❶export "is_prime") (❷param $n i32) (❸result i32)
  ❹ i32.const 0 ;; remove later
  )
)
```

Listing 3-1: WebAssembly is_prime function stub

We export this function to JavaScript as is_prime ❶. JavaScript passes in a single parameter param $n as an i32 ❷. When complete, the function returns a 32-bit integer to JavaScript ❸. To compile, this function expects to find a 32-bit integer on the stack when the function completes, so we add the line i32.const 0 ❹. Without this line, the compiler will throw an error when we run wat2wasm because it's expecting to return a number when the function completes, and it needs that number to be on the stack when the function ends.

This function is set for export alone and is not labelled for internal use. The (func) expression begins with an export expression, not a $is_prime label. If we wanted to call this function from within the WebAssembly module or from the JavaScript, we would label it as shown in Listing 3-2.

```
(func ❶$is_prime (export "is_prime") (param $n i32) (result i32)
```

Listing 3-2: Exporting the function

TRUTHINESS

The $is_prime ❶ function should return an i32 to the calling JavaScript, but we know that on the JavaScript end, what we really want is a boolean value of true or false. However, WebAssembly currently doesn't have a boolean type. Instead, it uses an i32 that must be interpreted by JavaScript as true or false. For non-boolean variables, JavaScript uses a concept not common to all programming languages called *truthy*, which means kinda true but not strictly true. Whenever you want a value that's returned from WebAssembly to evaluate to a boolean, it's good practice to use the JavaScript !! operator, which forces the value 0 to a boolean false and any other number will be coerced to true.

Creating Internal Functions

Let's add a little more code to the *is_prime.wat* file. No prime numbers are even except for the number 2, so we'll write a function that checks whether the input number is even by looking at the last bit in the integer. All odd numbers have a 1 in the integer's lowest order bit. Listing 3-3 shows the code for the $even_check function that we'll add to the *is_prime.wat* file.

```
(module
   ;; add the $even_check function to the top of the module
   (func $even_check (❶param $n i32) (result i32)
      local.get $n
      i32.const 2
   ❷ i32.rem_u   ;; if you take the remainder of a division by 2
      i32.const 0 ;; even numbers will have a remainder 0
   ❸ i32.eq      ;; $n % 2 == 0
   )
...
```

Listing 3-3: Defining the $even_check function

The $even_check function takes a single parameter $n ❶ and will return a value of 1 if $n is even and 0 if $n is odd. We use the remainder operation i32.rem_u ❷, which divides $n by 2 and finds the remainder. An even number will have a remainder of 0, so we compare the remainder returned from i32.rem_u with 0 using an i32.eq ❸ expression.

Now let's create another simple function to handle the exception case if the number being passed in is 2, which is the only even prime number. It takes a single parameter and returns a 1 (true) if the number passed in is 2 or 0 (false) if it isn't. We'll call this function $eq_2, as shown in Listing 3-4.

```
...
;; add the $eq_2 function after $even_check
(func $eq_2 (param $n i32) (result i32)
   local.get $n
   i32.const 2
❶ i32.eq    ;; returns 1 if $n == 2
)
...
```

Listing 3-4: The $eq_2 function checks whether the value passed in is 2.

We use i32.eq ❶ to determine whether $n has a value of 2, return 1 if it does, and return 0 if it doesn't. Writing the $eq_2 function is overkill, but because we're demonstrating how calling functions work, another example couldn't hurt.

In Listing 3-5, we add a $multiple_check function that checks whether the first parameter $n is a multiple of the second parameter $m. If the input number has multiples, it means it's divisible and therefore cannot be prime.

```
...
;; add $multiple_check after $eq_2
   (func $multiple_check (param $n i32) (param $m i32) (result i32)
   ❶ local.get $n
   ❷ local.get $m
   ❸ i32.rem_u     ;; get the remainder of $n / $m
      i32.const 0  ;; I want to know if the remainder is 0
   ❹ i32.eq        ;; that will tell us if $n is a multiple of $m
   )
...
```

Listing 3-5: Defining a $multiple_check function that checks whether $n is a multiple of $m

The $multiple_check function takes in two parameters, an integer
$n ❶ and a second integer $m ❷, and checks whether $n is a multiple of
$m. To do this, we get the remainder of $n / $m using i32.rem_u ❸ and
then check whether that remainder is 0 using i32.eq ❹. If the remainder
is 0, the $multiple_check function returns 1. If the remainder is anything
else, the $multiple_check returns 0.

Adding the is_prime Function

Now that we have all the internal functions defined, let's change the
definition of the is_prime exported function so it returns 1 if the number
passed in is prime and 0 if it's not. Listing 3-6 shows the new version of the
is_prime function.

is_prime.wat
(part 4 of 4)

```
...
;; add the is_prime exported function after $multiple_check
(func (export "is_prime") (param $n i32) (result i32)
❶ (local $i i32)
  ❷ (if (i32.eq (local.get $n) (i32.const 1)) ;; 1 is not prime
    (then
      i32.const 0
      return
    ))
  (if (call $eq_2 (local.get $n)) ;; check to see if $n is 2
    (then
      i32.const 1 ;; 2 is prime
      return
    )
  )

  (block $not_prime
    (call $even_check (local.get $n))
    br_if $not_prime ;; even numbers are not prime (except 2)

    (local.set $i (i32.const 1))

    (loop $prime_test_loop

      (local.tee $i (i32.add (local.get $i) (i32.const 2) ) ) ) ;; $i += 2
      local.get $n  ;; stack = [$n, $i]

      i32.ge_u ;; $i >= $n
      if  ;; if $i >= $n, $n is prime
        i32.const 1
        return
      end

      (call $multiple_check (local.get $n) (local.get $i))
      br_if $not_prime    ;; if $n is a multiple of $i this is not prime
      br $prime_test_loop ;; branch back to top of loop
    ) ;; end of $prime_test_loop loop
  )  ;; end of $not_prime block
```

```
  i32.const 0 ;; return false
  )
) ;; end of module
```

Listing 3-6: The $is_prime function definition

Before we added the code in Listing 3-6, the is_prime function didn't actually test for prime numbers. Previously, it always returned 0 (to be interpreted as false). Now that we've coded the is_prime function, it will return 1 if the number passed in is prime and 0 if it's not. At the beginning of this function, we create a local variable $i ❶, which we use later as a loop counter. We check whether $n is 1 and return 0 ❷ if it is because the number one isn't a prime number. We then eliminate half of the numbers by checking whether the number is 2, or even. If the number is 2, it's prime; if it's even but not 2, it's not prime. We divide the number by every odd number from 3 to $n-1. If $n is evenly divisible by any of those numbers, it's not prime. If it's not evenly divisible by any of those numbers, it's prime. The $is_prime function is rather large, so we'll review it a piece at a time.

Listing 3-7 is the portion of the code that tests whether the number is 2.

```
...
  ;; the beginning of the $is_prime function in listing 3-6
  (if ❶(call $eq_2 (local.get $n)) ;; check to see if $n is 2
❷ (then
      i32.const 1 ;; 2 is prime
      return
    )
  )
...
```

Listing 3-7: The $eq_2 number check from $is_prime in Listing 3-6

The if statement calls the $eq_2 ❶ function defined earlier and passes it $n. If the value of $n is 2, this function returns 1; if not, it returns 0. The then expression ❷ runs if the value returned by the call is 1, indicating that the number is prime.

Then we begin a block of code called $not_prime. If at any time the number is determined not to be a prime number, we exit this block, causing the function to exit with a return value of 0, denoting the input isn't prime. Listing 3-8 shows the beginning of that block.

```
...
  ;; code from the $is_prime function in listing 3-6
❶ (block $not_prime
  ❷ (call $even_check (local.get $n))
  ❸ br_if $not_prime ;; even numbers are not prime (except 2)
...
```

Listing 3-8: If the number is even, jump to $not_prime; from $is_prime in Listing 3-6

This block first calls $even_check ❷ to see whether the number is even. Because we verified earlier that this number isn't 2, any other even number wouldn't be a prime. If $even_check returns 1, the code leaves the $not_prime ❶ block using the br_if ❸ statement.

Next, Listing 3-9 begins the loop that checks the numbers that $n might be divisible by.

```
...
  ;; code from the $is_prime function in listing 3-6
❶ (local.set $i (i32.const 1))

❷ (loop $prime_test_loop
  ❸ (local.tee $i
    (❹i32.add (local.get $i) (i32.const 2) ) ) ) ;; $i += 2
    ❺ local.get $n   ;; stack = [$n, $i]

  ❻ i32.ge_u        ;; $i >= $n
  ❼ if              ;; if $i >= $n, $n is prime
      i32.const 1
      return
    end
...
```

Listing 3-9: Prime number test loop; from $is_prime in Listing 3-6

Right before the loop, we set the value of $i to 1 ❶ because we're looping over odd values when we increment through the loop. We call the loop $prime_test_loop ❷ so when we branch to $prime_test_loop ❷, it jumps back to that label. We use the local.tee ❸ command in combination with an i32.add ❹ command to increment the value of $i by 2 (because we're only testing odd numbers) and leave the value calculated by i32.add on the stack when $i is set. The local.tee command is like the local.set command in that it sets the value of the variable you pass to it to the value on top of the stack. The difference is that local.set pops that value off the top of the stack, whereas local.tee leaves the value on it. We want to keep the new value for $i on the stack to compare its value with $n, which we push onto the stack in the next line using a local.get ❺ expression.

The i32.ge_u ❻ expression pulls the last two values off the stack and checks whether the value we had in $i is greater than or equal to the value in $n (because a number can't be divisible by a number greater than it) and assumes these integers are unsigned (because negative numbers can't be prime). If this evaluates to true, the expression pushes 1 onto the stack, and if false, pushes 0 onto the stack.

The if ❼ statement that follows pulls one value off the stack and then executes the code between the if and end statements if the value pulled off the stack isn't 0. The upshot is, if $i is greater than or equal to $n, the number is prime. That means we only execute the code between the if and end statements if we incremented $i until its value is greater than or equal to $n without having ever found a number that evenly divides $n.

Listing 3-10 shows the code that checks whether $i evenly divides $n, which would mean $n isn't prime.

```
...
;; code from the $is_prime function in listing 3-6
❶ (call $multiple_check (local.get $n) (local.get $i))
  ❷ br_if $not_prime    ;; if $n is a multiple of $i this is not prime
  ❸ br $prime_test_loop ;; branch back to top of loop
  ) ;; end of $prime_test_loop loop
) ;; end of $not_prime block
❹ i32.const 0 ;; return false
)
```

Listing 3-10: Call $multiple_check inside the prime test loop; from $is_prime in Listing 3-6

The call ❶ expression at the beginning calls $multiple_check, passing it $n and $i. That returns 1 if $n is evenly divisible by $i and 0 if it's not. If the value returned is 1, the br_if ❷ statement jumps to the end of the $not_prime block, causing the is_prime function to return 0 ❹ (false). If $multiple_check returns 0, we branch back to the top of the loop ❸. We do this to continue testing numbers until $i is greater than $n, or we find a $i where $n is evenly divisible by $i.

With all of our WAT code written, we can use wat2wasm to compile our WebAssembly module:

```
wat2wasm is_prime.wat
```

The JavaScript

Once you've compiled the WebAssembly module, create a JavaScript file named *is_prime.js* and add the code in Listing 3-11 to load and call the WebAssembly is_prime function.

is_prime.js
```
const fs = require('fs');
const bytes = fs.readFileSync(__dirname + '/is_prime.wasm');
const value = parseInt(process.argv[2]);

(async () => {
  const obj =
    await WebAssembly.instantiate(new Uint8Array(bytes));
  if(❶!!obj.instance.exports.is_prime(value)) {
  ❷ console.log(`
     ${value} is prime!
    `);
  }
  else {
  ❸ console.log(`
     ${value} is NOT prime
    `);
  }
})();
```

Listing 3-11: The is_prime.js file calls the is_prime WebAssembly function.

When the is_prime function is called, passing in the value taken from a command line argument, the !! ❶ operator coerces the value from an integer into a true or false boolean value. If the value returned is true, we log out a message stating that the value is prime ❷. If the value returned is false, the message indicates that the value isn't prime ❸. Now we can run the JavaScript function using node like this to check if 7 is a prime number:

```
node is_prime.js 7
```

Here's the output you should see.

```
7 is prime!
```

We've created several functions in our WebAssembly module that we use to check whether or not a number is prime. You should now be familiar with the basics of creating functions and calling those functions from within a WAT module.

ACCESSING THE STACK FROM A FUNCTION

When the running code is inside a function, the wat2wasm compiler will throw an error if the code attempts to pop a value off the stack that your function didn't push on. Here's a small WebAssembly module that attempts to pop a value off the stack that was placed on it by the calling function (Listing 3-12).

```
;; wat2wasm will fail
(module
  (func $inner
    (result i32)
    (local $1 i32)
    ;; 99 is on the stack in the calling function
    local.set $1

    i32.const 2
  )
  (func (export "main")
  (result i32)

    i32.const 99 ;; push 99 onto stack - [99] ❶
    call $inner  ;; 99 is on the stack here ❷
  )
)
```

Listing 3-12: WAT can only access stack variables added in the current function.

The main function first pushes 99 onto the stack ❶. When we call the function labeled $inner, the value of 99 is on the stack ❷. The first statement is $inner is local.set, which requires at least one item be on the stack when the statement is called. However, wat2wasm doesn't care that you pushed an

(continued)

---

item onto the stack before calling the $inner function. If you fail to define a parameter, wat2wasm assumes that you don't have something on the stack and throws an error. If you want a function to have access to a variable, you need to create a parameter when you define the function. You don't have access to data on the stack put there by the calling function. You must pass in variables as parameters.

Declaring an Imported Function

In this section, we'll look at declaring functions as imports in more detail. We'll need to import the "print_string" function from JavaScript, as shown in Listing 3-13.

```
(import "env" "print_string" (func $print_string( param i32 )))
```

Listing 3-13: Declaring an imported function print_string

The import statement in Listing 3-13 tells the module to import an object called print_string passed inside an object called env. These names must correspond with the names in the JavaScript code. Within the JavaScript, you can call the object anything you like, but once you name it in the JavaScript, you must use the same name when you import it into WebAssembly.

Listing 3-14 shows what the import object looked like in the *helloworld .js* file.

helloworld.js
```
let importObject = {
❶ env: {
  ❷ buffer: memory,
  ❸ start_string: start_string_index,
  ❹ print_string: function(str_len) {
      const bytes = new Uint8Array( memory.buffer,
                                    start_string_index, str_len );
      const log_string = new TextDecoder('utf8').decode(bytes);
      console.log(log_string);
    }
  }
};
```

Listing 3-14: Defining the importObject

In the "hello world" app, we use a memory buffer ❷ to set string data. We also let the WebAssembly module know the location of the string data (start_string) ❸ inside the memory buffer. We put both objects inside an object called env to separate it from the JavaScript function. We then create the print_string function ❹ inside the env ❶ object as the JavaScript callback that prints a string from linear memory. At the time of this writing, there isn't a standardized convention for naming objects inside the importObject. We've chosen the env object to represent objects related to the embedded environment and for the function callbacks, but you can organize the importObject in any way you like.

JavaScript Numbers

When you create a JavaScript callback function, the only data type that function can receive is a JavaScript number. If you look at the print_string function we created in the "hello world" application, it passed a single variable. That variable is str_len, and it's the byte length of the string displayed in the console. Unfortunately, only numbers can be passed as parameters to JavaScript functions. Chapter 5 explains in detail what to do to pass other kinds of data back to JavaScript.

Passing Data Types

WebAssembly can pass three of the four main data types back to functions imported from JavaScript: they include 32-bit integers, 32-bit floating-point numbers, and 64-bit floating-point numbers. At the time of this writing, you can't pass 64-bit integers to a JavaScript function. The BigInt WebAssembly proposal will change this when it's implemented. Until then, you must choose the data type you want to convert it to and perform the conversion inside the WebAssembly module. If you pass a 32-bit integer or floating-point number to JavaScript, JavaScript converts it to a 64-bit float, which is the native JavaScript number type.

Objects in WAT

WAT doesn't support object-oriented programming (OOP). Creating classes and objects using WAT could potentially be accomplished using a combination of data structures, the function table, and indirect function execution, but that is beyond the scope of this book. In Chapter 6, we'll explore how to create more sophisticated data structures within linear memory that will allow you to group the data together into linear memory in a way that is similar to using a *struct* in C/C++. Unfortunately, implementing OOP features, such as object methods, class inheritance, and polymorphism, are beyond what we can accomplish in this book.

Performance Implications of External Function Calls

In this section, we'll explore the performance implications of calling imported and exported functions. When you call a JavaScript function in WAT, you lose some cycles to overhead. This number isn't extremely large, but if you execute an external JavaScript function in a loop that iterates 4,000,000 times, it can add up. To get an idea of the kind of performance hit an application suffers from calls to JavaScript versus internal WebAssembly function calls, we created a WebAssembly test module. It executes a simple increment 4,000,000 times in an external JavaScript function and 4,000,000 times in a WebAssembly function in the same module.

Because the code does very little, most of the difference in execution time can be attributed to the overhead of calling an external JavaScript function. Calling an internal WebAssembly function executed four to eight times faster on Chrome than internal WebAssembly calls and two to two and a half times faster in Firefox than internal calls. In our tests, Chrome performed worse than Firefox when crossing the JavaScript/WebAssembly boundary.

NOTE   *These tests only give rough approximations. They were conducted on a Windows PC and don't necessarily reflect overall performance differences. Different versions of the browsers may also give different results.*

Let's walk through this performance test. You first need to create a new WAT file. Create an empty file and name it *func_perform.wat*. Then open the file and create a module with one import and one global variable, as shown in Listing 3-15.

func_perform.wat (part 1 of 4)

```
(module
  ;; external call to a JavaScript function
❶ (import "js" "external_call" (func $external_call (result i32)))
❷ (global $i (mut i32) (i32.const 0)) ;; global for internal function
  ...
```

Listing 3-15: Importing a JavaScript external_call function

The import expression ❶ will import a function we'll define in the JavaScript. That function will return a value to the WebAssembly module. The global expression ❷ creates a mutable global variable with an initial value of 0. In general, it's considered bad practice to use mutable global variables, but this code is only intended as a means to test the difference in performance between a WebAssembly and JavaScript function call.

After we define the global variable, we define the WebAssembly function we'll be calling 4,000,000 times, as shown in Listing 3-16.

func_perform.wat (part 2 of 4)

```
...
❶ (func $internal_call (result i32) ;; returns an i32 to calling function
    global.get $i
    i32.const 1
    i32.add
❷  global.set $i  ;; The first 4 lines of code in the function increments $i

❸  global.get $i  ;; $i is then returned to the calling function
  )
...
```

Listing 3-16: Internal call to the WebAssembly function

The function $internal_call ❶ returns a 32-bit value to the calling function, which will be the incremented value of the $i global variable. All this function does is increment the value of $i ❷ and then push it back on to the stack ❸ to return it to the calling function.

Next, we need to create a function that JavaScript can call with an export expression. This function needs to call the $internal_call function 4,000,000 times. Listing 3-17 shows the code for that external function.

func_perform.wat
(part 3 of 4)

```
...
❶ (func (export "wasm_call")  ;; function "wasm_call" exported for JavaScript
  ❷ (loop $again               ;; $again loop
    ❸ call $internal_call       ;; call $internal_call WASM function
      i32.const 4_000_000
    ❹ i32.le_u                  ;; is the value in $i <= 4,000,000?
    ❺ br_if $again              ;; if so repeat the loop
    )
  )
...
```

Listing 3-17: Four million calls to an internal function

This function ❶ is exported to be called from the JavaScript code. It has a simple loop labeled $again ❷ that will call the $internal_call function ❸ 4,000,000 times. The loop does this by comparing the value returned by $internal_call (the value in the global $i) to 4_000_000. If the value of $i is less than 4,000,000 (i32.le_u) ❹, it branches back to the beginning of the $again loop ❺.

Now that we have a function that will test the internal call to the WebAssembly function, in Listing 3-18 we create an almost identical function that will make a call to an external JavaScript function.

func_perform.wat
(part 4 of 4)

```
...
❶ (func (export "js_call")
  (loop $again
  ❷ (call $external_call) ;; calls the imported $external_call function
    i32.const 4_000_000
    i32.le_u       ;; is the value returned by $external_call <= 4,000,000?
    br_if $again ;; if so, branch to the beginning of the loop
    )
  )
)   ;; end of module ❸
```

Listing 3-18: Four million calls to an external JavaScript function

There are only two differences between this function and the one in Listing 3-19. The first is the name of the function we export, "js_call" ❶, which calls the imported $external_call ❷ function. The second is that we put a closing parenthesis at the end to close the module expression ❸.

Once you've finished creating *func_perform.wat*, compile it into a WebAssembly module using the following command:

```
wat2wasm func_perform.wat
```

Now compile this module with wat2wasm. Then create an empty Java-Script file named *func_perform.js*. This JavaScript will load and call our WebAssembly module. Add the JavaScript in Listing 3-19.

```
const fs = require('fs');
const bytes = fs.readFileSync(__dirname + '/func_perform.wasm');
```

❶ let i = 0;
  let importObject = {
  js: {
❷ external_call: function () { // The imported JavaScript function
     i++;
   ❸ return i; // increment i variable and return it
   }
  }
};
...

Listing 3-19: The external_call function defined in the JavaScript importObject

We declare the variable i ❶ and initialize its value to 0. Inside import
Object we create a function "external_call" ❷ which we imported into the
WebAssembly earlier. The only thing this function does is increment and
then return the value in i ❸.

Next, we need to instantiate the *func_perform.wasm* module and execute
wasm_call and js_call, as shown in Listing 3-20.

```
...
(async () => {
```
❶ const obj = await WebAssembly.instantiate(new Uint8Array(bytes),
                                           importObject);
  // destructure wasm_call and js_call from obj.instance.exports
❷ ({ wasm_call, js_call } = obj.instance.exports);

  let start = Date.now();
❸ wasm_call(); // call wasm_call from WebAssembly module
  let time = Date.now() - start;
❹ console.log('wasm_call time=' + time); // execution time in ms

  start = Date.now();
❺ js_call();   // call js_call from WebAssembly module
  time = Date.now() - start;
❻ console.log('js_call time=' + time); // execution time in milliseconds
})();

Listing 3-20: Asynchronous IIFE definition inside JavaScript

Like the other apps in this book so far, we must instantiate the *func
_perform.wasm* module ❶ in the JavaScript. We use the JavaScript destruc-
turing syntax to create the wasm_call and js_call functions ❷. This destructuring is an ECMAScript 2015 syntax that's convenient for pulling multiple
variables out of an object. Alternatively, you could set wasm_call and js_call
variables to the values in obj.instance.exports.

After retrieving the functions from the WebAssembly module, we call
wasm_call ❸ and log the time it took to execute in milliseconds ❹ to the

console. Next, we call the js_call function ❺ and log ❻ the time it took to execute.

Run the JavaScript using node like so:

```
node func_perform.js
```

You should see something like this output logged to the console.

```
wasm_call time=7
js_call time=32
```

It took 7 milliseconds to call the WebAssembly function 4,000,000 times and 32 milliseconds for JavaScript. This might seem like a large difference, but a 25-millisecond difference spread over 4,000,000 calls is actually pretty small. If this function is only being called once per frame, the difference is trivial. However, if you have a loop that executes hundreds or thousands of times per frame render, it might be worth considering arranging your code differently for performance reasons. In the next section, we'll look at function tables and their performance.

Function Tables

JavaScript can set variables to functions, allowing an application to dynamically swap functions at runtime. WebAssembly doesn't have this feature, but it does have *tables*, which at the time of this writing can only hold functions. For that reason, we'll refer to them as *function tables*, although there are plans to support other types in the future. Function tables allow WebAssembly to dynamically swap functions at runtime, which allows compilers to support features such as function pointers and OOP virtual functions. For example, C/C++ programs use WebAssembly tables to implement function pointers. Currently, tables only support the anyfunc type (anyfunc is a generic WebAssembly function type), but in the future they might support JavaScript objects and DOM elements as well. Unlike import objects, JavaScript and WebAssembly can dynamically change tables at runtime. There is a performance cost to calling a function from a table rather than through an import because a function table entry must be called indirectly. Let's compare the performance of functions called through a table and those called directly.

Creating a Function Table in WAT

In this section, we'll create and export a simple function table in WAT. We'll build a module with four functions; two of which are imported from JavaScript, and two are defined inside the WebAssembly module. These functions will be very simple because the goal is to compare the performance of table function execution to a direct import. Create a new file named *table_export.wat* and enter the code in Listing 3-21.

```
table_export.wat    (module
                        ;; javascript increment function
                     ❶ (import "js" "increment" (func $js_increment (result i32)))
                        ;; javascript decrement function
                     ❷ (import "js" "decrement" (func $js_decrement (result i32)))

                     ❸ (table $tbl (export "tbl") 4 anyfunc) ;; exported table with 4 functions

                        (global $i (mut i32) (i32.const 0))

                     ❹ (func $increment (export "increment") (result i32)
                     ❺ (global.set $i (i32.add (global.get $i) (i32.const 1))) ;; $i++
                          global.get $i
                        )

                     ❻ (func $decrement (export "decrement") (result i32)
                     ❼ (global.set $i (i32.sub (global.get $i) (i32.const 1))) ;; $i--
                          global.get $i
                        )

                        ;; populate the table
                     ❽ (elem (i32.const 0) $js_increment $js_decrement $increment $decrement)
                        )
```

Listing 3-21: Exporting functions in a table

Two imports are in this module: a JavaScript increment function ❶ and a JavaScript decrement function ❷. However, you cannot add a JavaScript function to a function table from within JavaScript. There is a WebAssembly.Table function set that allows you to set functions in a table, only with a function defined in a WebAssembly module. We can work around this restriction by importing the JavaScript function into a WebAssembly module and adding it to the table there.

The table ❸ expression creates the table and names it $tbl, which we can reference within the WAT code. We export $tbl and tell table the expression that there are four objects in this table of type anyfunc (currently the only type of table object supported). We then create two WebAssembly functions: the $increment function ❹ sets the value of the global $i to $i+1 ❺ and the $decrement function ❻ sets the value of $i to $i-1 ❼.

The last thing we do in this module is set the values in the table using the elem expression ❽. As its first parameter, the elem expression takes the index of the first element we set. We set all four elements, so we use (i32 .const 0) because the first parameter is the starting index we want to update. We then follow that parameter with the four function variables we want in the table.

Alternatively, if we only wanted to set the first two items in the table, we wouldn't need to pass in all four function names and would do this:

```
(elem (i32.const 0) $js_increment $js_decrement) ;; set first 2 table func
```

To set the second two items, we would change the value of the first parameter to let the expression know we're starting with the third item in the table, as shown here:

```
(elem (i32.const 2) $increment $decrement)  ;; set table items 3 and 4
```

The first parameter of the elem statement in Listing 3-21 is an index of 0, similar to an array. When you've finished adding this code, compile *table_export.wat* into *table_export.wasm* using the wat2wasm command.

Sharing a Table Between Modules

Now that we have a *table_export.wasm*, let's create a second WebAssembly file that shares the same table. Create a new WAT file named *table_test.wat*. We'll begin the new WebAssembly module with a series of import statements and a type definition expression, as shown in Listing 3-22.

table_test.wat
(part 1 of 3)

```
(module
❶ (import "js" "tbl" (table $tbl 4 anyfunc))
     ;; import increment function
❷ (import "js" "increment" (func $increment (result i32)))
     ;; import decrement function
❸ (import "js" "decrement" (func $decrement (result i32)))

     ;; import wasm_increment function
❹ (import "js" "wasm_increment" (func $wasm_increment (result i32)))
     ;; import wasm_decrement function
❺ (import "js" "wasm_decrement" (func $wasm_decrement (result i32)))

     ;; table function type definitions all i32 and take no parameters
❻ (type $returns_i32 (func (result i32)))
...
```

Listing 3-22: Function imports in the WebAssembly module

The first import statement ❶ imports the table, with four anyfunc functions, in the *table_export.wat* file. Next, we import the JavaScript functions increment ❷ and decrement ❸, which we'll use to compare the performance of imported JavaScript functions against JavaScript functions defined in tables.

We then import the wasm_increment ❹ and wasm_decrement ❺ functions defined in the *table_export.wat* file in the table. With this we can test the performance of a call_indirect to a table element with a call to the same function imported directly with an import statement.

The last expression is a type expression ❻ which defines the signature of the functions in the table. I have to provide this $returns_i32 type as a static parameter to call_indirect. We can expect that call_indirect will be slower than call because the type of the indirectly called function must be dynamically checked to match this provided type.

Now, let's use the code in Listing 3-23 to define four global variables that we'll use to index into the function table.

```
...
❶ (global $inc_ptr i32 (i32.const 0)) ;; JS increment function table index
❷ (global $dec_ptr i32 (i32.const 1)) ;; JS decrement function table index

❸ (global $wasm_inc_ptr i32 (i32.const 2)) ;; WASM increment function index
❹ (global $wasm_dec_ptr i32 (i32.const 3)) ;; WASM decrement function index
...
```

Listing 3-23: Global variable function table indexes

These four global variables are indexes into the function table and give us an easier way to keep track of which index corresponds to which function. The $inc_ptr ❶ and $dec_ptr ❷ variables point to the JavaScript increment and decrement functions, and $wasm_inc_ptr ❸ and $wasm_dec_ptr ❹ point to the WebAssembly versions of the increment and decrement functions in the table.

Defining the Test Functions

With the imports and globals defined, we'll define the four test functions. All of these functions will do the same task using different methods: they'll call an increment function 4,000,000 times from a loop and then call a decrement function 4,000,000 times. One function will call the functions indirectly from the imported table; one will call them directly from an import; one will call a WebAssembly version from a table; and the last will call the increment and decrement functions from a direct import. In the end, we should be able to compare the performance of calling JavaScript functions through a table or directly, as well as compare the performance of calling a WebAssembly module function directly or through a table.

Listing 3-24 shows the four function definitions.

```
;; Test performance of an indirect table call of JavaScript functions
❶ (func (export "js_table_test")
    (loop $inc_cycle
        ;; indirect call to JavaScript increment function
        (call_indirect (type $returns_i32) (global.get $inc_ptr))
        i32.const 4_000_000
        i32.le_u  ;; is the value returned by call to $inc_ptr <= 4,000,000?
        br_if $inc_cycle ;; if so, loop
    )

    (loop $dec_cycle
        ;; indirect call to JavaScript decrement function
        (call_indirect (type $returns_i32) (global.get $dec_ptr))
        i32.const 4_000_000
        i32.le_u  ;; is the value returned by call to $dec_ptr <= 4,000,000?
        br_if $dec_cycle ;; if so, loop
    )
)
```

```
;; Test performance of direct call to JavaScript functions
❷ (func (export "js_import_test")
    (loop $inc_cycle
      call $increment  ;; direct call to JavaScript increment function
      i32.const 4_000_000
      i32.le_u  ;; is the value returned by call to $increment<=4,000,000?
      br_if $inc_cycle ;; if so, loop
    )

    (loop $dec_cycle
      call $decrement  ;; direct call to JavaScript decrement function
      i32.const 4_000_000
      i32.le_u  ;; is the value returned by call to $decrement<=4,000,000?
      br_if $dec_cycle ;; if so, loop
    )
  )

  ;; Test performance of an indirect table call to WASM functions
❸ (func (export "wasm_table_test")
    (loop $inc_cycle
      ;; indirect call to WASM increment function
      (call_indirect (type $returns_i32) (global.get $wasm_inc_ptr))
      i32.const 4_000_000
      i32.le_u  ;; is the value returned by call to $wasm_inc_ptr<=4,000,000?
      br_if $inc_cycle ;; if so, loop
    )

    (loop $dec_cycle
      ;; indirect call to WASM decrement function
      (call_indirect (type $returns_i32) (global.get $wasm_dec_ptr))
      i32.const 4_000_000
      i32.le_u  ;; is the value returned by call to $wasm_dec_ptr<=4,000,000?
      br_if $dec_cycle ;; if so, loop
    )
  )

  ;; Test performance of direct call to WASM functions
❹ (func (export "wasm_import_test")
    (loop $inc_cycle
      call $wasm_increment  ;; direct call to WASM increment function
      i32.const 4_000_000
      i32.le_u
      br_if $inc_cycle
    )

    (loop $dec_cycle
      call $wasm_decrement  ;; direct call to WASM decrement function
      i32.const 4_000_000
      i32.le_u
      br_if $dec_cycle
    )
  )
)
```

Listing 3-24: Performance testing

The first function we define for export is js_table_test ❶. This function runs 8,000,000 indirect calls to simple JavaScript functions. The function following js_table_test is js_import_test ❷. The js_import_test function calls the same functions js_table_test does. However, it does it directly from an import. This allows us to compare the performance of 8,000,000 runs of the same function with and without the use of a table. The other two functions, wasm_table_test ❸ and wasm_import_test ❹, are the same as the js versions of those functions but call WebAssembly module functions instead of JavaScript functions.

Once you've created your *table_test.wasm* file, create a new JavaScript file named *table.js* and add the code in Listing 3-25.

<table>
<tr><td>

table.js
(part 1 of 4)
</td><td>

```
const fs = require('fs');
const export_bytes = fs.readFileSync(__dirname+'/table_export.wasm');
const test_bytes = fs.readFileSync(__dirname + '/table_test.wasm');

let i = 0;
let increment = () => {
  i++;
  return i;
}
let decrement = () => {
  i--;
  return i;
}
...
```
</td></tr>
</table>

Listing 3-25: JavaScript increment and decrement functions

We'll test these functions by calling them directly using an import and indirectly using a table.

Creating the WebAssembly importObject in JavaScript

Now we need an importObject that we'll use for both of the WebAssembly modules. This object defines all of the functions, values, and tables we want to pass from the JavaScript into a WebAssembly module. In Listing 3-27, we'll also use it to pass a table from one WebAssembly module to another. We'll initially set the tbl, wasm_decrement, and wasm_increment objects to null because they're not yet being used by the *table_export.wasm* module. But they'll be needed when we load the *table_test.wasm* module. Listing 3-26 shows the importObject.

<table>
<tr><td>

table.js
(part 2 of 4)
</td><td>

```
...
const importObject = {
    js: {
  ❶ tbl: null, // tbl is initially null and is set for the second WASM module
  ❷ increment: increment, // JavaScript increment function
      decrement: decrement, // JavaScript decrement function
  ❸ wasm_increment: null, // Initially null, set to function by second module
```
</td></tr>
</table>

```
        wasm_decrement: null   // Initially null, set to function by second module
    }
};
...
```

Listing 3-26: JavaScript importObject

At this point, the tbl ❶ value we pass in through the importObject is null, because it's created in the *table_export.wasm* module, and we'll need to initialize that value with the table exported from *table_export.wasm*. The increment and decrement ❷ functions were defined earlier in the JavaScript. We haven't defined the wasm_increment and wasm_decrement ❸ functions yet because we'll need to put them into the import function after they're created in *table_export.wasm*.

Instantiating the WebAssembly Modules

Now let's look at how to instantiate the two WebAssembly modules in Listing 3-27.

table.js
(part 3 of 4)

```
...
❶ (async () => {
    // instantiate the module that uses a function table
❷ let table_exp_obj = await WebAssembly.instantiate(
       new Uint8Array(export_bytes), importObject);

    // set the tbl variable to the exported table
❸ importObject.js.tbl = table_exp_obj.instance.exports.tbl;

❹ importObject.js.wasm_increment =
       table_exp_obj.instance.exports.increment;
❺ importObject.js.wasm_decrement =
       table_exp_obj.instance.exports.decrement;
❻ let obj = await WebAssembly.instantiate(
            new Uint8Array(test_bytes), importObject);
...
```

Listing 3-27: Instantiating a WebAssembly module in asynchronous IIFE

As we've done previously, we use an asynchronous IIFE ❶ to instantiate the WebAssembly modules. However, now we instantiate two WebAssembly modules instead of just a single module to demonstrate how we can share functions and function tables between WebAssembly modules. When we instantiate the *table_export.wasm* module, we put the WebAssembly object into a variable called table_exp_obj ❷. In the past we've put all the WebAssembly module objects into a variable called obj, but because we're using more than one module in this app, we need more specific names.

We use the table_exp_obj to set the tbl variable ❸, defined earlier in the importObject, to the function table created in the *table_export.wasm* module. Next, we set the wasm_increment ❹ and wasm_decrement ❺ variables in the importObject. Then we instantiate the *table_test.wasm* module ❻.

The last block of code in this section, in Listing 3-28, performs the test and measures the time in milliseconds each test took to run.

```
...
// use destructuring syntax to create JS functions from exports
❶ ({ js_table_test, js_import_test,
    wasm_table_test, wasm_import_test } = obj.instance.exports);

   i = 0; // i variable must be reinitialized to 0
   let start = Date.now(); // get starting timestamp
❷ js_table_test();          // run function that tests JS table calls
   let time = Date.now() - start; // find out how much time it took to run
   console.log('js_table_test time=' + time);

   i = 0; // i must be reinitialized to 0
   start = Date.now(); // get starting timestamp
❸ js_import_test();    // run function that tests JS direct import calls
   time = Date.now() - start;
   console.log('js_import_test time=' + time);

   i = 0; // i must be reinitialized to 0
   start = Date.now(); // get starting timestamp
❹ wasm_table_test();   // run function that tests WASM table calls
   time = Date.now() - start; // find out how much time it took to run
   console.log('wasm_table_test time=' + time);

   i = 0; // i must be reinitialized to 0
   start = Date.now(); // get starting timestamp
❺ wasm_import_test(); // run function that tests WASM direct import calls
   time = Date.now() - start; // find out how much time it took to run
   console.log('wasm_import_test time=' + time);
})();
```

Listing 3-28: Calling the WebAssembly functions and recording the execution time

We use the JavaScript destructuring syntax to create four variables ❶, {js_table_test, js_import_test, wasm_table_test, wasm_import_test}, from the obj.instance.exports object's attributes. This is just a handy way to create all four of these function variables at once and set them to the functions of the same name exported by the WebAssembly module.

Then we run each of the functions one by one using node, like this:

```
node table.js
```

Here are the four lines you should see displayed to the console that show the js_table_test ❷, js_import_test ❸, wasm_table_test ❹, and wasm_import_test ❺ runtime:

```
js_table_test time=67
js_import_test time=60
wasm_table_test time=25
wasm_import_test time=20
```

The line displaying the js_import_test ❸ runtime shows that for this run, calling the JavaScript through an import executed about 10 percent faster than calling the same function using a table. Although this might not seem like a tremendous difference, it depends on your application's needs.

We then see the time in milliseconds it takes to call similar WebAssembly versions of the increment and decrement functions. This difference is a bit more significant: the table call takes about 25 percent longer than the direct import.

NOTE *If you get inconsistent test results, you might want to increase the number of runs from 4,000,000 to 20,000,000 or more. Four million worked well for us here, but results will vary based on your computer hardware.*

In this section, you learned how to share functions and function tables between different WebAssembly modules. You also learned the difference between calling a function directly from an import and calling one indirectly through a table, and the performance implications of calling a function using a table. Understanding how functions are called, imported, exported, and used in function tables are fundamental features of the language you'll need to understand before you master WebAssembly development.

Summary

In this chapter, we examined calling WebAssembly functions from JavaScript and JavaScript functions from WebAssembly. We covered what the performance implications of each type of call are. We also created an app that tests for prime numbers to demonstrate the kind of function that it makes sense to create in a WebAssembly module. We looked at passing parameters to functions defined in WebAssembly and how to create functions in WebAssembly that won't be available to JavaScript. We looked into what it takes to create functions that manipulate strings within WebAssembly and how to access those strings from JavaScript. We dove further into data types in WebAssembly and how they translate into data types in JavaScript. We reviewed tables and how to use them to indirectly call WebAssembly and JavaScript functions, including WebAssembly functions created in a second module. We also spent time investigating the performance implications of using tables and functions created in a second WebAssembly module. In the next chapter, we'll explore using WAT for low-level programming.

4

LOW-LEVEL BIT MANIPULATION

This chapter discusses some bit manipulation techniques for WebAssembly applications, which we'll apply to projects in later chapters to improve application performance. This topic can be challenging for readers not familiar with low-level programming, so if working with binary data isn't in your interest, you can continue on to the next chapter and simply refer back to this one as needed.

Before exploring bit manipulation techniques, we'll go over a few essential topics, which include the three different numeric bases—decimal, hexadecimal, and binary; the details of integer and floating-point arithmetic; and 2s complement as well as big-endian and little-endian byte order. Additionally, we'll examine high-order and low-order bits, bit masking, bit shifting, and bit rotation.

WebAssembly allows you to get as close to the metal as possible from within a web browser. If you want to write WebAssembly that executes at lightning speed, understanding how to manipulate your data at the level of bits is very useful. Bit manipulation is also essential to comprehend the data types WebAssembly works with, how they perform, and their limitations. WAT can manipulate data at the level of bits in a way that's similar to assembly languages. Low-level coding is a tricky subject, and if you're not already familiar with some of the concepts in this chapter, you might not grasp them all immediately. The good news is you don't need to know all of these low-level concepts to work with WebAssembly, but understanding low-level WebAssembly can help you write fast, high-performance code for the web. Many times, code a compiler optimizes will generate code that performs bit manipulation, so knowledge of how these bit manipulation operations work is also important when you're disassembling a WebAssembly binary to WAT code.

Binary, Decimal, and Hexadecimal

The *hexadecimal system* is a common numbering system in computer programming that uses base-16 instead of the base-10 decimal numbering system you've been using since you were two years old. Computer programmers work with hexadecimal (hex) because computers natively use binary, and hex more cleanly translates into binary than decimal. You won't learn how to convert from decimal to hex manually, because I'll assume you're either familiar with how to do it or have access to a calculator; most calculator apps offer a programmer mode that will do this conversion for you, like the one shown in Figure 4-1.

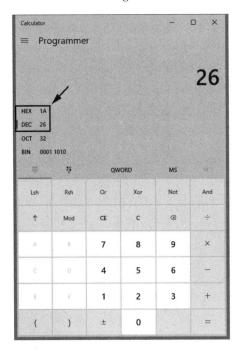

Figure 4-1: Microsoft Windows Calculator app in Programmer mode

I also provide a simple decimal to hex conversion tool at *https:// wasmbook.com/hex*, as well as an online calculator written in WAT at *https:// wasmbook.com/calculator.html*. Keep in mind that if you want to embed numeric data into a string in WAT, you need to use two-digit hex numbers, not decimals.

Integers and Floating-Point Arithmetic

Before discussing how we can use bit manipulation on types, we need to discuss the details of the types that WebAssembly supports. The two primary data types in WebAssembly are integers and floating-point numbers. These types are assigned to all local and global variables when they're declared, and you should use them for all parameters in function declarations. Integers represent whole numbers and can represent negative as well as positive numbers. However, using negative integer numbers requires a little more effort than negative floating-point numbers.

You can store integers and floating-point numbers in variables and in linear memory. If you're familiar with JavaScript, linear memory is like a typed, unsigned-integer array. We'll discuss linear memory more in Chapter 6.

NOTE *If you're familiar with low-level assembly languages, you can think of linear memory as similar to a memory heap. If you're not familiar with low-level languages, just ignore this note.*

In this section, we'll look at how integer and floating-point variables work, the different types of floating-point and integer variables, and how to do some basic binary manipulation on them. Let's first briefly discuss the four primary data types that WebAssembly supports. There are two integer data types (i32 and i64) as well as two floating-point data types (f32 and f64).

Integers

Integer arithmetic is usually faster than floating-point arithmetic for most math operations. WebAssembly currently supports 32-bit and 64-bit integers but, unfortunately, cannot share 64-bit integers with JavaScript as easily as the other data types.

i32 (32-Bit Integers)

The i32 data type is fast, small, and easily moved between WebAssembly and JavaScript. It can represent between 0 and 4,294,967,295 as unsigned data and between −2,147,483,648 to 2,147,483,647 for signed integers. If you're dealing with numbers that you know will be less than a billion in value and you don't need fractional numbers, using i32 is a great choice. Working with signed or unsigned values has more to do with the functions you perform on the data rather than the data in the variable. The i32 data type represents negative numbers using 2s complement.

2s Complement

The 2s complement is a widely used technique for representing negative numbers in a binary format. Computers only work in binary so only have memory with 1s and 0s. Binary can be translated into decimal fairly easily, but it's less obvious how to represent a negative number with only 1s and 0s. It's important to note that floating-point numbers have a dedicated sign bit and therefore don't use 2s complement.

To understand how 2s complement works, let's digress into a metaphorical comparison. Imagine you have a push button tally counter and each time you press a button, it advances a little number dial by one (Figure 4-2). This particular counter only has a single decimal digit display, so it starts at 0 and counts to 9, but when you click it a tenth time, it rolls back to 0. From your counter's perspective, adding 10 is the equivalent of adding 0, because your counter ends up in the same location as it started. Apropos of that, pressing the button 9 times is functionally the same as subtracting 1 for all numbers except 0.

Figure 4-2: Nine rolls over to 0 when 1 is added.

Using the high-value numbers as negatives is only useful if you know that your numbers will be in a range that doesn't include the chosen negative numbers. If you declare that 9 is equivalent to –1, but you need to count up to 9 with your counter, this number system won't work. The rolling-over system is the reason that a signed 8-bit integer supports numbers from –128 to 127. The unsigned 8-bit encoding of the number 255 (eight 1s) is the same as the signed 8-bit representation of –1 because adding 255 to any number causes the bits to roll over like an odometer and subtract one. The largest numbers become negative because they result in the bits rolling over. The code that performs a 2s complement conversion on binary digits uses a binary XOR to flip all of the bits and then adds the number 1 to the result, which results in the negative of the number. You'll see the code to this function when we look at XOR and bit flipping later in this chapter.

i64 (64-Bit Integers)

The i64 data type can represent positive integer numbers between 0 and 18,446,744,073,709,551,615 for unsigned integers and between −9,223,372,036,854,775,808 and 9,223,372,036,854,775,807 for signed integers. The i64 data type in WAT doesn't specify whether it's signed or unsigned when the variable is declared. Instead, WAT has to choose operations to perform on that data based on whether the user wants to treat the number as signed or unsigned. Not all operations require you to make that choice: for example, i64.add, i64.sub, and i64.mul all work the same whether the integers are signed or not. In contrast are the division functions, such as i64.div_s and i64.div_u. The division operation must treat the numbers differently if they're signed or unsigned and so must have the _s and _u suffix appended to the different versions of the operation.

As mentioned earlier, one problem with i64 data types is that you cannot directly move 64-bit integers back and forth between WebAssembly and JavaScript. JavaScript only uses 64-bit floating-point numbers, but 64-bit floats can accommodate 32-bit integers and 32-bit floating-point numbers. The bottom line is that transferring 64-bit integers to the JavaScript portion of your app can be a pain.

NOTE *At the time of this writing, WebAssembly support for JavaScript BigInt objects is in the final stages of development. When support is complete, it will be easier to pass 64-bit integers into JavaScript from WebAssembly and vice versa.*

Floating-Point Numbers

A floating-point number contains three parts in binary: a sign bit, followed by a series of bits to represent the exponent, and then the bits that represent the significant digits (sometimes called the *mantissa* or *significand*). Remember, there is no decimal point in binary; computer scientists had to invent a system for representing decimal points inside a binary number. The sign bit indicates whether the number is positive or negative. The exponent signifies how many positions to move a decimal point (left or right), and the significant digits are simply the numbers for your floating-point number. Let's look at how you could create floating-point numbers using base 10 by first using the exponent to raise a number: if you take a number like 345, and multiply it by 10 raised to a power of 2, it appends two zeros to the end of your number, as shown in Figure 4-3. This is effectively moving the decimal place two positions to the right.

SHIFT DECIMAL POINT RIGHT

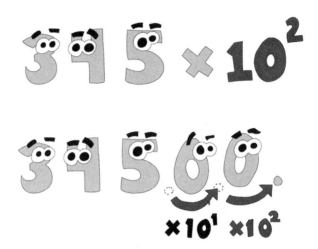

Figure 4-3: Shift the decimal point right with a positive exponent.

Using only base 10 numbers, you would say that you have an exponent of 2 followed by 3 decimal digits, so 2345 would be the number 34,500, or 345×10^2 depicted in Figure 4-4.

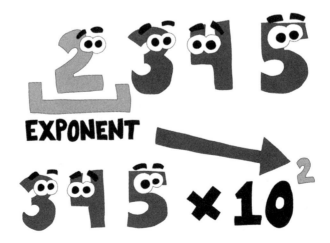

Figure 4-4: Using a decimal exponent

To get a fractional value, we need an exponent that is negative rather than positive, as shown in Figure 4-5: a negative exponent moves the decimal point to the left.

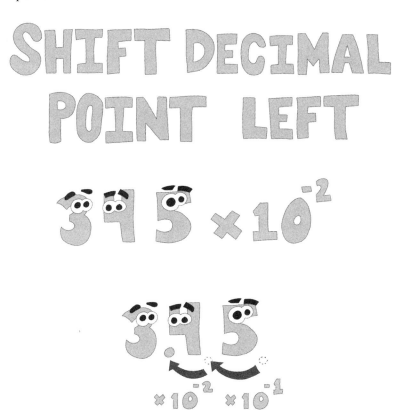

Figure 4-5: Shift the decimal point left with a negative exponent.

An exponent of negative 2 turns 345 into 3.45, resulting in a fractional value. Notice the problem with this system: so far we have no method for representing the negative nature of the first exponent bit. We said we could use 2345 to represent 345×10^2, but we didn't represent the minus sign. We can choose from one of two approaches: 2s complement and biased exponent. First, we could use a method like 2s complement and assign the higher digit values negative numbers, so 8345 could represent 345×10^{-2} because $10 - 2 = 8$. But this isn't the method the designers of floating-point numbers chose. Instead, they use a *biased exponent* where they simply subtract a particular chosen value from the exponent to give us the negative exponent. For example, if we decide to always subtract 5 from our exponent digit, 3345 would represent 345×10^{-2} because $3 - 5 = -2$.

Real floating-point numbers are binary, not decimal, but the basic principles are the same. In binary floating-point numbers, the most significant bit is a sign bit, which is 0 if the number is positive and 1 if it's negative. The eight bits that follow the sign bit represent the exponent. The mantissa represents a fractional number value between one and two. The leftmost bit represents a value of 0.5, followed by 0.25, 0.125, 0.0625, and so on, halving each time. Because the minimum value of the mantissa is 1, the actual value of the mantissa is always one greater than the sum of all these fraction bits. The layout of these bits is shown in Figure 4-6.

> **NOTE** *The exponent portion of a floating-point number doesn't use 2s complement, as integer numbers do. Instead, 127 is subtracted from the unsigned value in these eight bits to give the real exponent. This is also known as a biased exponent.*

Figure 4-6: 32-bit floating-point bits

The fact that the mantissa has a minimum value of 1 creates a problem for the number 0. Raising a non-zero value to any power can never result in a value of 0. To compensate for this, the exponent has two special values that allow for the representation of 0 and infinite values in the floating-point number. If all the bits in the exponent and mantissa are 0, then the number represented is 0, even though 0^0 is 1. Interestingly, floating-point numbers can represent 0 and –0 depending on the value in the sign bit. Infinity and –Infinity are values that have all of the exponent bits set to 1 and all of the mantissa bits set to 0. If the mantissa bits aren't 0, the floating-point is a NaN (not a number).

> **NOTE** *If you want to see what floating-point numbers look like in binary, I have a simple web app that allows you to enter binary values in the sign, mantissa, and exponent bits to see the floating-point value that results. You can also enter a floating-point value to see the bits that are set. You can find the app at* https://wasmbook.com/binary_float.html.

Subnormal Numbers

Subnormal numbers (sometimes called *denormalized numbers*) are another floating-point edge case in the IEEE-754 specification for floating-point numbers. Subnormal numbers are an edge case where the exponent bits are all 0. In the situation in which all the exponent bits are 0, the mantissa value no longer adds 1 to the value represented. This allows for even smaller decimal point values. We won't use subnormal numbers in this book, but you should at least be aware of their existence.

f64/number

The f64 data type is a double-precision 64-bit floating-point number. An f64 has 52 bits that represent the significant digits, an 11-bit exponent, and a sign bit. This data type allows for high precision but on most hardware executes more slowly than integers or smaller floating-point numbers. One of its benefits is that it's the same data type JavaScript uses for all of its numbers, making it a convenient data type for numbers that must be moved back and forth between JavaScript and WebAssembly.

f32

The f32 data type is smaller and faster than f64 but has far less precision, giving you fewer significant digits to work with. The f64 data type has roughly 16 decimal significant digits for you to play with where an f32 has only about seven. Because binary digits represent the significand, it doesn't line up perfectly with decimal digits. The number of significant decimal digits is only an approximation, but it does give you a sense of each type's limitations.

High- and Low-Order Bits

In this section, we'll look at bit significance. The low-order bit is the least significant bit of a binary number; significance simply means *representing the largest value*. In Figure 4-7, in the number 128, the digit 1 is the most significant digit and 8 is the least significant.

Figure 4-7: Most significant and least significant digits

The digit representing the largest numeric value is the most significant. Here, 1 is the most significant digit because it's in the 100th place, and there are no digits representing numbers in a higher position. The sad little 8 in the illustration is the least significant digit because it represents the 1s place.

Binary numbers also have higher-order digits. On a computer, one byte is always eight binary digits; even if the number is 00000001, the left seven binary digits are still in the byte. For example, the number 37 is 100101 in binary, but in computer memory, the value in the byte is 00100101. The most significant bit (high-order bit) in this byte is the leftmost 0, as shown in Figure 4-8.

Figure 4-8: High-order and low-order bit

The low-order bit in this byte is the 1 on the far right, and the high-order bit is the 0 on the far left.

Looking at just the high-order and low-order bits of a variable can reveal some information about a byte. The low-order bit in an integer indicates whether that integer has an even (0) or odd (1) value. The high-order bit of a signed integer determines whether that number is positive (0) or negative (1).

Bit Operations

WebAssembly offers data manipulation at a low level of abstraction. If you're willing to put in the work, you can frequently provide better code performance by manipulating data at the level of bits. Understanding how these operations work can also be useful when you're trying to improve your code's performance, even in high-level languages. We'll use many of the operations in this chapter in applications we write later in the book, so refer back to this chapter as needed. These operations are very general purpose, so it's difficult to give an example of when we would use them. However, as situations arise, it will be obvious which operation is suitable.

Shifting and Rotating Bits

In this section, we'll cover shifting and rotating bits. These are fundamental bit manipulation operations that we'll use from time to time in this book. A single byte of data is made up of eight bits and can hold a number from 0 to 255 in decimal, which is the same as 0 to FF in hexadecimal. Did you know that four bits are called a *nibble*? Single hexadecimal digits are made up of a single nibble (half a byte) and can be a value from 0 to 15 in decimal and 0 to F in hexadecimal.

The fact that four bits can store a single hexadecimal digit makes it relatively easy to work with hexadecimal numbers in WAT, especially when it comes to *shifting*. Shifting is a generic operation that's a building block for the optimizations we'll discuss in later chapters. Shifting is somewhat like pushing bits off a cliff and replacing them with 0s (or 1s for some signed right shifts). You can shift by any number of bits and in either the left or right direction. For example, the binary 1110 1001 is E9 in hexadecimal (and 233 in decimal). If we shift that number 4 bits to the right using the (i32.shr_u) expression, it returns the binary 0000 1110 or 0E in hexadecimal. Figure 4-9 shows a dramatization of a four-bit shift of E9.

Figure 4-9: Shifting hexadecimal E9 four bits to the right results in 0E.

Shifting data to the right can be a useful trick. Every bit you shift to the right is the functional equivalent of dividing by 2. Similarly, every bit you shift to the left is the functional equivalent of multiplying by 2. You can use shifting in combination with masking to isolate sections of binary data.

Left-shifting in WebAssembly is sign-independent, but to right-shift we use a signed or an unsigned shift operation. When you right-shift or left-shift a binary number, the bits shifted off are usually replaced on the opposite side of the integer with 0s. However, with a negative number, if you sign-shift to the right, 1s will be sign-shifted in from the left side to preserve the integer's sign. Sign-shifting a 2s complement representation preserves the sign (negativeness).

Bit rotation, unlike a shift, flips bits back around to the other side of the variable. If you rotate a bit to the right, the least significant bit is transferred to the front and ends up as the most significant bit, and all the other bits shift to the right. WAT does bit rotation with the rotl (rotate left) or rotr (rotate right) commands, depicted in Figure 4-10.

Figure 4-10: Rotating a bit to the right

Masking Bits with AND and OR

Bit masking is a method used to set some specified bits in an integer to 1 or 0, depending on the kind of mask we use, to isolate or override them. This can be very helpful when writing high-performance applications. Also, it's important to know that WebAssembly doesn't have the concept of boolean values. Comparisons in WebAssembly usually return a value of 1 for true and 0 for false. You must use the i32.and and i32.or when, in many languages, you would use boolean logic. In this section, we'll use the i32.and and i32.or to isolate or override bit values with bit masking.

When you mask with a bitwise AND, the 0 bits in your integer win the battle of the bits. The 0 bits in the mask act like masking tape that covers up any other bit in the integer, replacing them with 0s. The 1 bits in the mask allow the original value to show through. Figure 4-11 shows what it looks like to mask binary 1011 1110 (190) with 0000 0111 (7).

As you can see in Figure 4-11, all of the bits of our original value are covered by the 0s in the AND mask. When a bitwise AND operation is performed on two different integers, the 0 bit wins (Figure 4-12).

Figure 4-11: Masking bits with bitwise AND

Figure 4-12: Bitwise AND 0 wins the battle of the bits.

When you mask with OR, using an i32/i64.or, the results would be the exact opposite: 1 bits cover up any bits with 1s. You cannot use the OR mask to isolate bits as with an AND. Instead, you use it to set specific bits to 1. Figure 4-13 shows masking with OR.

Figure 4-13: Masking with a bitwise OR

As you can see in Figure 4-13, when you use a bitwise OR, the 1 bits in your mask cover any bits in your initial integer value. So in a bitwise OR situation, the 1 bit wins over the 0 bit (Figure 4-14).

Figure 4-14: In a bitwise OR, the 1 bit always wins.

XOR Bit Flip

The last binary operation we'll cover is XOR. With AND and OR, the results of a mask are clear. The XOR i32/i64.xor operation is a little different. If a 0 masks a 0, a 1 masks a 0, or a 0 masks a 1, the XOR operates just like a typical i32/i64.or. The weirdness occurs when you have two 1s, which results in the XOR setting the resulting bit to 0. This feature is handy for *bit flipping*, where you invert each bit to its opposite. Certain operations require you to change every 1 bit in an integer to a 0 and every 0 bit to a 1. Figure 4-15 shows how to flip every bit in a nibble with an XOR.

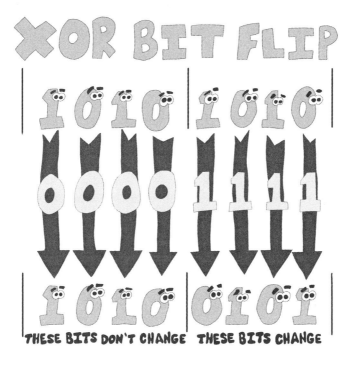

Figure 4-15: XOR bit flip

In our 2s complement discussion earlier, we noted that if you want to find the negative of any number, you can do so by flipping every bit and adding the number 1. You can flip all the bits using an XOR against an integer that has every bit set to 1. Let's write a short app that converts an integer value to its negative using 2s complement and bit flipping. Create a file named *twos_complement.wat* and add the code in Listing 4-1.

twos_complement
.wat

```
(module
  (func $twos_complement (export "twos_complement")
  (param $number i32)
  (result i32)
    local.get $number
❶ i32.const 0xffffffff  ;; all binary 1s to flip the bits
❷ i32.xor               ;; flip all the bits
    i32.const 1
```

```
  ❸ i32.add                    ;; add one after flipping all bits for 2s complement
  )
)
```

Listing 4-1: 2s complement function

This is a very simple module that takes an i32 parameter called $number. We push the i32 onto the stack, followed by a 32-bit number where all the bits are 1 ❶. When we call i32.xor ❷, all of the bits from the original number are flipped. Every 1 is turned into a 0 and every 0 into a 1. We then call i32.add ❸ to add a value of 1 to this number to get 2s complement, resulting in the negative number. This code works well as a demonstration of how 2s complement works; however, it would perform better if we just subtracted $number from 0 to negate it.

Big-Endian vs. Little-Endian

All numbers you're familiar with are arranged in a *big-endian* format, meaning the highest-order digits are on the left side and the lowest-order digits are on the right side. Most computer hardware uses *little-endian*, where the lowest-order digit is on the left and the high-order digit is on the right, so one hundred twenty-eight would be written as 821 instead. Keep in mind that endianness is about byte order, not digit order, so my little-endian decimal 821 example is an oversimplification that can't be directly translated to binary. Little-endian hardware orders the bytes in reverse of what is typical. The number 168,496,141 written in big-endian hex is 0A0B0C0D. The high-order byte is 0A, and the low-order byte is 0D because each hex digit is represented by a nibble or half a byte. If we order the bytes in little-endian order, they're arranged as 0D0C0B0A, as illustrated in Figure 4-16.

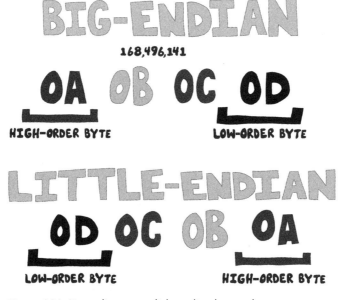

Figure 4-16: Big-endian versus little-endian byte order

Most hardware today arranges bytes in little-endian order for performance reasons. WebAssembly uses little-endian byte order regardless of the hardware. When you're initializing data using the (data) statement in WebAssembly, it's important to keep the byte order in mind.

Summary

This chapter covered a lot of low-level programming concepts. We looked at the different numeric bases (decimal, hexadecimal, and binary) used in low-level programming. We examined the details of integer and floating-point arithmetic, and touched on 2s complement as well as big-endian and little-endian byte order. We talked about bit manipulation, including discussions of high-order and low-order bits, bit masking, bit shifting, and bit rotation. These low-level options will become useful for applications in later chapters that enhance performance by manipulating bits.

In the next chapter, you'll learn several methods for managing strings as data structures, including null-terminated strings and length-prefixed strings. We'll also explore copying strings and converting numeric data into strings in decimal, hexadecimal, and binary formats.

5

STRINGS IN WEBASSEMBLY

This chapter discusses how to handle strings in WAT because WebAssembly doesn't have a built-in string data type as high-level languages do. To represent string data in WebAssembly, you must set linear memory to ASCII or Unicode character values. You need to know where you're setting your data in linear memory and how many bytes the string will use.

In this chapter, we'll look at the ASCII and Unicode character formats before we explore the relationship between string objects and how to store them in linear memory. You'll learn how JavaScript can retrieve the strings from linear memory and output them to the command line. Once you know how to pass string data from WebAssembly to JavaScript, we'll cover two popular methods for string management: null-terminated strings and length-prefixed strings, discussing the pros and cons of each technique. You'll learn how to copy a string from one location in linear memory to another using a byte-by-byte copy and a 64-bit copy. Then you'll convert integer data into number strings in decimal, hexadecimal, and binary formats.

NOTE *For the most part, you don't need to choose a specific address in linear memory to store your strings, as long as it falls within the number of pages you allocated. Unless otherwise mentioned, you can assume that a memory address was chosen arbitrarily.*

ASCII and Unicode

When working with strings in WebAssembly, you need to know which character set you're using, because different sets look different in linear memory. *American Standard Code for Information Interchange (ASCII)* is a 7-bit character encoding system that supports up to 128 characters with an 8th bit that might be used for error checking or is simply set to 0. The ASCII character set works well if your code is only supporting the English language.

Unicode Transformation Format (UTF) comes in 7-bit, 8-bit, 16-bit, and 32-bit flavors, which are called UTF-7, UTF-8, UTF-16, and UTF-32. UTF-7 and ASCII are identical. UTF-8 incorporates UTF-7 and allows for some additional Latin, Middle Eastern, and Asian characters by creating a flexible length format that allows for additional bytes when the starting byte of the format falls outside of the ASCII character set. UTF-16 is also a flexible length character set where most characters take up two bytes. Because some codes expand the number of bytes a character uses to four, UTF-16 supports more than 1.1 million characters. UTF-32 is a fixed 32-bit character set that supports more than 4 billion characters. In this book, we'll work exclusively with the ASCII/UTF-7 character set because it's simple to read and understand.

Strings in Linear Memory

The only way to pass a string from WebAssembly to JavaScript is to create an array of character data inside a memory buffer object like we did in Chapter 2 with the hello world app. You can then pass a 32-bit integer into JavaScript that represents the location of that character data in the memory buffer. The only problem with this scheme is that it doesn't tell JavaScript where the data ends. The C language manages this by using a null-terminating byte: a byte with a value of 0 (not a character 0) tells the program that the string ends in the previous byte. We'll look at three ways to pass strings between WAT and JavaScript, including null-termination, and then look at how to copy strings.

Passing the String Length to JavaScript

The most obvious way to work with strings is to pass a string position and a string length to JavaScript so JavaScript can extract the string from linear memory and can know when it ends. Create a new WAT file named *strings.wat* and add the code in Listing 5-1.

strings.wat
(part 1 of 11)

```
(module
;; Imported JavaScript function (below) takes position and length
❶ (import "env" "str_pos_len" (func $str_pos_len (param i32 i32)))
❷ (import "env" "buffer"    (memory 1))
;; 30 character string
❸ (data (i32.const 256) "Know the length of this string")
;; 35 characters
❹ (data (i32.const 384) "Also know the length of this string")

❺ (func (export "main")
;; length of the first string is 30 characters
 ❻ (call $str_pos_len (i32.const 256) (i32.const 30))
;; length of the second string is 35 characters
 ❼ (call $str_pos_len (i32.const 384) (i32.const 35))
 )
)
```

Listing 5-1: Passing strings from WebAssembly to JavaScript

This module imports a JavaScript function we'll create called "str_pos _len" ❶, which finds a string in the memory buffer using a combination of the string's position and its location in linear memory. We also need to import a memory buffer we'll declare in JavaScript ❷.

Next, we define two strings in memory: "Know the length of this string" ❸ and "Also know the length of this string" ❹. The two strings specify that we need to know the length of those strings because they're just character arrays in linear memory and we need to indicate where they begin and end. The first string has 30 characters and the second has 35. Later, in the "main" ❺ function, we call $str_pos_len twice. The first time ❻, we pass in the position of the first string in memory (i32.const 256) followed by the length of that string (i32.const 30). This tells the JavaScript we'll write in a moment to extract 30 bytes starting at memory position 256 into a string and display it to the console. The second time we call $str_pos_len ❼, we pass in the position of the second string in memory (i32.const 384) followed by the length of that string (i32.const 35). The JavaScript then displays the second string to the console. Compile the WebAssembly module using the command in Listing 5-2.

```
wat2wasm strings.wat
```

Listing 5-2: Compiling strings.wat

Once you've compiled your WebAssembly module, create a JavaScript file named *strings.js* and enter the code in Listing 5-3.

strings.js
(part 1 of 3)

```
const fs = require('fs');
const bytes = fs.readFileSync(__dirname + '/strings.wasm');

let memory = new WebAssembly.Memory( {initial: 1 });
```

```
let importObject = {
  env: {
    buffer: memory,
  ❶ str_pos_len: function(str_pos, str_len) {
    ❷ const bytes = new Uint8Array( memory.buffer,
                                    str_pos, str_len );
    ❸ const log_string = new TextDecoder('utf8').decode(bytes);
      ❹ console.log(log_string);
    }
  }
};

( async () => {
  let obj = await WebAssembly.instantiate( new Uint8Array(bytes),
                                           importObject );

  let main = obj.instance.exports.main;

  main();
})();
```

Listing 5-3: JavaScript that calls the WebAssembly string function

Inside the `importObject` we define `str_pos_len` ❶, which takes the position of the string in memory and its length. It uses the position of the length to retrieve an array of bytes ❷ of the length provided. We use a `TextDecoder` to convert that byte array into a string ❸. Then we call `console.log` ❹ to display the string. When you run the JavaScript, you should see the message in Listing 5-4.

```
Know the length of this string
Also know the length of this string
```

Listing 5-4: String length output

Next, we'll discuss null-terminated strings, which is a method for tracking string length that languages such as C/C++ use.

Null-Terminated Strings

The second method of passing strings is *null-terminated* (or *zero-terminated*) strings. Null-termination is a method for defining string length used by the C programming language. In a null-terminated string, you place a value of 0 as the last character in the array. The benefit of null-terminated strings is that you don't have to know the string's length as you're using it. The downside is that this requires more computation when processing strings because your program needs to take the time to locate the terminating null byte. Let's open the *strings.wat* file and add the code in Listing 5-5 for our null-terminated strings. First, we need to add an import of a `null_str` function that we'll define later in the JavaScript.

```
(module
❶ (import "env" "str_pos_len" (func $str_pos_len (param i32 i32)))
   ;; add line below
❷ (import "env" "null_str" (func $null_str (param i32)))
   ...
```

Listing 5-5: Modifying strings.wat *from Listing 5-1 to import the* null_str *function*

Notice that unlike str_pos_len ❶, the null_str ❷ function only requires one i32 parameter, because the code working with it only needs to know where the string begins in linear memory. It's up to the code to figure out where that null byte is located to manipulate it.

Next, between the import statement that defines the buffer and the (data) expression that defines the earlier strings, in Listing 5-6 we add two more data expressions that define null-terminated strings.

```
   ...
   (import "env" "buffer" (memory 1))
   ;; add the two lines below
❶ (data (i32.const 0) "null-terminating string\00")
❷ (data (i32.const 128) "another null-terminating string\00")

   (data (i32.const 256) "Know the length of this string")
   ...
```

Listing 5-6: Modifying strings.wat *from Listing 5-1 to add null-terminated string data*

The first data defines the string "null terminating string\00" ❶. Notice the last three characters \00. The \ character is the escape character in WAT. If you follow an escape character with two hexadecimal digits, it defines a numeric byte with the value you specify. That means that \00 represents a single byte with a value of 0. The second data expression creates the string "another null terminating string\00" ❷, which is also null-terminated and ending with \00.

In Listing 5-7, we add two lines in the beginning of the main function to call the imported $null_str JavaScript function, passing it the location in linear memory of the null-terminated strings.

```
   ...
   (func (export "main")
❶ (call $null_str (i32.const 0))    ;; add this line
❷ (call $null_str (i32.const 128))  ;; add this line

   (call $str_pos_len (i32.const 256) (i32.const 30))
   ...
```

Listing 5-7: Modifying strings.wat *from Listing 5-1 to call the* null_str *function*

We pass in a value of 0 ❶, which is the location in memory where we defined the string "null terminating string\00". Then we pass in the value 128 ❷, where we defined the string "another null terminating string\00".

Once you've made those changes in your WAT file, open *strings.js* to add some more code. First, add a new function to the env object nested in importObject, as shown in Listing 5-8.

strings.js   ...
(part 2 of 3) ❶ `const max_mem = 65535; // add this line`

```
let importObject = {
env: {
  buffer: memory,
  // add the null_str function to the importObject here
❷ null_str: function(str_pos) { // add this function
❸ let bytes = new Uint8Array( memory.buffer,
                              str_pos, max_mem-str_pos );

❹ let log_string = new TextDecoder('utf8').decode(bytes);
❺ log_string = log_string.split("\0")[0];
❻ console.log(log_string);
  }, // end of function
  str_pos_len: function(str_pos, str_len) {
...
```

Listing 5-8: The null_str function added to importObject in strings.js from Listing 5-3

The code starts by defining the maximum possible length of the string in the variable max_mem ❶. To find the string that's null terminated, we decode a chunk of linear memory with the maximum string length into one long string, and then use JavaScript's split function to get the null-terminated string. Inside the env object, we add another function called null_str ❷ that takes a single str_pos parameter. JavaScript then needs to extract an array of bytes from the memory buffer starting at the position specified by the str_pos parameter passed into the function. We cannot search through the memory buffer until we convert it into a string. But before converting it to a string, we need to convert it into an array of bytes ❸. Then we create a TextDecoder object to decode those bytes into one long string ❹.

We split the string into an array using the null byte "\0" ❺. Splitting on the null byte creates an array of strings that terminate in the null byte. Only the first item in the array is an actual string we defined. We're using the split as a quick and dirty way to take the string out of linear memory. We then set log_string to the first string in the array. We call the JavaScript console.log function ❻, passing it log_string to display that string to the console. Because we're calling it with two different strings from WebAssembly, we should now have the four messages in Listing 5-9 logged to the console.

```
null-terminating string
another null-terminating string
Know the length of this string
Also know the length of this string
```

Listing 5-9: Output from null-terminating strings

Length-Prefixed Strings

A third way to store a string in memory is to include the length of the string at the beginning of the string data. A string created with this method is called a *length-prefixed string* and can improve processing performance. The way we're prefixing limits the strings to a maximum length of 255 because a single byte of data can only hold a number between 0 and 255.

16-BIT PREFIXED STRING LENGTH

You could encode the length in two bytes of data, which would allow strings of more than 65,000 characters. Just keep in mind that you must arrange the bytes in little-endian order. If you want to use a 16-bit number to encode the length, you must put the low-order byte ahead of the high-order byte. For example, if you want your string to have a length of 1024 (0400 in hex), you would need to encode it in little-endian order. Because little-endian byte order is flipped, in the string it would need to be encoded as \00\04. To make matters even more complicated, JavaScript doesn't always use little-endian. In JavaScript, you need to check whether you're dealing with big-endian or little-endian.

Let's start by modifying the current *strings.wat* file, as shown in Listing 5-10, to add a new import line for the len_prefix function we'll define later in the JavaScript.

strings.wat
(part 5 of 11)

```
(module
  (import "env" "str_pos_len" (func $str_pos_len (param i32 i32)))
  (import "env" "null_str" (func $null_str (param i32)))
  ;; add the line below
❶ (import "env" "len_prefix" (func $len_prefix (param i32)))
  ...
```

Listing 5-10: Modifying strings.wat from Listing 5-1 to add the len_prefix function import

The len_prefix ❶ function will take the first byte of the string to find the length.

Next, we add two new strings that begin with a hexadecimal number indicating their length. Add the code in Listing 5-11 to *strings.wat*.

strings.wat
(part 6 of 11)

```
  ...
  (data (i32.const 384) "Also know the length of this string")

  ;; add the next four lines.  Two data elements and two comments
  ;; length is 22 in decimal, which is 16 in hex
❶ (data (i32.const 512) "\16length-prefixed string")
  ;; length is 30 in decimal, which is 1e in hex
❷ (data (i32.const 640) "\1eanother length-prefixed string")
```

```
(func (export "main")
...
```

Listing 5-11: Modifying strings.wat *from Listing 5-1 to add length-prefixed string data*

The first string, "\16length-prefixed string", has 22 characters, so we prefix it with \16 because 22 in decimal is 16 in hexadecimal ❶. The second string, "\1eanother length-prefixed string", is 30 characters long, so we prefix it with a hexadecimal \1e ❷.

Next, we need to add two calls to the imported $len_prefix function with the two memory locations where we just created the strings. The "main" function should now look like the code in Listing 5-12.

---

strings.wat
(part 7 of 11)

```
...
(func (export "main")
  (call $null_str (i32.const 0))
  (call $null_str (i32.const 128))

  (call $str_pos_len (i32.const 256) (i32.const 30))
  (call $str_pos_len (i32.const 384) (i32.const 35))

❶ (call $len_prefix (i32.const 512))    ;; add this line
❷ (call $len_prefix (i32.const 640))    ;; add this line

)
...
```

Listing 5-12: Modifying strings.wat *from Listing 5-1 to add calls to the* $len_prefix *function*

The first call to $len_prefix ❶ passes it the location of the data string "\16length-prefixed string" at memory location 512. The second call ❷ passes the location of the second length-prefixed string "\1eanother length-prefixed string" at memory location 640.

Before we can run this, we need to add a new function to our JavaScript importObject. Open *strings.js* and add the len_prefix function to the import Object, as shown in Listing 5-13.

---

strings.js
(part 3 of 3)

```
...
let importObject = {
  env: {
    buffer: memory,
    null_str: function (str_pos) {
      let bytes = new Uint8Array(memory.buffer, str_pos,
                                 max_mem - str_pos);

      let log_string = new TextDecoder('utf8').decode(bytes);
      log_string = log_string.split("\0")[0];
      console.log(log_string);
    }, // end null_str function
    str_pos_len: function (str_pos, str_len) {
      const bytes = new Uint8Array(memory.buffer,
        str_pos, str_len);
      const log_string = new TextDecoder('utf8').decode(bytes);
      console.log(log_string);
```

```
    },
  ❶ len_prefix: function (str_pos) {
    ❷ const str_len = new Uint8Array(memory.buffer, str_pos, 1)[0];
    ❸ const bytes = new Uint8Array(memory.buffer,
                                     str_pos + 1, str_len);
    ❹ const log_string = new TextDecoder('utf8').decode(bytes);
      console.log(log_string);
    }
  }
};
...
```

Listing 5-13: Add the `len_prefix` function to `importObject` in strings.js from Listing 5-3

The new `len_prefix` ❶ function takes in a string position and then takes the first byte from the position as a number in the constant `str_len` ❷. It uses the value in `str_len` to copy the proper number of bytes ❸ from linear memory so it can decode them into the `log_string` ❹ it will log to the console.

Now that we have our WAT and JavaScript, we can compile the WAT module using wat2wasm, as shown in Listing 5-14.

```
wat2wasm strings.wat
```

Listing 5-14: Compile strings.wat

Then we can run our JavaScript file using node, as shown in Listing 5-15.

```
node strings.js
```

Listing 5-15: Run strings.js using node

You should see the output in Listing 5-16.

```
null-terminating string
another null-terminating string
Know the length of this string
Also know the length of this string
length-prefixed string
another length-prefixed string
```

Listing 5-16: Output from strings.js

In the next section, you'll learn how to copy strings using WAT.

Copying Strings

The simplest way to copy a string from one location in linear memory to another is to loop over every byte of data, load it, and then store it in the new location. However, this method is slow. A more efficient method is to copy the strings eight bytes at a time using 64-bit integer loads and stores. Unfortunately, not all strings are multiples of eight bytes. To cover all cases as efficiently as possible, we'll need a combination of a byte-by-byte copy and a faster 64-bit copy.

Byte-by-Byte Copy

We'll first write a function that does a slower byte-by-byte copy: it takes as parameters a source memory location, a destination memory location, and the length of the string we want to copy.

NOTE   *On some platforms, performance of a function like this might suffer if the strings don't have the proper byte alignment. Some hardware architectures require that you load and store data to and from addresses that are multiples of the bus size. For example, sometimes a processor with a 32-bit bus can only read from addresses that are multiples of four (4 bytes = 32 bits).*

Let's continue to add code to our *strings.wat* file. In Listing 5-17, we add the function $byte_copy to the *strings.wat* file.

strings.wat (part 8 of 11)

```
...
(func $byte_copy
    (param $source i32) (param $dest i32) (param $len i32)
    (local $last_source_byte i32)

❶ local.get $source
   local.get $len
❷ i32.add     ;; $source + $len

   local.set $last_source_byte        ;; $last_source_byte = $source + $len

   (loop $copy_loop (block $break
❸ local.get $dest       ;; push $dest on stack for use in i32.store8 call
❹ (i32.load8_u (local.get $source)) ;; load a single byte from $source
❺ i32.store8                         ;; store a single byte in $dest

❻ local.get $dest
   i32.const 1
   i32.add
❼ local.set $dest                    ;; $dest = $dest + 1

   local.get $source
   i32.const 1
   i32.add
❽ local.tee $source                  ;; $source = $source + 1

   local.get $last_source_byte
   i32.eq
   br_if $break
   br $copy_loop
 )) ;; end $copy_loop
)
...
```

Listing 5-17: A slow byte-by-byte method of copying strings added to strings.wat (Listing 5-1)

This $byte_copy function copies the block of memory from $source ❶ to $source + $len ❷ into the memory location $dest ❸ to $dest + len one byte at a time. This loop loads a byte from $source using the (i32.load8_u) expression ❹. It then stores that byte in the $dest location using the i32.store8 command ❺. Then we increment the destination location ❻ in the $dest variable ❼ and we increment the $source ❽ variable to make those variables point to the next bytes in memory.

64-Bit Copy

Copying a string byte-by-byte is slower than it needs to be, whereas a 64-bit integer is eight bytes long, and copying eight bytes at a time is significantly faster than copying a single byte at a time. We'll write another function similar to $byte_copy that copies the data significantly faster by doing it eight bytes at a time. Unfortunately, not all strings have lengths that are multiples of eight. If a string has a length of 43 characters, we can copy the first 40 bytes using five separate eight-byte copies, but for the last three bytes, we'll need to go back to the byte-by-byte copy method.

It's important to note that these byte copies don't prevent out of bounds memory access. The code will attempt to copy data to or from somewhere it shouldn't. However, if you try to access data outside the bounds of linear memory, the WebAssembly security model will cause the read or write to fail, halting the code's execution. As stated earlier, these functions weren't intended to be general purpose, but instead are for demonstrating the different ways you can copy strings.

Add the 64-bit copy function $byte_copy_i64 in Listing 5-18 to your *strings.wat* file.

strings.wat
(part 9 of 11)

```
...
;; add this block of code to the strings.wat file
(func $byte_copy_i64
  (param $source i32) (param $dest i32) (param $len i32)
  (local $last_source_byte i32)

  local.get $source
  local.get $len
  i32.add

  local.set $last_source_byte

  (loop $copy_loop (block $break
❶ (i64.store (local.get $dest) (i64.load (local.get $source)))

  local.get $dest
❷ i32.const 8
  i32.add
  local.set $dest              ;; $dest = $dest + 8

  local.get $source
❸ i32.const 8
  i32.add
  local.tee $source            ;; $source = $source + 8

  local.get $last_source_byte
  i32.ge_u
```

```
      br_if $break
      br $copy_loop
  )) ;; end $copy_loop
)
...
```

Listing 5-18: A faster method of copying strings added to strings.wat (Listing 5-2)

The load and store functions are (i64.load) and (i64.store) ❶, which load and store 64 bits (8 bytes) at a time. This method runs four to five times faster than loading and storing a single byte at a time (on x64 architecture). The other significant difference is that $dest ❷ and $source ❸ are incremented by 8 instead of 1.

Combination Copy Function

As mentioned earlier, not all strings are multiples of eight. Therefore, we'll define a new, improved function in Listing 5-19 that copies eight bytes at a time using the $byte_copy_i64 function and then copies the remaining bytes using $byte_copy, which copies a single byte at a time.

---

strings.wat
(part 10 of 11)

```
...
(func $string_copy
    (param $source i32) (param $dest i32) (param $len i32)
    (local $start_source_byte i32)
    (local $start_dest_byte   i32)
    (local $singles           i32)
    (local $len_less_singles  i32)

    local.get $len
❶ local.set $len_less_singles  ;; value without singles

    local.get $len
    i32.const 7                  ;; 7 = 0111 in binary
❷ i32.and
    local.tee $singles           ;; set $singles to last 3 bits of length

❸ if                            ;; if the last 3 bits of $len is not 000
        local.get $len
        local.get $singles
        i32.sub
      ❹ local.tee $len_less_singles  ;; $len_less_singles = $len - $singles

        local.get $source
        i32.add
        ;; $start_source_byte=$source+$len_less_singles
      ❺ local.set $start_source_byte

        local.get $len_less_singles
        local.get $dest
        i32.add
      ❻ local.set $start_dest_byte  ;; $start_dest_byte=$dest+$len_less_singles

      ❼ (call $byte_copy (local.get $start_source_byte)
```

```
        (local.get $start_dest_byte)(local.get $singles))
  end

  local.get $len
❽ i32.const 0xff_ff_ff_f8 ;; all bits are 1 except the last three which are 0
❾ i32.and                 ;; set the last three bits of the length to 0
  local.set $len
❿ (call $byte_copy_i64 (local.get $source) (local.get $dest) (local.get $len))
  )
...
```

Listing 5-19: Copy eight bytes at a time when possible and a single byte at a time when not.

As stated earlier, the $string_copy function must combine the eight-byte and single-byte copy functions to copy the string as quickly as possible. The $len parameter is the entire length of the string in bytes. The local variable $len_less_singles ❶ is the number of bytes that can be copied with the 64-bit copy. We get this number by masking off the last three bits. The $singles variable is the remaining three bits that aren't in the multiples of eight and is set by performing a bitwise (i32.and) expression ❷ (hurray for bit masking) between $len and 7 (binary 111). The last three bits of the length indicate the number of remaining bytes if we used an eight-byte copy for the majority of the bytes. As an example, using an i32.and expression on the $len of 190 and 7 looks like Figure 5-1.

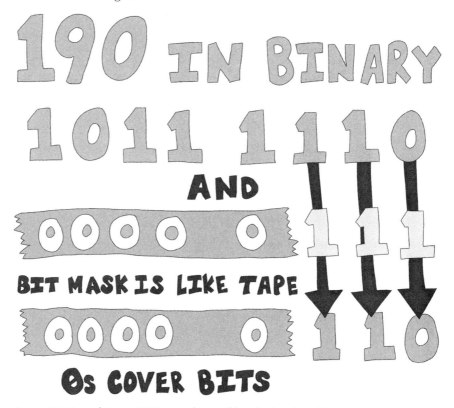

Figure 5-1: Using binary AND to mask out all but the last three bits

As you can see, calling i32.and passing the values 190 and 7 results in the binary 110, which is 6 in decimal. The i32.and expression sets all but the last three bits of our $len parameter to 0.

If the number of $singles isn't zero ❸, the code first copies the individual bytes that cannot be copied using the 64-bit copy. The if block sets $len_less_singles ❹ to $len - $singles: that is the number of bytes that must be copied individually. The local variable $start_source_byte ❺ is set to $source+$len_less_singles, setting it to the starting byte of the byte-by-byte copy ❼.

Then the variable $start_dest_byte ❻ is set to $dest+$len_less_singles, which sets it to the destination location for the byte-by-byte copy. The branch then calls $byte_copy to copy those remaining single bytes.

After the if block, the code must copy the bytes that it can with the 64-bit copy function (call $byte_copy_i64) ❿. We determine the number of bytes to copy with this function by using a bitwise (i32.and) ❾ expression of the length in $len with the 32-bit constant value 0xff_ff_ff_f8 ❽. The value 0xff_ff_ff_f8 in binary is all 1s except the last three bits, which are set to 0. Using the bitwise AND zeros out the last three bits of the length, which makes the length a multiple of eight.

Now that we have a string copy function, let's change the main function to test it. Change the main function so it contains only the code in Listing 5-20.

strings.wat
(part 11 of 11)

```
...
(func (export "main")
  ❶ (call $str_pos_len (i32.const 256) (i32.const 30))
  ❷ (call $str_pos_len (i32.const 384) (i32.const 35))

  ❸ (call $string_copy
        (i32.const 256) (i32.const 384) (i32.const 30))

  ❹ (call $str_pos_len (i32.const 384) (i32.const 35))
  ❺ (call $str_pos_len (i32.const 384) (i32.const 30))
  )
```

Listing 5-20: New version of the main function for strings.wat (Listing 5-2)

We removed the code that printed the null-terminated strings and the length-prefixed strings to the console. We keep the two lines that print the string at linear memory location 256 ❶, "Know the length of this string", and the string at memory location 384 ❷, "Also know the length of this string". Leaving these lines in will print the original value for the strings to the console before the copy.

The call to $string_copy ❸ copies 30 bytes from the first string to the second string. Then we print the second string location with the original string length. This will print "Know the length of this stringtring" ❹ to the console, which looks wrong because it ends with the word stringtring. The reason the last word doesn't end with string and has an additional five characters is that we needed to change the length to that of the string we copied from. If we'd been copying a null-terminated string or a length-prefixed string, this wouldn't have been a problem, because the null-byte or prefix would keep track of the length for us: but in this case, we need to know that the new length is 30.

When we call $str_pos_len passing in 384 as the index and 30 as the length ❺, it will properly print "Know the length of this string" to the console. We can recompile *strings.wat* using the command in Listing 5-21.

```
wat2wasm strings.wat
```

Listing 5-21: Compiling strings.wat

Run *strings.js* from the command line to see the output in Listing 5-22.

```
Know the length of this string
Also know the length of this string
Know the length of this stringtring
Know the length of this string
```

Listing 5-22: Output from strings.js *after adding a call to* $string_copy

In the next section, you'll learn how to turn numbers into strings.

Creating Number Strings

When you're working with strings, converting numeric data into string data is frequently required. High-level languages like JavaScript have functions that can do this for you, but in WAT you'll need to build your own functions. Let's look at what it takes to create strings from numbers in decimal, hexadecimal, and binary.

Create a WAT file named *number_string.wat* and add the code in Listing 5-23 to the beginning of the file.

number_string .wat (part 1 of 7)
```
(module
❶ (import "env" "print_string" (func $print_string (param i32 i32)))
❷ (import "env" "buffer" (memory 1))

❸ (data (i32.const 128) "0123456789ABCDEF")

❹ (data (i32.const 256) "               0")
❺ (global $dec_string_len  i32 (i32.const 16))
...
```

Listing 5-23: Imported objects and data in the WebAssembly module

The beginning of this module imports a $print_string ❶ function and one page of linear memory ❷ from JavaScript. Next, we define a data ❸ element with an array of characters that contains every hexadecimal character. Then we define a data element that will hold our string data ❹, followed by the length of that data string ❺.

In the next few listings, we define three functions that create number strings in three different formats. We use the first of these functions, $set_dec_string, to set the $dec_string linear memory area.

Listing 5-24 contains the code that turns an integer into a decimal string. The code can be a bit challenging to follow, so I'll give you an overview before showing the code. At a high level, when we assemble a string from a number, we need to look at the number one digit at a time and add the character form of that digit to our string. Let's say the number we're looking at is 9876. In the 1s place is the digit 6. We can find this digit by dividing the full number by 10 and using the remainder (called a *modulo*). In WAT, that code would be the type i32.rem_u (rem for remainder). Next, you use the character form of the number 6 and add it to your string. Other digits need to move along as if on a conveyor belt (illustrated in Figure 5-2). The way you do this in code is to divide by 10. Because this divide is on an integer, you don't get a fractional number, and the 6 is simply thrown away. You then use the remainder to get the next digit (7) and add that to the string. You continue on until all the digits are gone. Listing 5-24 shows the source code for the $set_dec_string function.

number_string
.wat (part 2 of 7)

```
...
(func $set_dec_string (param $num i32) (param $string_len i32)
  (local $index      i32)
  (local $digit_char i32)
  (local $digit_val  i32)

  local.get $string_len
❶ local.set $index     ;; set $index to the string length

  local.get $num
  i32.eqz              ;; is $num is equal to zero
  if                   ;; if the number is 0, I don't want all spaces
    local.get $index
    i32.const 1
    i32.sub
    local.set $index   ;; $index--

    ;; store ascii '0' to memory location 256 + $index
    (i32.store8 offset=256 (local.get $index) (i32.const 48))
  end

  (loop $digit_loop (block $break ;; loop converts number to a string
    local.get $index   ;; set $index to end of string, decrement to 0
    i32.eqz            ;; is the $index 0?
    br_if $break       ;; if so break out of loop

    local.get $num
    i32.const 10
❷ i32.rem_u            ;; decimal digit is remainder of divide by 10

❸ local.set $digit_val ;; replaces call above
    local.get $num
    i32.eqz            ;; check to see if the $num is now 0
    if
      i32.const 32         ;; 32 is ascii space character
      local.set $digit_char ;; if $num is 0, left pad spaces
    else
❹   (i32.load8_u offset=128 (local.get $digit_val))
      local.set $digit_char ;; set $digit_char to ascii digit
```

```
    end

    local.get $index
    i32.const 1
    i32.sub
    local.set $index
    ;; store ascii digit in 256 + $index
❺ (i32.store8 offset=256
    (local.get $index) (local.get $digit_char))

    local.get $num
    i32.const 10
    i32.div_u
❻ local.set $num        ;; remove last decimal digit, dividing by 10
    br $digit_loop       ;; loop
  )) ;; end of $block and $loop
)
...
```

Listing 5-24: A WebAssembly function that creates a decimal string from an integer

We start the function with $index ❶, a variable that points to the last byte in $dec_string. We set the values of this string from right to left, so the $index variable needs to be decremented every pass through the loop. Each pass through the loop, the number value set in $dec_string is the final base-10 digit. To get this value, we divide the $num ❻ value by 10 and get the remainder ❷ with modulo 10. This value is stored in the local variable $digit_val ❸ so we can later use it to set an ASCII character in the $dec_string data. We use $digit_val as an offset into the $digit_char string to load a character with i32.load8_u ❹. That character is then written to an address that is $dec_string+$index using i32.store8 ❺. Figure 5-2 illustrates the process.

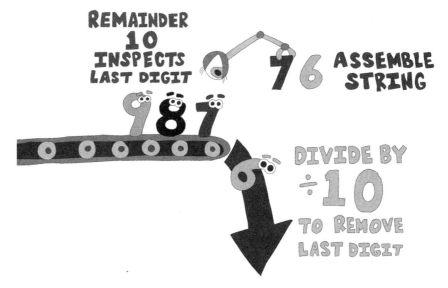

Figure 5-2: Look at digits one at a time and append characters one at a time.

Now that we have the function that does most of the work in our WebAssembly module, let's add a function to export to the JavaScript, as shown in Listing 5-25.

```
...
 (func (export "to_string") (param $num i32)
❶ (call $set_dec_string
      (local.get $num) (global.get $dec_string_len))
❷ (call $print_string
      (i32.const 256) (global.get $dec_string_len))
  )
)
```

Listing 5-25: The to_string function

The function is very simple. It calls $set_dec_string ❶ passing in the number we want to convert to a string and the length of the string we want including the left padding. It then calls the JavaScript print_string ❷ function passing in the location of the string we created in linear memory (i32.const 256) and the length of that string.

Now that we've completed the *number_string.wat* file, we can compile it using wat2wasm in Listing 5-26.

```
wat2wasm number_string.wat
```

Listing 5-26: Compiling number_string.wat

Next, we need to write the JavaScript that will run our WebAssembly module. Create a file named *number_string.js* and add the code in Listing 5-27.

```
  const fs = require('fs');
  const bytes = fs.readFileSync(__dirname + '/number_string.wasm');
❶ const value = parseInt(process.argv[2]);
  let memory = new WebAssembly.Memory({ initial: 1 });

  (async () => {
    const obj =
      await WebAssembly.instantiate(new Uint8Array(bytes), {
        env: {
          buffer: memory,
❷        print_string: function (str_pos, str_len) {
            const bytes = new Uint8Array(memory.buffer,
              str_pos, str_len);
            const log_string = new TextDecoder('utf8').decode(bytes);
            // log_string is left padded.
❸          console.log(`>${log_string}!`);
          }
        }
      });
    obj.instance.exports.to_string(value);
  })();
```

Listing 5-27: The JavaScript that calls the WebAssembly module to convert the number to a string

The JavaScript code loads the WebAssembly module and takes an additional argument ❶ that we'll convert into a number string and left pads the string up to 16 characters. The WebAssembly module will call the print_string ❷ JavaScript function, which writes the string to the console, appending a > character to the beginning of the string and a ! character to the end. We place these extra characters into the console.log ❸ output to show where the string coming from the WebAssembly module begins and ends. You can run the JavaScript using the node command in Listing 5-28.

```
node number_string.js 1229
```

Listing 5-28: Use node to call the number_string.js file, passing in 1229.

The result is that the number 1229 is converted to a string, and the output in Listing 5-29 is logged to the console.

```
>           1229!
```

Listing 5-29: The number 1229 is left padded to 16 characters, beginning with > and ending with !.

In the next section, we'll use similar techniques to create a hexadecimal string.

Setting a Hexadecimal String

Converting an integer to a hexadecimal string is very similar to converting an integer to a decimal number, as we did in the preceding section. We use a bit mask to look at specific hex digits and a shift to remove the digit, similar to our decimal conveyor belt (see Figure 5-2).

Recall from Chapter 4 that four bits of data is called a nibble and a hexadecimal digit corresponds to one nibble of data. At a high level, the code needs to look at the integer one nibble at a time as one hexadecimal digit. We look at the lowest order nibble, also the lowest order hex digit, and then add that digit to the string. Rather than finding the remainder, we use a mask to only look at the last digit. Instead of dividing by 10, we remove the last hex digit by shifting off four bits (one nibble).

In hexadecimal, each digit represents a number from 0 to 15 instead of 0 to 9, so each digit in hex must be one of the following: 0, 1, 2, 3, 4, 5, 6, 7, 8, 9, A, B, C, D, E, F where the value of A = 10, B = 11, C = 12, D = 13, E = 14, and F = 15. We often use hexadecimal as an alternative to binary numbers, which can get extremely long to represent; for example, the number 233 in decimal is 11101001 in binary. We can shorten 233 in the binary form into the hexadecimal E9 because 1110 is 14 or E in hex, and 1001 is 9 in both decimal and hex.

We mask E9 (binary 1110 1001) using (i32.and) with a value of binary 0000 1111 (0F) to find the least significant nibble. Using i32.and in that way results in E9 masked into 09, as shown in Figure 5-3.

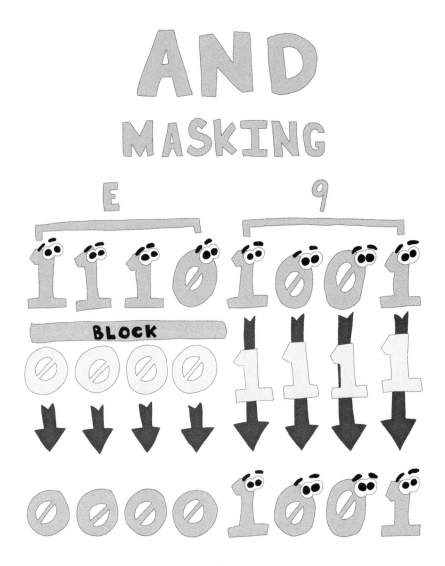

Figure 5-3: E9 byte masked to 09 with a mask of 0F (0000 1111)

We use a combination of a bit shift and an AND mask to convert the integer data into a hexadecimal string. Here, we create a hexadecimal version of the $set_dec_string function called $set_hex_string. This function sets a hexadecimal string based on a number passed into it. We can make this loop simpler than the loop in $set_dec_string because we can use simple bit manipulation to find the offset into $digits. The end of the function adds the extra ASCII characters 0x to indicate that the display string is in a hexadecimal format. Listing 5-30 shows what the $set_hex_string function looks like.

```
;; add this code before the $set_dec_string function
(global $hex_string_len  i32 (i32.const 16)) ;; hex character count
(data (i32.const 384) "                 0x0")    ;; hex string data

(func $set_hex_string (param $num i32) (param $string_len i32)
  (local $index       i32)
  (local $digit_char  i32)
  (local $digit_val   i32)
  (local $x_pos       i32)

  global.get $hex_string_len
  local.set $index ;; set the index to the number of hex characters

  (loop $digit_loop (block $break
    local.get $index
    i32.eqz
    br_if $break

    local.get $num
    i32.const 0xf ;; last 4 bits are 1
❶ i32.and        ;; the offset into $digits is in the last 4 bits of number

❷ local.set $digit_val  ;; the digit value is the last 4 bits
    local.get $num
    i32.eqz
❸ if                     ;; if $num == 0
      local.get $x_pos
      i32.eqz
      if
        local.get $index
      ❹ local.set $x_pos  ;; position of 'x' in the "0x" hex prefix
      else
        i32.const 32       ;; 32 is ascii space character
        local.set $digit_char
      end
    else
      ;; load character from 128 + $digit_val
    ❺ (i32.load8_u offset=128 (local.get $digit_val))
      local.set $digit_char
    end

    local.get $index
    i32.const 1
    i32.sub
❻ local.tee $index   ;; $index = $index - 1
    local.get $digit_char

    ;; store $digit_char at location 384+$index
❼ i32.store8 offset=384
```

```
      local.get $num
      i32.const 4
❽ i32.shr_u              ;; shifts 1 hexadecimal digit off $num
      local.set $num

      br $digit_loop
  ))

  local.get $x_pos
  i32.const 1
  i32.sub

  i32.const 120          ;; ascii x
❾ i32.store8 offset=384  ;; store 'x' in string

  local.get $x_pos
  i32.const 2
  i32.sub

  i32.const 48           ;; ascii '0'
❿ i32.store8 offset=384  ;; store "0x" at front of string
  ) ;; end $set_hex_string
...
```

Listing 5-30: Create a hexadecimal string from an integer. Add this before the $set_dec_string function.

In the $set_dec_string function, we use a modulo 10 to find each digit, and then shift that digit off by dividing it by 10. Instead of finding a remainder, the $set_hex_string function can use i32.and ❶ to mask all but the last four bits of $num. The value of that nibble is a single hexadecimal digit and is used to set $digit_val ❷.

If all remaining digits are 0 ❸, we set the position to put the hexadecimal string prefix of 0x in the local variable $x_pos ❹. Otherwise, if any remaining digits are 1 or greater, we use the value in $digit_val to load ❺ an ASCII value for that hexadecimal digit from the $digits string and store it into $digit_char. Then we decrement $offset ❻ and use that value to store the character in $digit_char into the $hex_string data ❼.

The loop then shifts off one hexadecimal digit (four bits) using i32.shr_u ❽, which shifts bits to the right. The last task this function does is append the 0x prefix to the string by using the value we set earlier in $x_pos as an offset and storing an ASCII x character in that position ❾. It then decrements the $x_pos position and stores the ASCII 0 ❿. The process looks a bit like Figure 5-4.

Figure 5-4: Creating a hexadecimal string from an integer

After adding the $set_hex_string function, we need to update the to_string function to call $set_hex_string and print the resulting string to the console. Update the to_string function to look like the code in Listing 5-31.

number_string .wat (part 5 of 7)

```
...
  (func (export "to_string") (param $num i32)
    (call $set_dec_string
      (local.get $num) (global.get $dec_string_len))
    (call $print_string (i32.const 256) (global.get $dec_string_len))

  ❶ (call $set_hex_string (local.get $num)
      (global.get $hex_string_len))
  ❷ (call $print_string (i32.const 384) (global.get $hex_string_len))
  )
)
```

Listing 5-31: Update to the to_string function calling $set_hex_string and $print_string

These two new statements call $set_hex_string ❶ to set the hexadecimal string in linear memory. We then call $print_string ❷ passing in the memory location of the hexadecimal string (i32.const 384) and the length of the string. No changes to the JavaScript file are necessary. All we need to do is recompile our WAT file, as shown in Listing 5-32.

```
wat2wasm number_string.wat
```

Listing 5-32: Compiling number_string.wat with wat2wasm

Once you've recompiled the WebAssembly module, you can run the *number_string.js* file using node, as shown in Listing 5-33.

```
node number_string.js 2049
```

Listing 5-33: Running number_string.js passing in the value 2049

Listing 5-34 shows the output.

```
>          2049!
>          0x801!
```

Listing 5-34: The second line is the output of the hexadecimal string conversion.

In the next section, we'll add a function to generate a string of binary digits from a 32-bit integer.

Setting a Binary String

The final format we'll cover is converting an integer to a string that represents the binary data. It's best to get an intuitive sense for binary numbers when you're working with low-level code. Having a better conceptual grasp on the numbers can sometimes help you create improvements in your code's performance by using bit manipulation as an alternative to decimal math. Computers work with binary, even if your code is working with decimal. Understanding what the computer is doing is often helpful when you're trying to improve your code's performance.

We'll create the $set_bin_string function, which uses a double loop to separate every 4-bit nibble with a space character to make it more readable. We'll use (i32.and) against the number 1 to see whether the last bit is a 1 or a 0, and then shift a single bit off the number every pass through the inner loop of the function. Listing 5-35 shows what the code looks like.

number_string .wat (part 6 of 7)
```
...
;; add this code before the $set_hex_string function
(global $bin_string_len  i32 (i32.const 40))
(data (i32.const 512) " 0000 0000 0000 0000 0000 0000 0000 0000")

(func $set_bin_string (param $num i32) (param $string_len i32)
  (local $index i32)
  (local $loops_remaining i32)
  (local $nibble_bits i32)

  global.get $bin_string_len
  local.set $index

❶ i32.const 8   ;; there are 8 nibbles in 32 bits (32/4 = 8)
  local.set $loops_remaining  ;; outer loop separates nibbles

❷ (loop $bin_loop (block $outer_break   ;; outer loop for spaces
    local.get $index
    i32.eqz
```

```
      br_if $outer_break        ;; stop looping when $index is 0

    i32.const 4
❸ local.set $nibble_bits        ;; 4 bits in each nibble

❹ (loop $nibble_loop (block $nibble_break ;; inner loop for digits
    local.get $index
    i32.const 1
    i32.sub
    local.set $index            ;; decrement $index

    local.get $num
    i32.const 1
❺ i32.and    ;; i32.and 1 results in 1 if last bit is 1 else 0
    if          ;; if the last bit is a 1
      local.get $index
      i32.const 49              ;; ascii '1' is 49
    ❻ i32.store8 offset=512    ;; store '1' at 512 + $index

    else                        ;; else executes if last bit was 0
      local.get $index
      i32.const 48              ;; ascii '0' is 48
    ❼ i32.store8 offset=512    ;; store '0' at 512 + $index
    end

    local.get $num
    i32.const 1
❽ i32.shr_u                     ;; $num shifted right 1 bit
    local.set $num              ;; shift off the last bit of $num

    local.get $nibble_bits
    i32.const 1
    i32.sub
    local.tee $nibble_bits      ;; decrement $nibble_bits
    i32.eqz                     ;; $nibble_bits == 0
❾ br_if $nibble_break          ;; break when $nibble_bits == 0

    br $nibble_loop
  )) ;; end $nibble_loop

    local.get $index
    i32.const 1
    i32.sub
    local.tee $index           ;; decrement $index
    i32.const 32               ;; ascii space
❿ i32.store8 offset=512        ;; store ascii space at 512+$index

    br $bin_loop
  )) ;; end $bin_loop
)
...
```

*Listing 5-35: Create a binary string from an integer. Add this code before the $set_hex
_string function.*

The $set_bin_string function has two loops. The outer loop puts a space between each of the nibbles. Because we are working with 32-bit numbers in this code, there are eight nibbles ❶ that we need to loop over. We label the outer loop $bin_loop ❷, and the block we break from is called $outer_break ❷.

Before the inner loop, we need to set the local variable $nibble_bits to 4 ❸. The code loops over four bits for each nibble in the inner loop. Inside the inner loop $nibble_loop ❹, we place a $nibble_block block that can break out of the inner loop ❹. Inside $nibble_loop, we use an (i32.and) ❺ expression along with an if/else statement to determine whether the last bit in the $num variable is 1 or 0. If it's 1, we use an i32.store8 ❻ statement to store an ASCII 1 in the linear memory address $index + 512. If it isn't 1, we store an ASCII 0 in that location ❼.

Next, we need to shift that bit off for the next pass through the loop. As we did in the $set_hex_string function, we're using a (i32.shr_u) ❽ expression for this shifting, but this time we're shifting off a single bit instead of four bits. After looping through the $nibble loop four times, we break ❾ out of it and store an ASCII space character at the linear memory position $offset + $bin_string ❿.

Now we can call $set_bin_string to print the value of our string from the to_string function. Update the to_string function with the code in Listing 5-36.

number_string *.wat (part 7 of 7)*

```
...
(func (export "to_string") (param $num i32)
  (call $set_dec_string
    (local.get $num) (global.get $dec_string_len))
  (call $print_string (i32.const 256) (global.get $dec_string_len))
  (call $set_hex_string
    (local.get $num) (global.get $hex_string_len))
  (call $print_string (i32.const 384) (global.get $hex_string_len))
❶ (call $set_bin_string
    (local.get $num) (global.get $bin_string_len))
❷ (call $print_string (i32.const 512) (global.get $bin_string_len))
  )
)
```

Listing 5-36: Adding $set_bin_string to the to_string function

The first of the two call statements we just added (call $set_bin_string ❶) sets the binary string using the function defined in Listing 5-35. The second call statement (call $print_string ❷) prints the binary string to the console. Now let's recompile the WebAssembly module, as shown in Listing 5-37.

```
wat2wasm number_string.wat
```

Listing 5-37: Recompiling number_string.wat with the binary string function

We can now run the *number_string.js* file using the node command in Listing 5-38.

```
node number_string.js 4103
```

Listing 5-38: Running number_string.js *with the binary string WebAssembly module*

The output in Listing 5-39 will be logged to the console.

```
>              4103!
>            0x1007!
> 0000 0000 0000 0000 0001 0000 0000 0111!
```

Listing 5-39: The binary string logged to the console

Summary

This chapter focused on how to work with strings in WAT. You learned about the ASCII and Unicode character formats. You stored string objects in linear memory and learned how to use JavaScript to retrieve the strings and output them to the command line. We covered how to pass string data from WebAssembly to JavaScript and examined two popular methods for string management, null-terminated strings and length-prefixed strings. You copied a string from one location in linear memory to another, using a byte-by-byte copy and a 64-bit copy. Then we explored how to convert integer data into number strings in decimal, hexadecimal, and binary format. In the next chapter, we'll focus on using linear memory in WAT.

6

LINEAR MEMORY

In this chapter, we'll examine what linear memory is, how to use it to share data between JavaScript and WebAssembly code, and how to create it from within JavaScript. We'll also update linear memory from WebAssembly and then use those updates from within the JavaScript code.

One common task in computer games is collision detection, detecting and appropriately reacting to two objects touching. The number of computations required grows exponentially as you add objects. Collision detection is a great candidate for building in WebAssembly. In this chapter, we'll create a list of circles defined randomly in the JavaScript, and then add that circle data to the WebAssembly linear memory. Then we'll use that data to determine whether any of those circles collide.

WebAssembly shines best when you can pass it tons of data that requires significant processing and let it run. A WebAssembly module can perform math faster than JavaScript. However, each interaction between JavaScript and the WebAssembly module has an associated cost. You can use linear memory to load significant amounts of data in JavaScript for processing within a WebAssembly module.

Linear Memory in WebAssembly

Linear memory acts as one giant array of data that can be shared between WebAssembly and JavaScript. If you're familiar with low-level programming, linear memory is similar to heap memory in native applications. If you're familiar with JavaScript, think of it as one giant ArrayBuffer object. Languages like C and C++ create local variables by allocating memory on the computer's stack. The stack-allocated local variables are released from memory as soon as the function finishes executing. This efficient process means that allocating and deallocating data on the stack is as simple as incrementing and decrementing a stack pointer. Your application simply increments the stack pointer, and voilà, you have a new allocated variable, as depicted in Figure 6-1.

Figure 6-1: The stack pointer

The stack works great for local variables. However, one limitation in WAT is that local variables that use the stack can only be one of four types, all of which are numeric. Sometimes, you might require more sophisticated data structures, such as strings, structures, arrays, and objects.

Allocation commands, like malloc in C and new in C++ and JavaScript, allocate onto the heap, and the memory management libraries included with those languages must look for a free section of memory on the heap large enough to hold the required block of memory. Over time that might result in memory fragmentation, where allocated memory segments are separated by unallocated memory, as illustrated in Figure 6-2.

WebAssembly linear memory is allocated in large chunks called *pages*, which, once allocated, cannot be deallocated. WebAssembly memory is also a bit more like assembly language memory management: once you've allocated your chosen number of pages to your WebAssembly module, you, as the programmer, must keep track of what you're using memory for and where it is. In the next few sections, we'll look more closely at how to use linear memory by exploring memory pages.

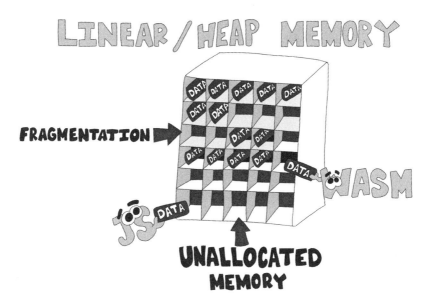

Figure 6-2: Linear memory passed data from JavaScript and WebAssembly

Pages

Pages are the smallest chunk of data that can be allocated for a WebAssembly module. At the time of this writing, all WebAssembly pages are 64KB in size. In the current version, WebAssembly 1.0, you cannot change that size, although the WebAssembly Community Group has an ongoing proposal to make the page size variable based on the application's needs. The maximum number of pages that an application can allocate at the time of this writing is 32,767, an overall maximum memory size of 2GB. This maximum memory allocation is plenty for web apps but is limiting for server-based applications. Increasing the page size could allow server apps to increase the maximum amount of linear memory they can allocate. For embedded WebAssembly applications, 64KB can be too large; for example, the ATmega328 only has 32KB of Flash memory. WebAssembly updates might remove this limitation by the time you read this.

NOTE *The WebAssembly Community Group is currently working to increase the maximum number of pages to 65,535, which would allocate 4GB of memory. It's likely that by the time this book is published, the maximum size of linear memory will be 4GB rather than 2GB.*

You can create the number of pages your app will use either inside the WebAssembly module or in the embedding environment for import.

Creating Pages in Your Code

To allocate a page of linear memory in WAT, use a simple (memory) expression, like the one in Listing 6-1.

```
(memory 1)
```

Listing 6-1: Declaring a page of memory in WAT

Passing 1 into the memory expression instructs the module to set aside one page of linear memory. To allocate the maximum amount of memory you can currently allocate to a WebAssembly module at runtime, use the expression in Listing 6-2.

```
(memory 32_767)
```

Listing 6-2: Declaring the maximum number of memory pages

Attempting to pass 32_767 into the (memory) expression results in a compile error. Memory created using the (memory) expression isn't accessible to the embedding environment unless you include an (export) expression.

Creating Memory in the Embedded Environment

The other way to create the linear memory is inside the embedding environment. If the embedding environment is JavaScript, the code to create that memory is new WebAssembly.Memory as in Listing 6-3.

```
const memory = new WebAssembly.Memory({initial: 1});
```

Listing 6-3: Creating a WebAssembly Memory object in JavaScript

You could then access it from the WebAssembly module using the (import) expression in Listing 6-4.

```
(import "js" "mem" (memory 1))
```

Listing 6-4: Importing a page of memory allocated in JavaScript

Using import requires you to create a Memory object in JavaScript using the WebAssembly.Memory class, and then to pass it into the WebAssembly module when you initialize it through an import object. Create a file called *pointer.js* and add the JavaScript code in Listing 6-5, which creates a WebAssembly Memory object.

pointer.js
```
const fs = require('fs');
const bytes = fs.readFileSync(__dirname + '/pointer.wasm');
const memory = new WebAssembly.Memory({❶initial: 1, ❷maximum: 4});

const importObject = {
  env: {
  ❸ mem: memory,
  }
};

( async () => {
```

```
    let obj = await WebAssembly.instantiate(new Uint8Array(bytes),
                                ❹ importObject);
    let pointer_value = obj.instance.exports.get_ptr();
    console.log(`pointer_value=${pointer_value}`);
})();
```

Listing 6-5: Initialize WebAssembly linear memory and pass it to the WebAssembly module.

On creation, this code passes in an object with two initialization values. The initial ❶ argument is required and by passing it 1, we instruct the JavaScript engine to set aside one page of linear memory (64KB). The second value maximum ❷ is optional and lets the browser know that we're likely to want to increase the size of the linear memory later, and we probably won't want to grow memory to more than four pages. You can increase the size of linear memory by calling the memory.grow method. You don't need to set a maximum value to grow your memory, but passing in a maximum value tells the browser to set aside more memory than the initial value because a call to grow is likely. If you attempt to grow your linear memory to more than the maximum value you pass in, the application will throw an error. After creating the memory object, we pass it to the WebAssembly module through the importObject in env.mem ❸. The JavaScript passes import Object into the module on instantiation ❹.

Pointers

A *pointer* is a variable that references a location in memory. Pointers have a variety of applications in computer science, but in this context, we'll use them to point to data structures in linear memory. Figure 6-3 shows a pointer pointing to memory location 5, which has a value of 99.

Figure 6-3: Pointer to the fifth byte in memory

WebAssembly pointers behave differently from those you might be familiar with in C or C++ that can point to local variables or variables on the heap. The C code in Listing 6-6 creates a pointer called ptr that points to the address of a local variable x.

```
int x = 25;
int *ptr = &x;
```

Listing 6-6: Example of setting pointer values in C

The pointer ptr is set to the address of the x variable, which is a local variable that has an address on the stack. WebAssembly doesn't have a distinct pointer type, such as C's int* integer pointer type. WebAssembly's linear memory is a large array of data. When you represent a pointer in WAT, you must put the data in the linear memory; the pointer is then an i32 index to that data. The variable x in Listing 6-6 receives an address in linear memory when compiling the program to WebAssembly. Unlike in C, WAT cannot create a pointer to a local or global variable. To get the C kind of pointer functionality in WebAssembly, you can set a global variable to a specific location in linear memory and use that global variable to set or retrieve the value stored in WebAssembly linear memory, as shown in Listing 6-7.

pointer.wat
```
(module
❶ (memory 1)
❷ (global $pointer i32 (i32.const 128))
❸ (func $init
   ❹ (i32.store
     ❺ (global.get $pointer)   ;; store at address $pointer
     ❻ (i32.const 99)          ;; value stored
       )
   )
❼ (func (export "get_ptr") (result i32)
❽ (i32.load (global.get $pointer)) ;; return value at location $pointer
   )
❾ (start $init)
)
```

Listing 6-7: Simulating pointers in WAT

This module creates a single page of linear memory ❶ and a global $pointer ❷ that points to the memory location 128. We create a function $init ❸ that sets the value of the memory location pointed to by $pointer to 99 using the (i32.store) ❹ expression. The first parameter passed to (i32.store) ❺ is the location in memory where the value is stored, and the second parameter ❻ is the value you want to store. To retrieve the value from this pointer location, you use the i32.load ❽ expression passing in the memory location you want to retrieve. We create a function "get_ptr" ❼ to retrieve this value. Then the (start $init) ❾ statement calls $init ❸ as a module initialization function. The start statement declares a given function to be the initialization function for the module. This function will automatically execute when the module is instantiated.

Once you've compiled the *pointer.wasm* file and executed it with node, you should see the following output:

```
pointer_value=99
```

JavaScript Memory Object

Now that we have some idea of how linear memory works, we'll create a WebAssembly memory object, initialize the data from within a WebAssembly module, and then access that data from JavaScript. When you're working with linear memory, there's a good chance that you'll want to access it from WebAssembly and the embedding environment. In this case, the embedding environment is JavaScript, so we'll define the linear memory there to have access to it before the WebAssembly module is initialized. This WAT module is similar to Listing 6-7 but will be importing linear memory from JavaScript.

Creating the WebAssembly Memory Object

Create a file named *store_data.wat* and add the code in Listing 6-8 to it.

store_data.wat
```
(module
❶ (import "env" "mem" (memory 1))
❷ (global $data_addr (import "env" "data_addr") i32)
❸ (global $data_count (import "env" "data_count") i32)

❹ (func $store_data (param $index i32) (param $value i32)
     (i32.store
      (i32.add
       (global.get $data_addr) ;; add $data_addr to the $index*4 (i32=4 bytes)
       (i32.mul (i32.const 4) (local.get $index)) ;; multiply $index by 4
      )
      (local.get $value) ;; value stored
     )
   )


❺ (func $init
     (local $index i32)

   ❻ (loop $data_loop
        local.get $index

        local.get $index
        i32.const 5
        i32.mul

      ❼ call $store_data ;; called with parameters $index and $index * 5

        local.get $index
        i32.const 1
        i32.add          ;; $index++

        local.tee $index
      ❽ global.get $data_count
        i32.lt_u
        br_if $data_loop
     )
```

```
❾ (call $store_data (i32.const 0) (i32.const 1))

  )

❿ (start $init)
)
```

Listing 6-8: Creating a linear memory object in WebAssembly

The module in Listing 6-8 imports its linear memory ❶ from the Java-
Script embedding environment, which we'll define in a moment. From
JavaScript it imports the address of the data we'll load in the global variable
$data_addr ❷. It also imports $data_count ❸, which contains the number of
i32 integers we'll store when the module initializes. The $store_data ❹ func-
tion takes in an index and a value, and sets the data location ($data_addr +
$index * 4) to $value (we multiply by 4 because the i32 type is four bytes).
Using $data_addr, an imported global variable, allows the JavaScript to
decide the location in the memory module to store these values.

As in Listing 6-6, the $init ❺ function executes on module initializa-
tion because of the (start $init) ❿ statement. Unlike the prior $init function, this function initializes the data in a loop ❻. A loop can be a useful
way to initialize data in certain parts of linear memory to the same value
or some value that might be calculated in the loop. This loop sets several
32-bit integers based on the $data_count ❽ global variable that the module
imports from JavaScript. When this loop calls $store_data ❼, it passes in an
index that is the number of times the loop has completed and a value that is
$index * 5. I chose the value $index * 5 so when we display the data, you'll see
the data values counting up by 5.

After the loop, we add one more call to $store_data ❾ to set the first data
value in the array to 1. If we don't initialize it with a value, the memory buffer begins with all data set to 0. Because the loop sets the first data value to
0, it wouldn't be clear where the set data begins when we look at the data in
JavaScript. Setting it to 1 makes the beginning of the data set more apparent
when we display it from the JavaScript in the next section.

After you've finished creating the *store_data.wat* file, compile it using
wat2wasm to generate a *store_data.wasm* file.

Logging to the Console with Colors

Before writing the *store_data.js* portion, let's briefly look at a node module
called *colors* that allows you to log lines to the console using your choice of
colors. In later sections, we'll use this package to make it easier to see different results in our output data. To install colors, use the npm command, as
shown in Listing 6-9.

```
npm i colors
```

Listing 6-9: Using npm to install the colors module

Now we can require our app to use it, which allows us to modify the string type in JavaScript to include attributes that set colors, bold text, and several other features. Create a file named *colors.js* and add the code in Listing 6-10.

colors.js

```
const colors = require('colors');

console.log('RED COLOR'.red.bold);  // logs bold red text
console.log('blue color'.blue);      // logs blue text
```

Listing 6-10: Log to console in color

When you run *colors.js* using node, as shown in Listing 6-11, the logged output will appear with the colors we specified.

```
node colors.js
```

Listing 6-11: Run color.js and log with colors to the console.

You should now see the output in Listing 6-12 with the first line in red and the second in blue.

```
RED COLOR
blue color
```

Listing 6-12: The colors module applied

We'll use the colors module in future apps to improve the output's appearance in the console. In the book, the red output will be black but in bold. Let's move forward by creating a *store_data.js* file in the next section.

Creating the JavaScript in store_data.js

Now we need a *store_data.js* JavaScript file to execute the *store_data.wasm* module. We create that JavaScript file using Listing 6-13.

store_data.js
(part 1 of 2)

```
const colors = require('colors'); // allow console logs with color
const fs = require('fs');
const bytes = fs.readFileSync(__dirname + '/store_data.wasm');

// allocate a 64K block of memory
❶ const memory = new WebAssembly.Memory({initial: 1 });
// 32-bit data view of the memory buffer
❷ const mem_i32 = new Uint32Array(memory.buffer);

❸ const data_addr = 32; // the address of the first byte of our data

// The 32-bit index of the beginning of our data
❹ const data_i32_index = data_addr / 4;
❺ const data_count = 16; // the number of 32-bit integers to set

❻ const importObject = { // The objects WASM imports from JavaScript
   env: {
     mem: memory,
```

```
            data_addr: data_addr,
            data_count: data_count
        }
    };
    ...
```

Listing 6-13: A WebAssembly linear memory buffer and importObject *with global imports*

We create three constants, the first of which creates a new WebAssembly
.Memory ❶ object that we'll use when we initialize the WebAssembly module. The constant mem_i32 ❷ provides a 32-bit integer view into the memory
buffer. It's crucial to keep in mind that this isn't a copy of the data in the
buffer but instead is a specific way to view that buffer as an array of 32-bit
unsigned integers. When we change the values in the memory buffer from
inside the WebAssembly module, we can use this mem_i32 view to look at the
changes to those values. The constant data_addr ❸ is the byte location of the
data we set in the WebAssembly module. This location is the *byte index m*,
not the 32-bit integer array number.

Because a 32-bit integer is four bytes, we need a starting data index that
is the data_addr constant divided by 4. We set that value in data_i32_index ❹.
Then we have the number of 32-bit integer values set in the module defined
by const data_count ❺. The last const in this section of code is the import
Object ❻. The importObject contains three imported data objects for the
WebAssembly module.

The final portion of the JavaScript in Listing 6-14 uses an IIFE to
instantiate the WebAssembly module and output the values in linear memory to the console.

store_data.js
(part 2 of 2)
```
...
( async () => {
❶ let obj = await WebAssembly.instantiate(new Uint8Array(bytes),
                                            importObject );

❷ for( let i = 0; i < data_i32_index + data_count + 4; i++ ) {
    let data = mem_i32[i];
    if (data !== 0) {
    ❸ console.log(`data[${i}]=${data}`.red.bold);
    }
    else {
    ❹ console.log(`data[${i}]=${data}`);
    }

  }
})();
```

*Listing 6-14: Outputting the data values inside linear memory after the IIFE instantiates the
WebAssembly module*

This final portion of the JavaScript instantiates the *store_data.wasm* ❶
module, passing in the importObject we created in Listing 6-13. After initializing the WebAssembly module, the data in the memory buffer will
change because the $init function within the WAT code runs during the

initialization. We then loop ❷ over the mem_i32 array starting at the first address in the memory buffer and displaying four integers after the data is set. This loop displays the value in mem_i32 in the browser by logging it to the console in red ❸ if the value isn't 0 and in the default console color ❹ if it is.

Use node to run *store_data.js*; you should see the output in Listing 6-15 logged to the console.

```
data[0]=0
data[1]=0
data[2]=0
data[3]=0
data[4]=0
data[5]=0
data[6]=0
data[7]=0
data[8]=1
data[9]=5
data[10]=10
data[11]=15
data[12]=20
data[13]=25
data[14]=30
data[15]=35
data[16]=40
data[17]=45
data[18]=50
data[19]=55
data[20]=60
data[21]=65
data[22]=70
data[23]=75
data[24]=0
data[25]=0
data[26]=0
data[27]=0
```

Listing 6-15: Data output

The first data element that was set by the WebAssembly module is data[8], which is where the red output begins. The value 8 is the value in the data _i32_index constant, which is one fourth the value in data_addr. There are 16 integers set in the code, because we've set the const data_count to a value of 16. In the data in Listing 6-15, all data elements that are 0 weren't set in the WebAssembly module. You can see that the first eight numbers as well as the last four are 0, and they all appear in the default console color.

Collision Detection

Previously, we created the memory buffer object inside JavaScript, but we initialized it from the WebAssembly module. This time, we'll initialize the memory buffer inside JavaScript with values generated in the JavaScript. We'll also create more interesting data structures that will handle our collision detection data. When modifying the data in the WebAssembly memory buffer, we want to group the data into structures to make it manageable. We'll create a set of random circle definitions in JavaScript, defined with an x- and y-coordinate, and a radius. The JavaScript will then set those values in the WebAssembly memory buffer. To organize objects in linear memory, you use a combination of a base address, a stride, and an offset.

Base Address, Stride, and Offset

When working with linear memory inside our WebAssembly module, we need to understand our data structures at a low level. In our JavaScript, we work with the data in linear memory as a JavaScript typed array. Inside the WebAssembly module, linear memory is more like a memory heap, or a large array of bytes. When we want to create an array of data structures, we need to know the *starting address* (base address) of that array, the *stride* (distance in bytes between each structure), and the *offset* of any structure's attributes (how far into a structure can we find our attribute).

We'll work with a structure in our linear memory that has four attributes: an x- and y-coordinate, a radius, and a hit flag. We'll set the stride as a *unit stride*, as shown in Figure 6-4, which means that the distance between each structure in our array matches the size of the structure.

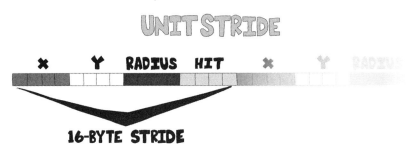

Figure 6-4: Setting a unit stride

To get the memory address of the specific data structure we want to access, we multiply the structure's index by the stride and add the base address. The *base address* is the starting address of our array of structures.

As an alternative to unit stride, you could pad your stride. If a developer decided to align their structure addresses to power-of-two, they might add unused bytes (called *padding*) to the end of their structures. For example, if we wanted our structure to align with 16-byte addresses, we could add four bytes of padding to the end of our structure, giving it a stride of 16, as shown in Figure 6-5.

However, we have no need for padding in this example. Each attribute of our data structure has an offset. For example, say we have two 32-bit integer attributes, x and y, that are the first two attributes in the data structure, respectively. The first attribute, x, is at the beginning of the data structure and so has an offset of 0. Because the x attribute is a 32-bit integer, it takes up the first four bytes of the data structure. That means the y offset begins on the fifth byte with an offset of 4 (bytes 0, 1, 2, and 3). Using a base address (the starting address of our data structure), stride, and offset for each attribute, we can construct an array of data structures.

Figure 6-5: Padding a stride

NOTE   *The syntax for load and store has a modifier called offset, which allows you to offset the address parameter by some constant integer value. This isn't quite the same as the attribute offset we refer to here.*

Loading Data Structures from JavaScript

Let's start by creating the JavaScript file for a new example app named *data_structures.js*. In this app, we'll create data structures that represent circles in memory. Later, we'll perform a collision detection check between those circles. Add the code in Listing 6-16 to *data_structures.js*.

data_structures.js
(part 1 of 3)

```
const colors = require('colors'); // allow console logs with color
const fs = require('fs');
const bytes = fs.readFileSync(__dirname + '/data_structures.wasm');
  // allocate a 64K block of memory
❶ const memory = new WebAssembly.Memory({initial: 1});

  // 32-bit view of memory buffer
  const mem_i32 = new Uint32Array(memory.buffer);

  const obj_base_addr = 0; // the address of the first byte of our data
❷ const obj_count = 32;    // the number of structures
❸ const obj_stride = 16;   // 16-byte stride

  // structure attribute offsets
❹ const x_offset = 0;
❺ const y_offset = 4;
  const radius_offset = 8;
  const collision_offset = 12;

  // 32-bit integer indexes
  const obj_i32_base_index = obj_base_addr / 4; // 32-bit data index
  const obj_i32_stride = obj_stride / 4;        // 32-bit stride

  // offsets in the 32-bit integer array
❻ const x_offset_i32 = x_offset / 4;
  const y_offset_i32 = y_offset / 4;
```

```
      const radius_offset_i32 = radius_offset / 4;
      const collision_offset_i32 = collision_offset / 4;

❼ const importObject = { // The objects WASM imports from JavaScript
     env: {
       mem: memory,
       obj_base_addr: obj_base_addr,
       obj_count: obj_count,
       obj_stride: obj_stride,
       x_offset: x_offset,
       y_offset: y_offset,
       radius_offset: radius_offset,
       collision_offset: collision_offset,
     }
  };
  ...
```

Listing 6-16: Setting the constants to define the structure of the collision detection program

First, we create a series of const values used to create structures in the
WebAssembly memory buffer. As in Listing 6-16, this code creates a single
64KB page of WebAssembly memory ❶ and a 32-bit unsigned integer view
into that data. The obj_base_addr constant sets the base address of the data
structures to 0, the very first byte of memory in the page.

We set the obj_count ❷ const to the number of structures set in this
code. The obj_stride ❸ constant holds the number of bytes in the structure. We set this to 16 because we have four 32-bit integers in this structure,
which is 16 bytes. The next group of const declarations contains the attribute offsets.

The x_offset ❹ is the offset of x from the start of the structure, so is the
number of bytes into each structure in the x value location. The y_offset ❺
is the number of bytes into the structure in the y value location, and has a
value of 4 because the x value is a 32-bit integer, pushing the y value into
the fifth byte in the structure. We then set the offset for the radius ❻ attribute and collision ❼ attribute.

We calculate the integer index and stride by dividing the byte address
by 4 and the stride by 4. The reason is that the byte address and stride are
the number of bytes, and the integer index is 32-bit integers (4 bytes). We
also need to find the indexes into the integer array, which we calculate by
dividing the byte indexes by 4 ❻ as well. The importObject ❼ has been modified to include the new const values we've added.

With the constants defined, we'll create a series of randomly sized
circles for the program to use. As mentioned earlier, a circle is defined by
x- and y-coordinates and a radius. We'll randomly define the circles' x- and
y-coordinates with values from 0 to 99 and a radius that is between 1 and
11. The code in Listing 6-17 loops over the memory object, setting values in
the memory buffer to random values for each of the structures.

data_structures.js
(part 2 of 3)
```
  ...
  for( let i = 0; i < obj_count; i++ ) {
  ❶ let index = obj_i32_stride * i + obj_i32_base_index;
```

```
❷ let x = Math.floor( Math.random() * 100 );
  let y = Math.floor( Math.random() * 100 );
  let r = Math.ceil( Math.random() * 10 );

❸ mem_i32[index + x_offset_i32] = x;
  mem_i32[index + y_offset_i32] = y;
  mem_i32[index + radius_offset_i32] = r;
}
...
```

Listing 6-17: Initializing the circles with random x- and y-coordinates and a radius

The loop gets an index for each of the structures ❶ for the collision detection circles. The x, y, and radius r values ❷ are set to random values. Those random values are then used to set the memory values ❸ based on the object index and the attribute offsets.

Displaying the Results

Next, we need to instantiate the *data_structures.wasm* module, which runs the $init function, which runs collision detection between each of the circles we randomly generated in this data test. Listing 6-18 shows the code added to *data_structures.js*.

data_structures.js
(part 3 of 3)
```
...
( async () => {
❶ let obj = await WebAssembly.instantiate(new Uint8Array(bytes),
                                            importObject );

❷ for( let i = 0; i < obj_count; i++ ) {
  ❸ let index = obj_i32_stride * i + obj_i32_base_index;

  ❹ let x = mem_i32[index+x_offset_i32].toString().padStart(2, ' ');
    let y = mem_i32[index+y_offset_i32].toString().padStart(2, ' ');
    let r = mem_i32[index+radius_offset_i32].toString()
                  .padStart(2,' ');
    let i_str = i.toString().padStart(2, '0');
    let c = !!mem_i32[index + collision_offset_i32];

    if (c) {
    ❺ console.log(`obj[${i_str}] x=${x} y=${y} r=${r} collision=${c}`
          .red.bold);
    }
    else {
    ❻ console.log(`obj[${i_str}] x=${x} y=${y} r=${r} collision=${c}`
          .green);
    }
  }
})();
```

Listing 6-18: After WebAssembly runs, the code loops over linear memory looking for circle collisions.

This IIFE function instantiates the WebAssembly module ❶ and then loops over the objects in the mem_i32 array ❷. This loop gets an index for the structure using the stride, the index, and the base index value ❸. We then use this calculated index to get the x, y, radius, and collision values from the mem_i32 ❹ array. These values are logged to the console in red ❺ if there was a collision or green ❻ if there wasn't.

We now have JavaScript that loads a series of structures that define circles with x- and y-coordinates randomly chosen with values between 0 and 100. Each circle also has a radius with a value randomly chosen between 1 and 10. The WebAssembly memory buffer is initialized with these values. The JavaScript will set the appropriate offset and stride values in the import Object. In addition to the x, y, and radius in each structure, there are four bytes set aside to hold a collision value. This value is 1 if the circle collides with another circle and 0 if it doesn't. The WebAssembly module's initialization (start) function calculates the collisions. Once the WebAssembly module initializes, the console displays the results of this collision check. At this point, we've not yet defined the WebAssembly module. Let's do that next.

Collision Detection Function

In other sections, we've defined the WAT code before the JavaScript. In this section, the JavaScript initializes the values that define the circles in the array of structures. For that reason, we'll be writing the JavaScript first in this section. When you're doing collision detection between two circles, you use the Pythagorean theorem to determine whether the distance between the centers of your circles is greater than the sum of the circles' radii. The WAT code in this section loops over each of the circles we've defined in the WebAssembly memory, comparing it to every other circle to see whether they collide. The details of collision detection aren't the focus of this section, so we won't go into it too deeply. It's simply a means to demonstrate how you can separate your data into structures and use that data to perform computations with your WAT code.

The first portion of the WAT code defines the imports from the JavaScript. Listing 6-19 shows the beginning of the WAT module.

data_structures
.wat (part 1 of 6)

```
(module
  (import "env" "mem" (memory 1))
❶ (global $obj_base_addr  (import "env" "obj_base_addr") i32)
❷ (global $obj_count     (import "env" "obj_count") i32)
❸ (global $obj_stride     (import "env" "obj_stride") i32)

  ;; attribute offset locations
❹ (global $x_offset       (import "env" "x_offset") i32)
❺ (global $y_offset       (import "env" "y_offset") i32)
❻ (global $radius_offset  (import "env" "radius_offset") i32)
❼ (global $collision_offset (import "env" "collision_offset") i32)
  ...
```

Listing 6-19: Importing global variables that define the data structure

The global variables passed into the WebAssembly module define the layout of the linear memory and the data structures within it. The $obj_base_addr ❶ global variable is the location in memory where the circle structures are defined. The $obj_count ❷ global variable is the number of circles defined in linear memory. The $obj_stride ❸ global variable is the number of bytes between each of the circle definitions. Then we import values for each of the attributes. The $x_offset ❹, $y_offset ❺, $radius_offset ❻, and $collision_offset ❼ are the number of bytes between the start of the object's x, y, radius, and collision flag values. These must be set inside this module.

Next, we'll define the $collision_check function. The details of how this function works are only valuable if you're interested in how circle collision detection works. But as an overview, it uses the Pythagorean theorem to determine whether the distance between two circles is less than the sum of the circle's radii. To briefly explain, let's label the radius of the first circle R_1, the radius of the second circle R_2, and the distance between the circles D, as shown in Figure 6-6. No collision occurs if $R_1 + R_2$ is less than D.

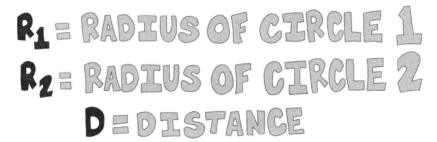

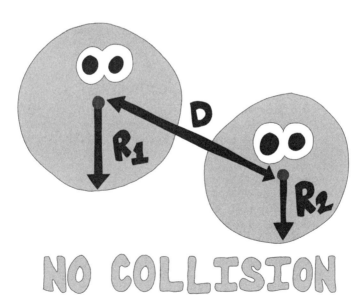

Figure 6-6: There is no collision if $R_1 + R_2$ is less than the distance between the circles.

If the distance is less than $R_1 + R_2$, we have a collision, as shown in Figure 6-7.

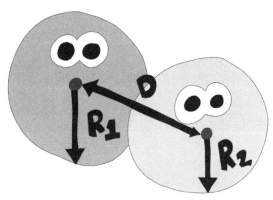

Figure 6-7: $R_1 + R_2$ is greater than the distance between the circles.

Listing 6-20 shows the code for the $collision_check function.

data_structures
.wat (part 2 of 6)

```
...
❶ (func $collision_check
     (param $x1 i32) (param $y1 i32) (param $r1 i32)
     (param $x2 i32) (param $y2 i32) (param $r2 i32)
     (result i32)

     (local $x_diff_sq i32)
     (local $y_diff_sq i32)
     (local $r_sum_sq i32)

     local.get $x1
     local.get $x2
     i32.sub
     local.tee $x_diff_sq
     local.get $x_diff_sq
     i32.mul
   ❷ local.set $x_diff_sq  ;; ($x1 - $x2) * ($x1 - $x2)

     local.get $y1
```

```
        local.get $y2
        i32.sub
        local.tee $y_diff_sq
        local.get $y_diff_sq
        i32.mul
          ❸ local.set $y_diff_sq  ;; ($y1 - $y2) * ($y1 - $y2)

        local.get $r1
        local.get $r2
        i32.add
        local.tee $r_sum_sq
        local.get $r_sum_sq
        i32.mul
          ❹ local.tee $r_sum_sq   ;; ($r1 + $r2) * ($r1 + $r2)

        local.get $x_diff_sq
        local.get $y_diff_sq
          ❺ i32.add  ;; pythagorean theorem A squared + B squared = C squared

          ❻ i32.gt_u ;; if distance is less than sum of the radii return true
    )
    ...
```

Listing 6-20: A WebAssembly collision detection function

This function takes in the x, y, and radius attributes of two circles ❶ and then returns 1 if they overlap and 0 if they don't. It first finds the x distance between the two circles by subtracting $x2 from $x1. It then squares that value and stores it in $x_diff_sq ❷; then it finds the y distance between the two circles by subtracting $y2 from $y1. It squares the result of that subtraction and stores it in $y_diff_sq ❸. What we're building toward is the Pythagorean theorem $A^2 + B^2 = C^2$ ❺. In this scenario, $x_diff_sq is A^2, and $y_diff_sq is B^2. The sum of these two values is C^2, which is compared with the sum of the radii squared ❹. If $radius^2$ is greater than C^2, the circles overlap and the function returns 1; otherwise, the function returns 0. The function makes this decision using the i32.gt_u ❻ expression.

After the $collision_check function, we need a few helper functions. The $get_attr helper function takes an object base address parameter and an attribute offset parameter and returns the value in linear memory at that address location. Listing 6-21 shows that function.

data_structures
.wat (part 3 of 6)
```
    ...
  ❶ (func $get_attr (param $obj_base i32) (param $attr_offset i32)
      (result i32)
      local.get $obj_base
      local.get $attr_offset
    ❷ i32.add       ;; add attribute offset to base address
    ❸ i32.load      ;; load the address and return it
    )
    ...
```

Listing 6-21: Retrieving an object attribute from linear memory

In the function definition ❶, the $obj_base parameter is the base address for the object, and $attr_offset is the offset of the specific attribute we want to retrieve. The function adds those values together ❷. Then it loads the value from that address ❸ to return it as a result.

The next helper function is $set_collision, which sets the collision flag for two of the circle objects to true. Listing 6-22 shows that function.

data_structures
.wat (part 4
of 6)

```
...
❶ (func $set_collision
    (param $obj_base_1 i32) (param $obj_base_2 i32)
    local.get $obj_base_1
    global.get $collision_offset
❷  i32.add    ;; address = $obj_base_1 + $collision_offset
    i32.const 1
❸  i32.store ;; store 1 as true in the collision attribute for this object

    local.get $obj_base_2
    global.get $collision_offset
❹  i32.add    ;; address = $obj_base_2 + $collision_offset
    i32.const 1
❺  i32.store ;; store 1 as true in the collision attribute for this object
  )
...
```

Listing 6-22: Set the collision attribute for a given object

This function takes in two object base parameters ❶ to set the collision flags for those objects in memory. It does this by adding $obj_base_1 to $collision_offset ❷ and then setting the value in linear memory at that location to 1 ❸. It then adds $obj_base_2 to $collision_offset ❹ and sets the value at that location to 1 ❺.

Now that we have the other functions defined, we can add the $init function to the WAT code, as shown in Listing 6-23.

data_structures
.wat (part 5
of 6)

```
...
(func $init
❶ (local $i i32)     ;; outer loop counter
  (local $i_obj i32) ;; address of ith object
  (local $xi i32)(local $yi i32)(local $ri i32) ;; x,y,r for object i

❷ (local $j i32)     ;; inner loop counter
  (local $j_obj i32) ;; address of the jth object
  (local $xj i32)(local $yj i32)(local $rj i32) ;; x,y,r for object j

  (loop $outer_loop
  (local.set $j (i32.const 0))  ;; $j = 0

  (loop $inner_loop
    (block $inner_continue
    ;; if $i == $j continue
❸   (br_if $inner_continue (i32.eq (local.get $i) (local.get $j) ) )
```

```
    ;; $i_obj = $obj_base_addr + $i * $obj_stride
    (i32.add (global.get $obj_base_addr)
❹        (i32.mul (local.get $i) (global.get $obj_stride) ) )

    ;; load $i_obj + $x_offset and store in $xi
❺ (call $get_attr (local.tee $i_obj) (global.get $x_offset) )
    local.set $xi

    ;; load $i_obj + $y_offset and store in $yi
    (call $get_attr (local.get $i_obj) (global.get $y_offset) )
    local.set $yi

    ;; load $i_obj + $radius_offset and store in $ri
    (call $get_attr (local.get $i_obj) (global.get $radius_offset) )
    local.set $ri

    ;; $j_obj = $obj_base_addr + $j * $obj_stride
❻ (i32.add (global.get $obj_base_addr)
            (i32.mul (local.get $j)(global.get $obj_stride)))

    ;; load $j_obj + $x_offset and store in $xj
    (call $get_attr (local.tee $j_obj) (global.get $x_offset) )
    local.set $xj

    ;; load $j_obj + $y_offset and store in $yj
    (call $get_attr (local.get $j_obj) (global.get $y_offset) )
    local.set $yj

    ;; load $j_obj + $radius_offset and store in $rj
    (call $get_attr (local.get $j_obj) (global.get $radius_offset) )
    local.set $rj

    ;; check for collision between ith and jth objects
❼ (call $collision_check
      (local.get $xi)(local.get $yi)(local.get $ri)
      (local.get $xj)(local.get $yj)(local.get $rj))

    if ;; if there is a collision
    ❽ (call $set_collision (local.get $i_obj) (local.get $j_obj))
    end
)

❾ (i32.add (local.get $j) (i32.const 1)) ;; $j++

    ;; if $j < $obj_count loop
    (br_if $inner_loop
      (i32.lt_u (local.tee $j) (global.get $obj_count)))
)

❿ (i32.add (local.get $i) (i32.const 1)) ;; $i++

;; if $i < $obj_count loop
(br_if $outer_loop
```

```
      (i32.lt_u (local.tee $i) (global.get $obj_count) ) )
  )
)
...
```

Listing 6-23: A double loop that checks for a collision between every object in linear memory

The function begins with two groups of local variables. One group contains a counter, the address of the objects, and the x, y, and r local variables for use with the outer loop ❶. The second batch of local variables is for use within the inner loop ❷. The meat of this function is a double loop that compares every circle with every other circle in the linear memory looking for circles that collide with each other. The beginning of the inner loop checks whether $i is the same value as $j ❸. If it is, the code skips the check on this particular $j object, because otherwise, every circle would collide with itself.

The next line of code calculates the linear memory address of the ith object ❹ as $obj_base_addr + $i * $obj_stride. It then sets the value of $i_obj using the local.tee expression in the (call $get_attr) ❺ expression in the next line. This call to $getattr ❺ retrieves the value for x from the ith object and then sets $xi.

The next four lines load values into $yi and $ri in the same way. Then $xj, $yj, and $rj ❻ are set using a call to $get_attr as well. These values are passed into a call to $collision_check ❼, which returns 1 if the $i and $j circles collide and 0 if they don't. The if statement that follows executes a call to $set_collision ❽ if there was a collision, which then sets the collision flags on those two objects to 1. The end of the loop increments $j ❾ and branches back to the top of the inner loop if $j is less than $obj_count. The end of the outer loop increments $i ❿ and branches back to the top of the outer loop if $i is less than $obj_count.

The last item we call in this module is the (start $init) statement, as shown in Listing 6-24, which executes the $init function when the module is initialized.

data_structures .wat (part 6 of 6)
```
...
  (start $init)
)
```

Listing 6-24: The start indicates the function that will execute when the module is initialized.

Now that we have all the code in the *data_structures.wat* file, we can compile the WebAssembly file using wat2wasm, as shown in Listing 6-25.

```
wat2wasm data_structures.wat
```

Listing 6-25: Compile data_structures.wat

Once we have a compiled *data_structures.wasm* file, we can run *data_structures.js* using node, as shown in Listing 6-26.

```
node data_structures.js
```

Listing 6-26: Run data_structures.js.

The output will look something like Listing 6-27.

```
obj[00] x=48 y=65 r= 4 collision=true
obj[01] x=46 y=71 r= 6 collision=true
obj[02] x=12 y=75 r= 3 collision=true
obj[03] x=54 y=43 r= 2 collision=false
obj[04] x=16 y= 6 r= 1 collision=false
obj[05] x= 5 y=21 r= 9 collision=true
obj[06] x=71 y=50 r= 5 collision=false
obj[07] x=11 y=13 r= 5 collision=true
obj[08] x=43 y=70 r= 7 collision=true
obj[09] x=88 y=60 r= 9 collision=false
obj[10] x=96 y=21 r= 9 collision=true
obj[11] x= 5 y=87 r= 2 collision=true
obj[12] x=64 y=39 r= 3 collision=false
obj[13] x=75 y=74 r= 6 collision=true
obj[14] x= 2 y=74 r= 8 collision=true
obj[15] x=12 y=85 r= 7 collision=true
obj[16] x=60 y=27 r= 5 collision=false
obj[17] x=43 y=67 r= 2 collision=true
obj[18] x=38 y=53 r= 3 collision=false
obj[19] x=34 y=39 r= 5 collision=false
obj[20] x=42 y=62 r= 2 collision=true
obj[21] x=72 y=93 r= 7 collision=false
obj[22] x=78 y=79 r= 8 collision=true
obj[23] x=50 y=96 r= 7 collision=false
obj[24] x=34 y=18 r=10 collision=true
obj[25] x=19 y=44 r= 8 collision=false
obj[26] x=92 y=82 r= 7 collision=true
obj[27] x=59 y=56 r= 3 collision=false
obj[28] x=41 y=75 r= 9 collision=true
obj[29] x=28 y=29 r= 6 collision=true
obj[30] x=32 y=10 r= 1 collision=true
obj[31] x=83 y=15 r= 6 collision=true
```

Listing 6-27: Output from data_structures.js

In the actual output, any circle that collides with another circle should be in red text, and any circle that collides with no other circles should be in green text. We now have an application that uses JavaScript to load randomly generated data for circles into WebAssembly linear memory. The initialization function in the WebAssembly module then loops over all of that data and updates the linear memory wherever one of those circles collides with another circle. Collision detection is a great use case for WebAssembly because it allows you to load a lot of data into linear memory and let your WebAssembly module work in a fast and efficient way.

Summary

In this chapter, you learned what WebAssembly linear memory is and how to create it from within the WebAssembly module or JavaScript. Next, we initialized the linear data from within the WebAssembly module and accessed it from JavaScript. Then we created data structures within linear memory using a base address, stride, and attribute offsets, and initialized these data structures from within JavaScript using random data.

The final project was an array of circle data structures with x- and y-coordinates and a radius. These were passed into a WebAssembly module, which used a double loop to loop over the circle data structures looking for circles that overlap with each other. If two circles were found to overlap, the WebAssembly module set a collision flag inside the linear memory for both circles. JavaScript then looped over all of those circles, displaying their x- and y-coordinates, their radius, and whether they collided with any other circles.

At this point, you should understand how to manipulate and set linear memory from within WAT and JavaScript. You should also be able to use linear memory from within your applications to create data structures and process large quantities of data in WebAssembly that you can then display using JavaScript. In the next chapter, we'll look at how to manipulate the Document Object Model (DOM) from WebAssembly.

7

WEB APPLICATIONS

This chapter will help you understand how WebAssembly interacts with the DOM through JavaScript. Although it might seem cumbersome, it's a necessary evil to understand WebAssembly and its strengths and weaknesses. If you're using a WebAssembly toolchain, you need to know how much additional code that toolchain will generate as JavaScript glue code. From this point forward, most of the examples will run from a web page instead of using node from the command line.

We'll begin by creating a simple static web server using Node.js. WebAssembly web applications cannot be loaded directly from the filesystem in a web browser; instead, they require you to run a web server. Node.js provides all the tools we need to create a web server. We'll then write our first WebAssembly web application.

The second web application we'll write reuses functions we wrote in Chapter 5 to take in a number from an input element in the HTML and pass it into WebAssembly, which converts the number into a decimal, hexadecimal, and binary string.

By the end of this chapter, you'll understand the basics of writing a web application that loads and instantiates a WebAssembly module and then calls functions from within that module. The applications will also write data from those modules to DOM elements. The examples in this chapter aren't representative of the types of applications you would typically write with WebAssembly. They only demonstrate how a web page can load, instantiate, and interact with WebAssembly modules.

The DOM

Modern web-based applications are so sophisticated it's easy to forget that an HTML page, at its core, is a simple document. The web was conceived as a means to share documents and information, but it soon became apparent that we needed a standard method for dynamically updating those documents using a language like JavaScript or Java. The DOM was designed as a language-independent interface for manipulating HTML and XML documents. Because an HTML document is a tree structure, the DOM represents a document as a logical tree. The DOM is how JavaScript and other languages modify the HTML in a web application.

The WebAssembly 1.0 release has no means of directly manipulating the DOM, so the JavaScript must make all modifications to the HTML document. If you're using a toolchain, such as Rust or Emscripten, manipulation of the DOM is usually done from JavaScript glue code. As a general rule, the WebAssembly portion of a web application should focus on working with numeric data, but with the DOM most of the data processing will likely be string manipulation. The performance of string manipulation from within WebAssembly is entirely dependent on the library you use for the task. For this reason, DOM heavy work is usually best kept in the JavaScript portion of the app.

Setting Up a Simple Node Server

To set up a static web server with Node.js, create a folder for your project and open it in VS Code or your choice of IDE. We need to install two packages using npm. Install the first package, connect, using the command in Listing 7-1.

```
npm install connect --save-dev
```

Listing 7-1: Use npm to install the connect package.

Install the second package, `serve-static`, using the command in Listing 7-2.

```
npm install serve-static --save-dev
```

Listing 7-2: Use npm to install `serve-static`.

With the packages installed, create a file named *server.js* and enter the code in Listing 7-3 to define a static web server.

server.js
```
var connect = require('connect');
var serveStatic = require('serve-static');
connect().use(serveStatic(__dirname + "/")).listen(8080, function(){
  console.log('localhost:8080');
});
```

Listing 7-3: Node.js http server code

We've created a static server that serves files from the current directory, but we don't yet have any files to serve. Use VS Code to create a file named *index.html* and enter some HTML, something like the code in Listing 7-4.

index.html
```
<html>
  <head></head>
  <body>
    <h1>OUR SERVER WORKS!</h1>
  </body>
</html>
```

Listing 7-4: A simple web page

Now you can run your Node.js web server using the following command:

```
node server.js
```

A web server starts running on port 8080. Test this by entering *localhost: 8080* into your browser; you should see something like Figure 7-1.

Figure 7-1: Testing our simple static server

Now that we have a working Node.js web server, let's create our first WebAssembly web app.

Our First WebAssembly Web Application

We'll begin with a simple web app that takes two number inputs, adds them together, and then displays those values. The final version of this app is available at *https://wasmbook.com/add_message.html*.

This app demonstrates how WebAssembly interacts with the DOM. You'll find that we don't change the way the WebAssembly module works, but instead change the embedding environment while the WebAssembly remains none the wiser.

To create a web app, we must run a web server, write an HTML page with JavaScript that will interact with the DOM, and load the WebAssembly module using the `instantiateStreaming` function (instead of using `instantiate` as we did in previous chapters). We'll define a WebAssembly module that adds two integers together and an HTML file that loads and runs that WebAssembly module. In Listing 1-8, JavaScript ran the `AddInt` function using Node.js to load and execute the WebAssembly module. In this app, the HTML file will contain that JavaScript, and a browser will be required to run the app.

Listing 7-5 shows the WAT module with the adding functionality. Create the file *add_message.wat* and add the code in Listing 7-5.

*add_message
.wat*

```
(module
❶ (import "env" "log_add_message"
    (func $log_add_message (param i32 i32 i32)))

❷ (func (export "add_message")
  ❸ (param $a i32) (param $b i32)
    (local $sum i32)

    local.get $a
    local.get $b
  ❹ i32.add
    local.set $sum

  ❺ (call $log_add_message
    ❻ (local.get $a) (local.get $b) (local.get $sum))
  )
)
```

Listing 7-5: The add_message.wat file adds two numbers and calls a JavaScript log function.

This WAT module should look very familiar at this point. It imports `log_add_message` ❶ from the JavaScript and defines the function `add_message` ❷ that will be exported to the embedding environment. It also takes two `i32` parameters ❸. These two parameters are added ❹ together and stored in a local variable `$sum`. It then calls the JavaScript function `log_add_message` ❺, passing in the `$a` and `$b` parameters, as well as `$sum` ❻, the sum of those two parameters.

At this point, you might be wondering how the WebAssembly interacts with the DOM. The unfortunate truth is that WebAssembly 1.0 doesn't directly interact with the DOM. It must rely on the embedding environment (JavaScript) to perform all the interaction. All the differences between calling a WebAssembly module from Node.js and a web page will be in the embedding environment. The WebAssembly module can only make function calls to the embedding environment. We'll create JavaScript functions inside the HTML page. The WebAssembly module will call these JavaScript functions, which will update the DOM. Compile *add_message.wat* using `wat2wasm`.

Defining the HTML Header

Now we'll create our HTML page. When we've previously used Node.js as our embedding environment, we could work in pure JavaScript, but for a static website, you need an HTML page. A web browser doesn't execute JavaScript directly in the same way as Node.js. Web browsers load HTML pages, which embed JavaScript inside <script> tags. I'll assume you have some familiarity with the basics of HTML, but this example should be fairly easy to follow if not. Create a new file *add_message.html* and add the code in Listing 7-6.

add_message .html (part 1 of 3)

```
<!DOCTYPE html>
<html lang="en">
<head>
  <meta charset="UTF-8">
  <meta name="viewport"
        content="width=device-width, initial-scale=1.0">
  <title>Add Message</title>
...
```

Listing 7-6: The HTML header for the add_message *app is mostly HTML boilerplate.*

This is the HTML opening tag and header information. It simply sets some font configuration and displays the app name, `Add Message`, as the title.

The JavaScript

Before ending the head element, we include a `script` tag for the JavaScript. Similar to when we used Node.js, JavaScript code is required to instantiate and execute functions in the WebAssembly module. An HTML page uses a script tag to contain this JavaScript, as shown in Listing 7-7.

add_message .html (part 2 of 3)

```
...
  <script>
❶ //const sleep = m => new Promise(r => setTimeout(r, m));
    var output = null;
    var add_message_function;

❷ var log_add_message = (a, b, sum) => {
      if (output == null) {
        console.log("page load not complete: log_add_message");
        return;
      }
    ❸ output.innerHTML += `${a} + ${b} = ${sum}<br>`;
```

```
  };

  let importObject = {
    env: {
  ❹ log_add_message: log_add_message,
    }
  };


  (async () => {
❺ // await sleep(5000);
    let obj = await
❻ WebAssembly.instantiateStreaming(fetch('add_message.wasm'),
                                    importObject);
    add_message_function = obj.instance.exports.add_message;
❼ let btn = document.getElementById("add_message_button");
    btn.style.display = "block";
  })();

❽ function onPageLoad() {
    //(async () => {
❾ //await sleep(5000);
❿ output = document.getElementById("output");
    //})();
  }
</script>
...
```

Listing 7-7: The JavaScript that loads a WebAssembly module is inside a script tag.

When building a web page, we need to be aware of when all the web page elements have completed loading and the time it takes to stream and instantiate our WebAssembly module.

This application writes messages to the paragraph tag output. The output paragraph hasn't yet loaded when the JavaScript executes, because it's further down the HTML page. The WebAssembly module will be streamed and loaded asynchronously, so you can't be sure whether the WebAssembly module is instantiated before or after the page load completes.

To test that this function works no matter what order these events occur, we create a sleep ❶ function at the beginning to force the JavaScript to wait. This function is commented out here. To test load order, uncomment sleep here as well as inside the IIFE or the onPageLoad function.

We create the add_message_function variable as a placeholder that will change to point to the add_message function inside our WebAssembly module as soon as the module is instantiated.

Next, we define log_add_message ❷, which contains an arrow function that checks whether output is set to something other than null. The default value for output is null, but as soon as the page is loaded, output is set to the paragraph element with an id of output; so this function will log a message if the function runs before the page has finished loading. The log_add _message ❹ function is imported by and called from the WebAssembly module, which passes to log_add_message the two parameters to add and the sum of those parameters. This function then writes those values to the output ❸ HTML paragraph tag from Listing 7-8.

In the IIFE, the sleep ❺ function is commented out, but you can restore it for testing. However, when loading a WebAssembly module from a web page, you use WebAssembly.instantiateStreaming ❻ combined with a call to fetch to retrieve the module. Once the module is instantiated, the add_message_button ❼ element is retrieved from the DOM and made visible when we set its style.display attribute to block. The user will now be able to click this button to run the WebAssembly function.

NOTE   *Unfortunately, Safari 14.0 hasn't implemented instantiateStreaming, so you'll need to polyfill WebAssembly.instantiateStreaming using WebAssembly.instantiate.*

Additionally, we define the onPageLoad ❽ function, which executes when the HTML body is finished loading. This function sets the output ❿ variable defined near the top of Listing 7-7 to the paragraph tag with an id of output. Prior to the page loading, the output variable has a value of null. If a function that requires the output tag executes before the page has finished loading, it can check for null before using it. This prevents the code from trying to use the paragraph tag before it has loaded. We included an optional sleep ❾ function, which can be used to delay setting the output variable. That allows us to simulate what happens when the page takes longer than expected to finish loading.

The HTML Body

The HTML body tag contains the DOM elements that will be displayed on our web page. Add the code in Listing 7-8 inside *add_message.html* below the script tag.

add_message .html (part 3 of 3)

```
...
</head>
❶ <body onload="onPageLoad()"
        style="font-family: 'Courier New', Courier, monospace;">
❷ <input type="number" id="a_val" value="0"><br><br>
❸ <input type="number" id="b_val" value="0"><br><br>
❹ <button id="add_message_button" type="button" style="display:none"
❺ onclick="add_message_function(
                document.getElementById('a_val').value,
                document.getElementById('b_val').value )">
    Add Values
  </button>
  <br>
❻ <p id="output" style="float:left; width:200px; min-height:300px;">
  </p>
</body>
</html>
```

Listing 7-8: The DOM elements in the HTML body tag

The body ❶ tag includes an onload attribute that calls the JavaScript onPageLoad function. This ensures that the output variable in our JavaScript isn't set until the output paragraph tag exists.

Then we have two input elements with the id inputs a_val ❷ and b_val ❸. The values in these inputs are passed to the WebAssembly when the button ❹ element is clicked. The button attribute onclick ❺ is set to call the add_message_function, which calls the add_message function in the WebAssembly module once the module is instantiated. The add_message function is called, passing in the values in the two input fields (a_val and b_val) above the button. In addition, we have a paragraph tag with an id of output ❻ that we'll populate with values from the WebAssembly module.

Our Completed Web App

We should now be able to run our web application. As mentioned earlier, we must serve the web page from a web server, so first make sure the web server in Listing 7-3 is running by using the command in Listing 7-9.

```
node server.js
```

Listing 7-9: Run the simple web server.

If you receive the error in Listing 7-10, you already have a web server running on that port.

```
Error: listen EADDRINUSE: address already in use :::8080
```

Listing 7-10: The web server error if the port is already in use

Getting this error likely means you're running *server.js* from a different command line. With your web server running, open the following URL in a browser: *http://localhost:8080/add_message.html*.

You should see something like the screen in Figure 7-2.

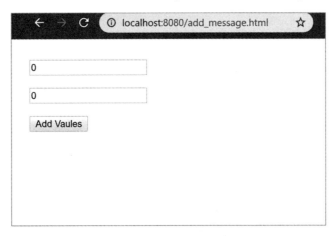

Figure 7-2: The add_message.html web app

Set values in the two number fields, and click **Add Values** to see the results of that addition (Figure 7-3).

Figure 7-3: Two addition messages added with the app

Notice that the WebAssembly module called JavaScript functions, as was done in other chapters. You didn't have to learn any new commands in WAT in this chapter. Because working directly with the DOM isn't possible from within Wasm 1.0, we made all our changes to the DOM inside the JavaScript. Even though this was the first time we used an HTML page, it didn't affect what WebAssembly does. WebAssembly 1.0 is fairly limited and is most useful for increasing performance for math-heavy applications. This characteristic will change with later WebAssembly releases as more features are added. But for now, you need to keep these limitations in mind as you decide which applications are best suited for this new technology.

Hex and Binary Strings

We'll continue and create a second app that uses our functions from Chapter 5 to convert numeric data into decimal, hexadecimal, and binary strings, and display them to a web page. See the final app at *https://wasmbook.com/hex_and_binary.html*.

The HTML

The HTML is pretty much the same as Listing 7-6 but with different title contents. Create a file named *hex_and_binary.html* and add the code in Listing 7-11.

hex_and_binary.html (part 1 of 3)

```
<!DOCTYPE html>
<html lang="en">

<head>
  <meta charset="UTF-8">
  <meta name="viewport"
```

```
                    content="width=device-width, initial-scale=1.0">
                <title> ❶ Hex and Binary</title>
        ...
```

Listing 7-11: The boilerplate at the beginning of hex_and_binary.html

The title tag here contains Hex and Binary ❶. Next, in Listing 7-12, we add the script tag and the JavaScript code that will instantiate and call the WebAssembly module.

```
...
<script>
  // allocate a 64K block of memory
  const memory = new WebAssembly.Memory({ initial: 1 });
  var output = null;

  // function will change when WebAssembly module is instantiated
❶ var setOutput = (number) => {
    // this message will appear if you run the function
    // before the WebAssembly module is instantiated.
  ❷ console.log("function not available");
    return 0;
  };

  // This function will be called from a button click and runs
  // the setOutput function in the WebAssembly module.
❸ function setNumbers(number) {
  ❹ if (output == null) {
      // if page has not fully loaded return
      return;
    }

    // calling WebAssembly setOutput function generates the HTML
    // string and puts it in linear memory returning its length
  ❺ let len = setOutput(number);

    // we know the position and length of the HTML string in
    // linear memory so we can take it out of the memory buffer
  ❻ let bytes = new Uint8Array(memory.buffer, 1024, len);

    // convert the bytes taken from linear memory into a
    // JavaScript string and use it to set the HTML in output
  ❼ output.innerHTML = new TextDecoder('utf8').decode(bytes);
  }


❽ function onPageLoad() {
    // when the page load is complete, set the output variable
    // to the element with an id of "output"
  ❾ output = document.getElementById("output");
    var message_num = 0;
  }

  let importObject = {
    env: {
```

```
            buffer: memory
        }
    };

    (async () => {
        // use WebAssembly.instantiateStreaming in combination with
        // fetch instead of WebAssembly.instantiate and fs.readFileSync
        let obj = await WebAssembly.instantiateStreaming(
                        fetch('hex_and_binary.wasm'),
                        importObject);
        // reset the setOutput variable to the setOutput
        // function from the WASM module
❿       setOutput = obj.instance.exports.setOutput;
        let btn = document.getElementById("set_numbers_button");
        btn.style.display = "block";
    })();

  </script>
</head>
...
```

Listing 7-12: JavaScript for the hex_and_binary.html file

The script tag first creates the variable setOutput ❶ and sets it to an arrow function that logs "function not available" ❷ to the console. This message will display if the user clicks the **Set Numbers** button before the WebAssembly module has finished loading.

Next, we define the setNumbers ❸ function that will be called when the user clicks the **Set Numbers** button. If the page load hasn't finished, the output is still null ❹ at the button click, and we return from this function. The setNumbers function then calls setOutput ❺ in the WebAssembly module, which creates an HTML string from the number passed in and returns the length of that string, which we'll use to retrieve the string from linear memory. We take the bytes that will be used to create the display string from the linear memory buffer ❻.

Then the output tag's innerHTML ❼ attribute is set to the display string generated from those bytes using a TextDecoder object, which displays the string in the web page.

We define the onPageLoad ❽ function, which the body tag executes once it has finished loading. That function sets the output ❾ variable used to display the output string from the WebAssembly module. It also instantiates the WebAssembly module and sets the setOutput ❿ variable to the setOutput function in the WebAssembly module, so we can call setOutput from the JavaScript.

Finally, we need the body tag, which contains an output tag to display the output from the WebAssembly function call, a number input to take in the user input, and a button to click that will call the setNumbers function. Listing 7-13 shows that code.

hex_and
_binary.html
(part 3 of 3)

```
...
<!-- body tag calls onPageLoad when the body load is complete -->
❶ <body onload="onPageLoad()"
        style="font-family: 'Courier New', Courier, monospace;">
```

```
❷ <div id="output"><!-- displays output from WebAssembly -->
    <h1>0</h1>
    <h4>0x0</h4>
    <h4> 0000 0000 0000 0000 0000 0000 0000 0000</h4>
  </div>
  <br>
  <!-- user enters input to convert to hex and binary here -->
❸ <input type="number" id="val" value="0"><br><br>
  <!-- when user clicks this button, the WASM function is run -->
❹ <button id="set_numbers_button" type="button" style="display:none"
❺   onclick="setNumbers( document.getElementById('val').value )">
    Set Numbers
  </button>
</body>
</html>
```

Listing 7-13: The UI elements of the HTML page

The onload ❶ attribute tells the browser to execute onPageLoad when the
body has completed loading. The tag ❷ <div id="output"> is where the output
from the WebAssembly module will be displayed. The number input tag ❸,
<input type="number" id="val" value="0"> is where the user enters the number
to convert to hexadecimal and binary. The button ❹ calls the WebAssembly
module when it's clicked using the onclick ❺ attribute. Now that we have
our HTML page, we can create the WAT file for this application.

The WAT

There's a lot of WAT code in this app, so we'll break it into four sections.
Also, you'll need to copy several functions from Chapter 5. Create a file
named *hex_and_binary.wat* and add the code in Listing 7-14.

hex_and_binary
.wat (part 1 of 4)
```
(module
  (import "env" "buffer" (memory 1))

  ;; hexadecimal digits
❶ (global $digit_ptr i32 (i32.const 128))
  (data (i32.const 128) "0123456789ABCDEF")
  ;; the decimal string pointer, length and data section
❷ (global $dec_string_ptr  i32 (i32.const 256))
  (global $dec_string_len  i32 (i32.const 16))
  (data (i32.const 256) "              0")

  ;; the hexadecimal string pointer, length and data section
❸ (global $hex_string_ptr  i32 (i32.const 384))
  (global $hex_string_len  i32 (i32.const 16))
  (data (i32.const 384) "           0x0")

  ;; the binary string pointer, length and data section
❹ (global $bin_string_ptr  i32 (i32.const 512))
  (global $bin_string_len  i32 (i32.const 40))
  (data (i32.const 512) " 0000 0000 0000 0000 0000 0000 0000 0000")

  ;; the h1 open tag string pointer, length and data section
```

```
❺ (global $h1_open_ptr i32  (i32.const 640))
  (global $h1_open_len i32  (i32.const 4))
  (data (i32.const 640) "<H1>")

    ;; the h1 close tag string pointer, length and data section
❻ (global $h1_close_ptr i32  (i32.const 656))
  (global $h1_close_len i32  (i32.const 5))
  (data (i32.const 656) "</H1>")

    ;; the h4 open tag string pointer, length and data section
❼ (global $h4_open_ptr i32  (i32.const 672))
  (global $h4_open_len i32  (i32.const 4))
  (data (i32.const 672) "<H4>")

    ;; the h4 close tag string pointer, length and data section
❽ (global $h4_close_ptr i32  (i32.const 688))
  (global $h4_close_len i32  (i32.const 5))
  (data (i32.const 688) "</H4>")

    ;; the output string length and data section
❾ (global $out_str_ptr i32 (i32.const 1024))
  (global $out_str_len (mut i32) (i32.const 0))

...
```

Listing 7-14: String data definitions at the beginning of the module

We define a series of data sections, pointers, and data lengths that will
be used to assemble decimal, hexadecimal, and binary strings from integer
data. The $digit_ptr ❶ global variable is a pointer to the data segment that
contains the 16 hexadecimal digits 0 to F defined at linear memory location 128. This data is used for all three conversions from integer to string.
We also have a length and pointer global variable, as well as a data segment
for our decimal ❷, hexadecimal ❸, and binary ❹ string. Much of the code
we'll use is taken from sections in Chapter 5.

Next, we have several strings that represent HTML tags. There are
opening ❺ and closing ❻ H1 tag pointers, length and data segments, as well
as opening ❼ and closing ❽ data for H4 tags. These strings will be used to
assemble our HTML output string that will be stored in the linear memory
position 1024 ❾, which I chose because it was unused.

As we copy string data to the output string, we'll need to keep track of
the new length of this string and pass that value to the JavaScript; so we use
the global variable $out_str_len to keep track of the output string length.
Instead of including the code for the original functions from Chapter 5, I
include an ellipsis (...) and a comment indicating the listing number that
has the function code to copy. Copy and paste the function code from the
original listing for all six of the functions in Listing 7-15.

hex_and
_binary.wat
(part 2 of 4)
```
...
❶ (func $set_bin_string (param $num i32) (param $string_len i32)
    ;; $set_bin_string defined in listing 5-35
  ...
```

```
   )

❷ (func $set_hex_string (param $num i32) (param $string_len i32)
     ;; $set_hex_string defined in listing 5-30
   ...
   ) ;; end $set_hex_string

❸ (func $set_dec_string (param $num i32) (param $string_len i32)
     ;; $set_dec_string defined in listing 5-24
   ...
   )

❹ (func $byte_copy
     (param $source i32) (param $dest i32) (param $len i32)
     ;; $byte_copy defined in listing 5-17
   ...
   )

❺ (func $byte_copy_i64
     (param $source i32) (param $dest i32) (param $len i32)
     ;; $byte_copy_i64 defined in listing 5-18
   ...
   )

❻ (func $string_copy
     (param $source i32) (param $dest i32) (param $len i32)
     ;; $string_copy defined in listing 5-19
   ...
     )
   ...
```

Listing 7-15: Functions reused from Chapter 5

First are the number-to-string conversion functions. The $set_bin
_string ❶ function converts a number into a binary string. As parameters
it takes an i32 $num to be converted into a binary string and $string_len as
the length of the output string, which includes nibble padding with spaces
(Listing 5-35). Next is $set_hex_string ❷, which converts the number and
length to a hexadecimal string prefixed with a 0x to indicate that the string
represents a hexadecimal number (Listing 5-30). Then $set_dec_string ❸
converts a number to a decimal string (Listing 5-24).

Next are the three copy functions that copy a byte at a time, eight bytes
at a time, and strings. Each takes three parameters: the $source parameter
is the string that we're copying from, the $dest parameter is the string we're
copying to, and $len is the length of the string. First is the $byte_copy ❹ function, which copies data one byte at a time (Listing 5-17). The $byte_copy_i64 ❺
function copies eight bytes at a time (Listing 5-18). The $string_copy ❻ func-
tion copies bytes eight at a time using $byte_copy_i64 until there are less than
eight bytes remaining and then copies the remaining bytes one by one using
$byte_copy (Listing 5-17).

There is one final copy command not in Listing 7-15. This is the $append_out function that will always append a given source string to the output string by copying it to the end of the current output string. Add the code in Listing 7-16 to *hex_and_binary.wat*.

```
...
    ;; append the source string to the output string
❶ (func $append_out (param $source i32) (param $len i32)
❷ (call $string_copy
      (local.get $source)
      (i32.add
        (global.get $out_str_ptr)
        (global.get $out_str_len)
      )
      (local.get $len)
    )

    ;; add length to the output string length
    global.get $out_str_len
    local.get $len
    i32.add
❸ global.set $out_str_len
  )
...
```

Listing 7-16: The $append_out function appends to the output string.

The $append_out ❶ function appends the source string to the end of the output string using $string_copy ❷ and then adds the length of the string just appended to the $out_str_len ❸, which represents the output string length.

The final function in this module is setOutput, which creates the string we use to set the output div tag. This is exported so it can be called from JavaScript. Add the code in Listing 7-17 to the end of the WAT file.

```
...
(func (export "setOutput") (param $num i32) (result i32)
    ;; create a decimal string from $num value
❶ (call $set_dec_string
      (local.get $num) (global.get $dec_string_len))
    ;; create a hexadecimal string from $num value
❷ (call $set_hex_string
      (local.get $num) (global.get $hex_string_len))
    ;; create a binary string from $num value
❸ (call $set_bin_string
      (local.get $num) (global.get $bin_string_len))

    i32.const 0
❹ global.set $out_str_len ;; set $out_str_len to 0

    ;; append <h1>${decimal_string}</h1> to output string
❺ (call $append_out
      (global.get $h1_open_ptr) (global.get $h1_open_len))
    (call $append_out
```

```
        (global.get $dec_string_ptr) (global.get $dec_string_len))
      (call $append_out
        (global.get $h1_close_ptr) (global.get $h1_close_len))

      ;; append <h4>${hexadecimal_string}</h4> to output string
    ❻ (call $append_out
        (global.get $h4_open_ptr) (global.get $h4_open_len))
      (call $append_out
        (global.get $hex_string_ptr) (global.get $hex_string_len))
      (call $append_out
        (global.get $h4_close_ptr) (global.get $h4_close_len))

      ;; append <h4>${binary_string}</h4> to output string
    ❼ (call $append_out
        (global.get $h4_open_ptr) (global.get $h4_open_len))
      (call $append_out
        (global.get $bin_string_ptr) (global.get $bin_string_len))
      (call $append_out
        (global.get $h4_close_ptr) (global.get $h4_close_len))

      ;; return output string length
    ❽ global.get $out_str_len
    )
)
```

Listing 7-17: The setOutput function exported to be called from JavaScript

The first three calls made by the set_output function in Listing 7-17 are to $set_dec_string ❶, $set_hex_string ❷, and $set_bin_string ❸. These functions take the number passed into setOutput and convert it into a decimal string, a hexadecimal string, and a binary string in linear memory. Once these strings are set, the global variable $out_str_len ❹ is set to 0, which resets the output string so that appending to the output string writes over the string currently in memory. After we reset the value, we can begin to append to the output string.

Next are nine calls to $append_out, grouped into three blocks. The first three calls append an opening and closing H1 tag with the decimal ❺ string inside it. This creates the HTML string to display the decimal numeric value in our web page. The next block of three appends the hexadecimal ❻ string inside an H4 element, and then the binary ❼ string is appended inside an H4 element. Finally, the length of the output string is loaded on the stack using a call to global.get $out_str_len ❽, which returns it to the calling JavaScript.

Compile and Run

The WAT module is complete, so use wat2wasm to compile your *hex_and_binary.wasm* file, as shown in Listing 7-18.

```
wat2wasm hex_and_binary.wat
```

Listing 7-18: Compiling hex_and_binary.wat using wat2wasm

Verify that you're running your *server.js*, and open *hex_and_binary.html* in a browser using the address *http://localhost:8080/hex_and_binary.html*.

Figure 7-4 shows something similar to what you should see onscreen.

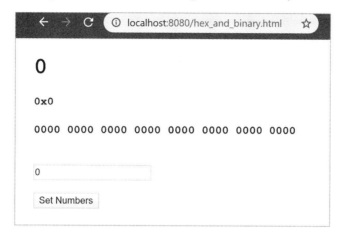

Figure 7-4: Converting decimal to hexadecimal and binary

Enter a number and give it a go. For example, in Figure 7-5, I entered the number 1025 and clicked Set Numbers.

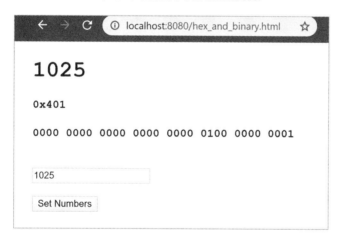

Figure 7-5: Convert 1025 to hexadecimal and binary

This application used several WebAssembly functions we created in Chapter 5 to convert a decimal number to hexadecimal and binary strings. We added some additional functionality that created HTML tags in the WebAssembly module so we could pass HTML to the JavaScript and display it on the web page. As you can tell, working with strings and manipulating the DOM from WAT is rather cumbersome. If you're working with a tool-chain, much of this hard work is done for you. Some of this functionality might compile into JavaScript glue code.

Summary

WebAssembly 1.0 doesn't directly work with user interfaces. Its sweet spot is math-intensive applications. When interacting with the DOM from a web application built on top of WebAssembly, manipulating the DOM is primarily a task for the JavaScript portion. Working with strings from within WebAssembly entirely depends on the implementation. WebAssembly is still an excellent choice for many web applications, especially graphical applications, such as games. But in its current state, it's not designed to work directly with the DOM.

We began this chapter by creating a simple JavaScript web server to run using Node.js. You can't load a WebAssembly web app from the filesystem but instead must serve your page using a web server. We wrote our first WebAssembly web application, which added two numbers together and then logged those numbers to the DOM in a paragraph tag called output.

The primary difference between web applications and Node.js applications is in the embedding environment. Node.js command line apps are written entirely in JavaScript, where the web application has its JavaScript inside an HTML web page. Node.js can load the WebAssembly module directly from the filesystem, whereas the web application uses instantiate Streaming and fetch to instantiate a WebAssembly module streaming it from a web server. A Node.js application would have logged its output to the console, whereas the HTML page updated the innerHTML of a DOM element.

The second application we wrote displayed the decimal, hexadecimal, and binary representations of a number passed into the WebAssembly module. This was done by assembling a string containing the HTML elements to be displayed in the application. This application reused several functions created in Chapter 5 for string manipulation. The JavaScript in this application wrote the string to the innerHTML of a div tag on our web page.

Neither of the applications we wrote is a particularly good use case for WebAssembly. My goal in this chapter was to create our first few WebAssembly web apps, not necessarily to make web applications that made sense to create using WebAssembly. In the next chapter, we'll render to the HTML canvas and examine collision detection between a large number of objects on that canvas. These tasks, commonly found in web games, better represent what WebAssembly 1.0 can do to improve your web application's performance.

8

WORKING WITH THE CANVAS

In this chapter, you'll learn how to use WebAssembly with the HTML canvas element to create fast and efficient animations in a web application. We'll manipulate pixel data inside the WebAssembly linear memory, and then transfer that pixel data in linear memory directly onto the HTML canvas. We'll continue with our random collider objects example (Listing 6-16) by generating the objects in JavaScript linear memory and then using WebAssembly to move these objects, detect collisions, and render them. Because the number of possible collisions grows exponentially with the number of objects, this kind of graphical collision detection is an excellent test of WebAssembly's capabilities. By the end of this chapter, we'll have an application that can test collisions between thousands of different colliders dozens of times per second. In this case, our objects will be squares drawn in green if there is no collision and red if a collision occurs.

As discussed earlier, web browsers were originally designed for displaying simple online documents, meaning any changes to the position of any of the document's elements frequently resulted in the entire page being rerendered. That is a performance nightmare for any application that requires high-frame-rate graphical effects (such as games). Since then browsers have evolved into sophisticated application-hosting environments, necessitating the development of a more sophisticated rendering model: the *canvas*. The canvas element was introduced in 2004 by Apple for its Safari web browser and adopted as a part of the HTML standard in 2006. Within the bounds of the canvas element, web developers can render 2D images and animations with significantly better performance than could be done by manipulating the DOM, as had been done previously. Using the canvas with WebAssembly can help us render animations to the browser with lightning speed.

Rendering to the Canvas

Entire books have been written on the HTML canvas API, so we'll only touch on a few of the features needed for this WebAssembly demonstration. As with the DOM, WebAssembly cannot interact directly with the canvas. Instead, we must render pixel data directly from linear memory onto the canvas element. That allows us to write a canvas application with minimal JavaScript code. Before writing the WebAssembly code, we'll write the HTML and JavaScript portion. To see what the finished app looks like, browse to *https://wasmbook.com/collide.html*.

Defining the Canvas in HTML

As usual, we'll break the HTML file into sections and examine it a piece at a time. This first piece defines the canvas, which is the area in the web page where animations are rendered. Create a file named *collide.html* and add the code in Listing 8-1.

collide.html
(part 1 of 5)

```
<!DOCTYPE html>
<html lang="en">
<head>
  <meta charset="UTF-8">
  <meta name="viewport" content="width=device-width, initial-scale=1.0">
  <title>Collision detection</title>
</head>
<body>
❶ <canvas ❷id="cnvs" ❸width="512" ❹height="512"></canvas>
...
```

Listing 8-1: HTML to define the canvas

The element you need to pay attention to here is the canvas ❶ element. We give the canvas element an id of cnvs ❷ so that later we can use a call to document.getElementById to retrieve the canvas element. We set the width ❸ and height ❹ to 512, chosen because 512 is 2^9 or hexadecimal 0x200. This choice makes it easy to work with the width and height using binary logic, which can help improve the app's performance if we design our code properly.

Defining JavaScript Constants in HTML

At the beginning of our JavaScript, we'll add constant values for configuring some top level settings in the WebAssembly module. The values will be shared between the JavaScript and the WebAssembly. Defining these values inside the JavaScript makes it simpler to update the configuration. We begin the code with some canvas-related constants that set parameters for interaction between the WebAssembly and the HTML canvas element. We also have a cluster of constants related to the organization of the data in linear memory that define our base address, stride, and offset for the objects we're rendering. In addition, we must define a new `ImageData` object that sets aside a section of the linear memory buffer as an object that the app can directly draw to the canvas. Add the code in Listing 8-2 to your HTML file.

collide.html
(part 2 of 5)

```
...
<script>
❶ const cnvs_size = 512;  // square canvas where width and height = 512

❷ const no_hit_color = 0xff_00_ff_00; // no hit color (green)
   const hit_color = 0xff_00_00_ff;    // hit color (red)

   // pixels count is canvas_size x canvas_size because it's a square canvas
❸ const pixel_count = cnvs_size * cnvs_size;

❹ const canvas = document.getElementById("cnvs");
❺ const ctx = canvas.getContext("2d");
   ctx.clearRect(0, 0, 512, 512);

   // the number of bytes needed for that pixel data is the number of pixels * 4
❻ const obj_start = pixel_count * 4; // 4 bytes in every pixel.
   const obj_start_32 = pixel_count;  // 32-bit offset to the starting object
   const obj_size = 4;        // how many pixels is the square object
   const obj_cnt = 3000;      // 3000 objects
   const stride_bytes = 16;   // there are 16 bytes in each stride

   const x_offset  = 0;       // x attribute is bytes 0-3
   const y_offset  = 4;       // y attribute is bytes 4-7
   const xv_offset = 8;       // x velocity attribute is bytes 8-11
   const yv_offset = 12;      // y velocity attribute is bytes 12-15

❼ const memory = new WebAssembly.Memory({initial: 80});
   const mem_i8 = new Uint8Array(memory.buffer);        // 8-bit view
   const mem_i32 = new Uint32Array(memory.buffer);      // 32-bit view

❽ const importObject = {
   env: {
      buffer: memory,

      cnvs_size: cnvs_size,
      no_hit_color: no_hit_color,
```

```
        hit_color: hit_color,
        obj_start: obj_start,
        obj_cnt: obj_cnt,
        obj_size: obj_size,

        x_offset: x_offset,
        y_offset: y_offset,
        xv_offset: xv_offset,
        yv_offset: yv_offset
    }
};

// An ImageData object can be blitted onto the canvas
const image_data =
❾ new ImageData( new Uint8ClampedArray(memory.buffer, 0, obj_start),
                cnvs_size,
                cnvs_size );
...
```

Listing 8-2: Configuring image data in JavaScript

We have a single cnvs_size ❶ constant that holds the height and width of the canvas element because they're the same. We then have two constants that define hexadecimal color values. The first, no_hit_color ❷, defines the color an object will be when it doesn't collide with another object. The second, hit_color, defines the color an object will be when it collides with another object. The meaning of these hexadecimal numbers is covered in more detail in "Bitmap Image Data" on page 162. Then we define the pixel_count ❸, which we can get by squaring the canvas_size because we have a square canvas.

Next, we deal with the Canvas API interface, the *drawing context*, which allows JavaScript to interact with the canvas. There are a few options for working with the HTML canvas. We'll work with the "2d" canvas context because it's relatively simple. Here we create a canvas ❹ element constant with a call to document.getElementById to retrieve a context from the HTML canvas. We then call the function getContext ❺ on that canvas constant to create a constant containing the context interface, which we've named ctx. We'll use this ctx object to render a bitmap generated in WebAssembly to the canvas element.

NOTE *WebAssembly also works well with the webgl and webgl2 canvas contexts, which render 3D models to the canvas. Unfortunately, WebGL is beyond the scope of this book.*

Following the canvas-related constants is a group of linear memory object-related constants. These constants begin with the obj_start ❻ constant and follow the base, stride, and offset format we discussed in Chapter 6. The base address in obj_start must show an address that follows all of our pixel data at the beginning of linear memory. We set obj_start to pixel_count * 4 because each pixel takes up four bytes of data, and the object data immediately follows a section of that size. In this area, we use some constants to define our stride size and the offsets for each of the object attributes. We define the linear memory ❼ with an initial size of 80 pages, enough to fit all the objects and pixel data we require. Then we create an 8-bit and a 32-bit view of that data object. All the constants we've created so far must be passed into the WebAssembly module using the importObject ❽.

Lastly, we create a new ImageData ❾ object, which is a JavaScript interface that we can use to access the underlying pixel data in our canvas element. The Memory ❼ object that we created in Listing 8-2 has an attribute called buffer, which is a typed array containing the data in linear memory. The buffer attribute is a data buffer that can represent the pixel data displayed on a canvas. To create a new ImageData object, the memory.buffer object must be passed into the ImageData object as a Uint8ClampedArray along with the width and height of the canvas.

Creating Random Objects

Next, we'll create the random objects, similar to how we did so previously in the book. We continue to use random data because it allows us to focus on the WebAssembly rather than the data. However, WebAssembly doesn't have a random number function, so creating our randomized objects inside JavaScript is much simpler. The objects have four attributes: an x- and y-coordinate (position), as well as an x and y velocity (motion). We use a 32-bit integer to represent the value of each of these attributes. Listing 8-3 shows the code that loops to create data for several objects represented by the object_cnt constant we defined earlier.

collide.html
(part 3 of 5)

```
...
❶ const stride_i32 = stride_bytes/4;
❷ for( let i = 0; i < obj_cnt * stride_i32; i += stride_i32 ) {

    // value less than canvas_size
  ❸ let temp = Math.floor(Math.random() * cnvs_size);

    // set object x attribute to random value
  ❹ mem_i32[obj_start_32 + i] = temp;

    //random value less than canvas_size
  ❺ temp = Math.floor(Math.random()*cnvs_size);

    // set object y attribute to random value
  ❻ mem_i32[obj_start_32 + i + 1] = temp;

    // random value between -2 and 2
  ❼ temp = (Math.round(Math.random() * 4) - 2);

    // set x velocity to random value
  ❽ mem_i32[obj_start_32 + i + 2] = temp;

    // random value between -2 and 2
  ❾ temp = (Math.round(Math.random() * 4) - 2);

    // set y velocity to random value
```

```
 ❿ mem_i32[obj_start_32 + i + 3] = temp;
}
...
```

Listing 8-3: Setting linear memory data

The code in this loop accesses the data in linear memory through the 32-bit integer view in mem_i32. Because the loop is working with 32-bit numbers, we create a 32-bit version of stride_bytes, which we call stride_i32 ❶. We set it to the value stride_bytes / 4, because there are four bytes per i32. The for loop loops until index i is equal to the number of objects set in obj_count multiplied by the number of 32-bit integers in our stride defined by stride_i32 ❷. This creates the circle data structure in linear memory.

Inside the loop, we set four 32-bit integers to random numbers that will represent the position and velocity of each object. First, we set the position attributes. We get a random number between 0 and the canvas width ❸ held in cnvs_size and store it in the location of the x position attribute ❹ in linear memory. Next, a random number between 0 and the canvas height ❺ is generated and stored in the y attribute ❻ location in linear memory. Then we set the velocity attributes by generating a number between –2 and 2 ❼, storing it in the location of the x velocity ❽ attribute, and do the same ❾ for the y velocity ❿ attribute.

Bitmap Image Data

We can render bitmap image data directly to the HTML canvas element using the putImageData function, passing in the ImageData object we defined earlier. The HTML canvas is a grid of pixels; each of which can be represented by three bytes with one byte dedicated to each of the three colors: red, green, and blue. In the bitmap format, a pixel is represented with a single 32-bit integer where each byte of the integer represents one of the colors. The fourth byte of the integer represents the *alpha value*, which is used for pixel opacity. When the alpha byte is 0, the pixel is fully transparent, and when it's 255, it's fully opaque. In WebAssembly linear memory, we'll create an array of 32-bit integers that represents an array of pixel data. This type of array makes WebAssembly a very convenient tool for manipulating data to be rendered to the HTML canvas.

In the script tag, we'll store the WebAssembly module function that generates this bitmap data in the variable animation_wasm. We also need a JavaScript function that calls that WebAssembly function. Then we call ctx.putImageData to render that image data to the canvas element. Listing 8-4 contains the next chunk of JavaScript code you need to add to the HTML file.

collide.html
(part 4 of 5)
```
...
❶ var animation_wasm; // the webassembly function we will call every frame

❷ function animate() {
  ❸ animation_wasm();
  ❹ ctx.putImageData(image_data, 0, 0); // render pixel data
```

```
❺ requestAnimationFrame(animate);
  }
...
```

Listing 8-4: The JavaScript animate function renders the animation frame.

The animation_wasm ❶ variable holds the WebAssembly function that generates the image data. The animate ❷ function that follows calls the WebAssembly module's animation_wasm ❸ function, which generates the image_data for the next frame in the animation. The image_data object is then passed into a call to ctx.putImageData ❹, which renders the image generated by WebAssembly in the canvas element. The last function, requestAnimation Frame ❺, is a little more complicated, so we'll examine it in more detail in the next section.

The requestAnimationFrame Function

Animation is an optical illusion: a series of still images displayed in rapid sequence tricks the eye into believing there is motion. Every television screen, computer monitor, and film you've ever watched works this way. JavaScript provides the handy requestAnimationFrame function: when you call requestAnimationFrame, the function passed to requestAnimationFrame is called the next time a frame is rendered. To requestAnimationFrame, we pass the function we want to call the next time our computer is ready to render a frame of animation.

We call this function at the end of the JavaScript, passing in the animate function that we defined in Listing 8-4. We call requestAnimationFrame a second time from the end of the animate function to register the function as a callback on the frame render that follows. That second call must be made because the requestAnimationFrame function doesn't register a function to be called every time a frame is rendered; it's only registered for the next frame render. The animate function needs to call the WebAssembly module, which performs the collision detection and object move computations. WebAssembly calculates the image data placed on the canvas. However, it's unable to render that data to the canvas directly. That's why we must call putImageData from our JavaScript animation function to render the pixel data to the canvas. The call to putImageData moves the chunk of linear memory we set aside to represent pixel data over to the canvas element.

The first time we call requestAnimationFrame is immediately after instantiating the WebAssembly module in the last line of the code. Listing 8-5 shows the final portion of the HTML code.

collide.html
(part 5 of 5)
```
...
(async () => {
  let obj = await
❶ WebAssembly.instantiateStreaming( fetch('collide.wasm'),
                                     importObject );
❷ animation_wasm = obj.instance.exports.main;
❸ requestAnimationFrame(❹animate);
})();
</script>
```

```
</body>
</html>
```

Listing 8-5: Instantiate the WebAssembly module and call requestAnimationFrame.

Inside the asynchronous IIFE we begin by calling the instantiate
Streaming ❶ function. We set the animation_wasm ❷ variable we defined in
Listing 8-4 to an exported function in the WebAssembly module named
main. Recall that we called the animation_wasm function from the animate function. Finally, a call to requestAnimationFrame ❸ passes in the animate ❹ function defined earlier. Because animate also calls requestAnimationFrame on itself,
the browser calls animate every time it refreshes.

The WAT Module

Now that we've defined the HTML, we need to write the WebAssembly
module in WAT, which will manage the object movement, collision detection, and bitmap image data. Create a file named *collide.wat*. We'll write the
collision code and canvas rendering code as straightforwardly as possible.
To accomplish this, we'll write it with many functions, some of which might
result in less than ideal performance. In the next chapter, we'll revisit this
code in an attempt to optimize it. But in this chapter, we'll focus on clarity
and simplicity over high performance. The module will define global variables that import values from the JavaScript. We'll need to define a series of
functions that clear the canvas, calculate the absolute value of an integer, set
individual pixels, and draw the collider objects. Then we'll need to define
the main function that will use a double loop to move each collider object
and test to see whether it collides with another object.

Imported Values

The beginning of the module, as shown in Listing 8-6, imports the constants passed into the module through the importObject we defined in our
JavaScript. These values include our memory buffer, the canvas size, object
colors, and the base, offset, and stride values we can use to access objects in
linear memory.

collide.wat
(part 1 of 12)

```
(module
❶ (global $cnvs_size     (import "env" "cnvs_size")     i32)

❷ (global $no_hit_color (import "env" "no_hit_color") i32)
   (global $hit_color     (import "env" "hit_color")     i32)
❸ (global $obj_start     (import "env" "obj_start")     i32)
❹ (global $obj_size      (import "env" "obj_size")      i32)
❺ (global $obj_cnt       (import "env" "obj_cnt")       i32)

❻ (global $x_offset      (import "env" "x_offset")      i32)  ;; bytes 00-03
   (global $y_offset      (import "env" "y_offset")      i32)  ;; bytes 04-07
❼ (global $xv_offset     (import "env" "xv_offset")     i32)  ;; bytes 08-11
   (global $yv_offset     (import "env" "yv_offset")     i32)  ;; bytes 12-15
```

❽ (import "env" "buffer" (memory 80))   ;; canvas buffer
   ...

Listing 8-6: Declaring the imported global variables and memory buffer

We first import the global variable $cnvs_size ❶, defined as 512 in the JavaScript, which represents the width and height of the canvas. Next are two color values, $no_hit_color ❷, representing the 32-bit color of a noncolliding object, and $hit_color, representing the color of a colliding object. Remember that we defined them as the hexadecimal value for green and red.

Then we have an $obj_start ❸ variable that contains the base location for the object data. The $obj_size ❹ variable is the width and height of the objects in pixels, which will be square. The $obj_cnt ❺ variable contains the number of objects the application will render and checks for collisions. Next is the offset for the two coordinates, $x_offset ❻ and $y_offset, and the two attributes for the velocity values ❼, $xv_offset and $yv_offset. The final import ❽ in this code block imports the memory buffer that we defined in JavaScript.

Clearing the Canvas

Next, we'll define a function that clears the entire bitmap image buffer. If the canvas isn't cleared every time the frame is rendered, the old impression of each object will remain in memory and the objects will smear across the screen. The $clear_canvas function sets every color value to 0xff_00_00_00, representing black with full opacity. Listing 8-7 shows the code for the $clear_canvas function.

collide.wat
(part 2 of 12)
```
...
;; clear the entire canvas
(func $clear_canvas
  (local $i        i32)
  (local $pixel_bytes  i32)

  global.get $cnvs_size
  global.get $cnvs_size
  i32.mul                    ;; multiply $width and $height

  i32.const 4
  i32.mul                    ;; 4 bytes per pixel

❶ local.set $pixel_bytes     ;; $pixel_bytes = $width * $height * 4

❷ (loop $pixel_loop
  ❸ (i32.store (local.get $i) (i32.const 0xff_00_00_00))

    (i32.add (local.get $i) (i32.const 4))
  ❹ local.set $i             ;; $i += 4 (bytes per pixel)

    ;; if $i < $pixel_bytes
```

```
❺ (i32.lt_u (local.get $i) (local.get $pixel_bytes))
❻ br_if $pixel_loop ;; break loop if all pixels set
  )
)
...
```

Listing 8-7: The $clear_canvas function definition

The $clear_canvas function calculates the number of pixel bytes by squaring the canvas size (because we chose a square canvas) and then multiplying by 4 because four bytes are used for each pixel. Next, we store this value, which is the number of bytes dedicated to pixel memory, in the local variable $pixel_bytes ❶. The function then loops ❷ over each pixel, storing a hexadecimal value 0xff_00_00_00 ❸, where all the pixel colors are 0 with 0xff (full opacity) used for the alpha value. The function increments the index stored in $i by 4 ❹ because four bytes are in an i32 integer. The code checks whether the $i index is less than the number of pixel bytes ❺ and if it is, branches back to the top of the loop ❻, because if $i is less than the number of pixels, it means there are objects that need to be cleared.

Absolute Value Function

In this app, we'll use the box collision detection strategy, as opposed to the circle collision detection we used earlier in the book, because our objects are square. We'll need to switch to the rectangle collision detection algorithm, which requires the code to find the absolute value of a signed integer. In Listing 8-8, we'll write a small $abs function that can take a signed integer and look to see whether the parameter passed in is negative, and if so, make it a positive number to give us that absolute value.

collide.wat
(part 3 of 12)

```
...
;; this function returns an absolute value when a value is passed in
(func $abs
    (param $value      i32)
    (result            i32)

❶ (i32.lt_s (local.get $value) (i32.const 0)) ;; is $value negative?
❷ if ;; if $value is negative subtract it from 0 to get the positive value
     i32.const 0
     local.get $value
  ❸ i32.sub
  ❹ return
   end
❺ local.get $value   ;; return original value
)
...
```

Listing 8-8: The absolute value function $abs

The $abs function first looks at the value passed in and checks whether the signed value of that integer is less than 0 ❶. If it is less than 0 ❷, the function subtracts ❸ that number from 0, negating it and returning the positive number ❹. If the number wasn't negative, the function returns the original number ❺.

Setting a Pixel Color

To draw the object to the canvas, we need to be able to set a pixel's color in linear memory given an x- and y-coordinate and the color value. That function will need a bounds check because we're writing to an area of linear memory set aside to represent the area of the canvas. Without this check, if we try to write to a memory location that isn't on the canvas, the function will be writing to an area of linear memory that we might be using for some other purpose.

The function tests coordinates against the bounds of the canvas and returns if those coordinates are out of bounds. This determines where, in linear memory, it needs to update the pixel data. Before we look at the code, let's quickly examine how coordinates on the canvas translate into linear memory.

The canvas is a 2D surface with rows and columns. Figure 8-1 shows a simple canvas four pixels high and four pixels wide.

4x4 Canvas

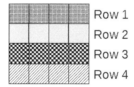

Figure 8-1: A 4 × 4 canvas

Each row in the canvas has been textured differently for reasons that will become clear shortly. The canvas has x- and y-coordinates, where the x-coordinate of the first column is 0 and increments from left to right; the y-coordinate also begins at 0 and increments from top to bottom. Figure 8-2 illustrates our 4 × 4 canvas with x- and y-coordinates.

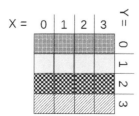

Figure 8-2: The 4 × 4 canvas
in x- and y-coordinates

This is how the canvas is arranged on a computer monitor, but computer memory isn't arranged in rows and columns. Memory is one dimensional with a single address representing each pixel. For this reason, our pixel data is arranged in memory as shown in Figure 8-3.

16 pixels in linear memory

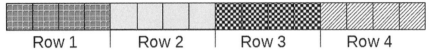

Figure 8-3: The 16 pixels of the canvas in linear memory

The rows are arranged one after the other in a 16-pixel data array. If you look at how the linear memory has arranged the pixels from the perspective of the x- and y-coordinates, it looks like Figure 8-4.

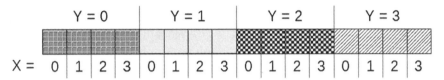

Figure 8-4: The x- and y-coordinates in linear memory

Our $set_pixel function already has the x- and y-coordinates, and needs to find the memory address. We do this using the equation $y * 4 + $x, which gives us the linear memory values in Figure 8-5.

Figure 8-5: The formula for translating from x-, y-coordinates to linear memory

Once we have the memory location, we can update linear memory using i32.store to set the value at that address to the color value in the parameter $c. Listing 8-9 shows the source code.

collide.wat
(part 4 of 12)

```
...
;; this function sets a pixel at coordinates $x, $y to the color $c
(func $set_pixel
    (param $x      i32)   ;; x coordinate
    (param $y      i32)   ;; y coordinate
    (param $c      i32)   ;; color value

    ;; is $x > $cnvs_size
❶ (i32.ge_u (local.get $x) (global.get $cnvs_size))
    if    ;; $x is outside the canvas bounds
      return
    end
```

```
❷ (i32.ge_u (local.get $y) (global.get $cnvs_size))   ;; is $y > $cnvs_size
   if     ;; $y is outside the canvas bounds
     return
   end

   local.get $y
   global.get $cnvs_size
❸ i32.mul

   local.get $x
❹ i32.add       ;; $x + $y * $cnvs_size (get pixels into linear memory)

   i32.const 4
❺ i32.mul       ;; multiply by 4 because each pixel is 4 bytes

   local.get $c  ;; load color value

❻ i32.store     ;; store color in memory location
)
...
```

Listing 8-9: The function that sets an individual pixel to a given color

This function first does a bounds check so the user can't try to set the color of a pixel that isn't on our canvas. To verify that the x-coordinate is in the bounds of the canvas, we check whether $x is greater than $cnvs_size ❶, and if it is, return the function without updating memory. We do the same with the y-coordinate ❷.

After the bounds check, we need to retrieve the location in integers of the target pixel. We get this by multiplying $y by $cnvs_size ❸ to get the number of pixels in memory that are in the rows before the pixel and adding ❹ $x to that value. Because the location value is in 32-bit integers (four bytes per pixel), we need to multiply that number by 4 ❺ to get the byte location of our pixel in linear memory. This memory location is where we store $c using a call to the i32.store ❻ statement.

Drawing the Object

The collider objects are green squares if they don't collide with another object and red if they do. We set the size of these squares to 4 in the JavaScript code's constant section, so each is four pixels wide and four pixels high. We draw these pixels using a loop that increments the x value until it reaches the position of the object plus width. Doing so draws the first row of pixels. Once the x-coordinate value has exceeded the maximum x, the code increments the y-coordinate value. We then draw the second row of pixels and repeat until it exceeds the maximum y value of a pixel in this object. The code then breaks out of the loop. We end up with an object of 4 × 4 pixels. Let's add the code for this function to our WAT file, as shown in Listing 8-10.

```
                ...
                ;; draw multi pixel object as a square given coordinates $x, $y and color $c
                (func $draw_obj
                  (param $x i32)      ;; x position of the object
                  (param $y i32)      ;; y position of the object
                  (param $c i32)      ;; color of the object

                  (local $max_x        i32)
                  (local $max_y        i32)

                  (local $xi           i32)
                  (local $yi           i32)

                  local.get $x
❶                 local.tee $xi
                  global.get $obj_size
                  i32.add
❷                 local.set $max_x          ;; $max_x = $x + $obj_size

                  local.get $y
                  local.tee $yi
                  global.get $obj_size
                  i32.add
❸                 local.set $max_y          ;; $max_y = $y + $obj_size

                  (block $break (loop $draw_loop

                    local.get $xi
                    local.get $yi
                    local.get $c
❹                   call $set_pixel         ;; set pixel at $xi, $yi to color $c

                    local.get $xi
                    i32.const 1
                    i32.add
❺                   local.tee $xi           ;; $xi++

                    local.get $max_x
❻                   i32.ge_u                ;; is $xi >= $max_x

                    if
                      local.get $x
❼                     local.set $xi         ;; reset $xi to $x

                      local.get $yi
                      i32.const 1
                      i32.add
❽                     local.tee $yi         ;; $yi++

                      local.get $max_y
❾                     i32.ge_u              ;; is $yi >= $max_y
```

```
        br_if $break

    end
    br $draw_loop
  ))
)
...
```

Listing 8-10: The $draw_obj function draws a square of pixels calling the $set_pixel function.

The $draw_obj function takes as parameters the x- and y-coordinates, and color in the form of param i32 variables $x, $y, and $c. It draws pixels starting at the $x position for the x-coordinate and $y for the y-coordinate. It needs to loop over each pixel until it reaches a $max_x and $max_y position for the x- and y-coordinates. The function begins by using local.tee ❶ to set the value of $xi to the value passed to the function as $x. It then adds the object's size ($obj_size) to find the $max_x ❷ value. Thereafter, the function finds $max_y ❸ in the same way.

We find the starting and ending x-coordinates, and then do the same task for the y-axis ❹. I chose 512 as the width and height of the canvas because I assumed this kind of mask would offer better performance than using an i32.rem_u for a canvas bounds check. In Chapter 9, we'll test this hypothesis to see whether this was a valid assumption or a premature optimization. Chapter 4 went into detail as to how bit masking works.

The minimum and maximum x and y values enter a loop that draws each pixel using a call $set_pixel expression ❺. The loop increments $xi ❻ and compares it with $max_x, resetting $xi to $x and incrementing $yi ❾ if $xi is greater than or equal to $max_x ❼. Then, when $yi has exceeded $max_y, the object is fully drawn and the code exits the loop.

Setting and Getting Object Attributes

Let's create a few helper functions to set and get object attribute values inside linear memory. These functions take in an object number and an attribute offset and return the value from linear memory. In the case of $set_obj_attr, the function also takes a value and sets the object attribute to that value. In the case of $get_obj_attr, the function returns the value in linear memory for that object and attribute. Add the code in Listing 8-11 for $set_obj_attr to your WAT module.

collide.wat
(part 6 of 12)

```
...
;; set the attribute of an object in linear memory using the object number,
;; the attributes offset and a value used to set the attribute
(func $set_obj_attr
  (param $obj_number i32)
  (param $attr_offset i32)
  (param $value      i32)

  local.get $obj_number
```

```
  i32.const 16
❶ i32.mul                  ;;  16 byte stride multiplied by the object number

  global.get $obj_start    ;;  add the starting byte for the objects (base)
❷ i32.add                  ;;  ($obj_number*16) + $obj_start

  local.get $attr_offset   ;; add the attribute offset to the address
❸ i32.add                  ;; ($obj_number*16) + $obj_start + $attr_offset

  local.get $value

  ;; store $value at location ($obj_number*16)+$obj_start+$attr_offset
❹ i32.store
)
...
```

Listing 8-11: Setting an object in memory based on a stride value of 16

Most of the code in this function calculates the address in linear
memory where the attribute for the specific object is stored. Recall from
Chapter 6 that we calculated the memory location of our attribute using a
base address ($obj_start in this function), a stride of 16, an object number
($obj_number), and an attribute offset ($attr_offset). This function uses the
formula $obj_number*16 ❶ + $obj_start ❷ + $attr_offset ❸ to determine
the memory location of the attribute we want to modify. It then calls the
i32.store ❹ statement to store that value in memory.

Next, we'll create the corresponding $get_obj_attr, which needs to cal-
culate the address of the attribute value. You might be familiar with the
software development principle *Don't Repeat Yourself (DRY)*. DRY code is an
excellent way to write maintainable code that is easy for other developers to
read and update. Unfortunately, there are times when DRY code can reduce
performance. In this example, we'll redo some of the calculations we did in
the previous function. When we venture into the performance optimization
chapter, we'll make our code even less DRY (sometimes called *wet code*) than
it was in this chapter. Some techniques that produce DRY code can add lay-
ers of abstraction that require additional computing cycles. For example,
a function call requires additional cycles to push values onto the stack and
jump to new locations in the code. Optimizing compilers can frequently
mitigate the impact of abstractions used in the code, but it can be helpful
to understand how they do this and why DRY code isn't always the most efficient during execution.

In other assembly languages, macros are a great way to maintain performance while keeping your code relatively DRY. Unfortunately, wat2wasm
doesn't currently support macros. Listing 8-12 shows the code for the
$get_obj_attr function.

collide.wat
(part 7 of 12)
```
...
;; get the attribute of an object in linear memory using the object
;; number, and the attributes offset
(func $get_obj_attr
  (param $obj_number  i32)
```

```
    (param $attr_offset i32)
    (result i32)

    local.get $obj_number
    i32.const 16
❶ i32.mul                    ;; $obj_number * 16

    global.get $obj_start
❷ i32.add                    ;; ($obj_number*16) + $obj_start

    local.get $attr_offset
❸ i32.add                    ;; ($obj_number*16) + $obj_start + $attr_offset

❹ i32.load                   ;; load the pointer above
    ;; returns the attribute
)
...
```

Listing 8-12: Gets an object in memory based on a stride value of 16

To get the offset bytes for an object, we start by multiplying $obj_number by the stride value of 16 ❶. Then we add ❷ the base address, which is stored in the global variable $obj_start. That's followed by adding the offset, stored in $attr_offset ❸. At this point, the top of the stack has the location in memory of the attribute we want to retrieve, so calling the expression i32.load ❹ pushes that value onto the stack.

The $main Function

The $main function will be called from the JavaScript code once per frame render. Its job is to move every object based on that object's velocity, detect a collision between objects, and then render the object in red if it collides with another object and green if it doesn't. The $main function is very long, so we'll break it into several parts.

Defining Local Variables

The first part of the $main function, shown in Listing 8-13, defines all the local variables and calls the $clear_canvas function.

collide.wat
(part 8 of 12)

```
...
;; move and detect collisions between all of the objects in our app
(func $main (export "main")
❶ (local $i          i32)  ;; outer loop index
   (local $j          i32)  ;; inner loop index
❷ (local $outer_ptr  i32)  ;; pointer to outer loop object
   (local $inner_ptr  i32)  ;; pointer to inner loop object

❸ (local $x1         i32)  ;; outer loop object x coordinate
   (local $x2         i32)  ;; inner loop object x coordinate
   (local $y1         i32)  ;; outer loop object y coordinate
   (local $y2         i32)  ;; inner loop object y coordinate
```

```
❹ (local $xdist       i32)   ;; distance between objects on x axis
   (local $ydist       i32)   ;; distance between objects on y axis

❺ (local $i_hit        i32)   ;; i object hit boolean flag
❻ (local $xv           i32)   ;; x velocity
   (local $yv           i32)   ;; y velocity

❼ (call $clear_canvas)        ;; clear the canvas to black
   ...
```

Listing 8-13: The beginning of the $main function declares the local variables and clears the canvas.

This function has a double loop that compares every object with every other object. To do this, we define two loop variables, $i ❶ and $j, which will be loop counters for our outer and inner loops, respectively. We need to loop over every object using the $i variable and compare it to every other object using the $j variable. Then we use two pointer variables, $outer_ptr ❷ and $inner_ptr, that point to the linear memory location for those two collider objects.

The next four local variables are the x- and y-coordinates ❸ for the inner and outer loop objects. The distance between the x- and y-coordinates of the two objects are stored in the $xdist ❹ and $ydist local variables. The $i_hit ❺ local variable is a boolean flag that is set to 1 if the $i object collides with another object and 0 if it doesn't. Two variables, $xv ❻ and $yv, store the velocity of the $i object. After the local variables are declared, the function performs the first action: clear all the canvas pixels to black using the statement (call $clear_canvas) ❼.

The $move_loop

The next part of the $main function defines a loop that moves every object in linear memory each frame. This part of the function will retrieve the $x, $y, $xv, and $yv attributes for the $i object. The $xv and $yv variables are the x and y velocity variables, and they're used to move the object by changing the $x and $y coordinate values. The code also forces the x and y values to stay within the bounds of the canvas. Immediately after the move loop, the $i variable is reset to 0. Add the code in Listing 8-14 to the WAT module.

collide.wat
(part 9 of 12)

```
...
❶ (loop $move_loop
      ;; get x attribute
      (call $get_obj_attr (local.get $i) (global.get $x_offset))
      local.set $x1

      ;; get y attribute
      (call $get_obj_attr (local.get $i) (global.get $y_offset))
      local.set $y1

      ;; get x velocity attribute
      (call $get_obj_attr (local.get $i) (global.get $xv_offset))
      local.set $xv
```

```
    ;; get y velocity attribute
    (call $get_obj_attr (local.get $i) (global.get $yv_offset))
    local.set $yv

    ;; add velocity to x and force it to stay in the canvas bounds
❷ (i32.add (local.get $xv) (local.get $x1))
    i32.const 0x1ff  ;; 511 in decimal
❸ i32.and            ;; clear high-order 23 bits
    local.set $x1

    ;; add velocity to y and force it to stay in the canvas bounds
    (i32.add (local.get $yv) (local.get $y1))
    i32.const 0x1ff  ;; 511 in decimal
    i32.and            ;; clear high-order 23 bits
❹ local.set $y1

    ;; set the x attribute in linear memory
❺ (call $set_obj_attr
    (local.get $i)
    (global.get $x_offset)
    (local.get $x1)
  )

    ;; set the y attribute in linear memory
    (call $set_obj_attr
    (local.get $i)
    (global.get $y_offset)
    (local.get $y1)
  )

  local.get $i
  i32.const 1
❻ i32.add
❼ local.tee $i        ;; increment $i

  global.get $obj_cnt
  i32.lt_u            ;; $i < $obj_cnt

❽ if  ;; if $i < $obj_count branch back to top of $move_loop
    br $move_loop
  end

 )

  i32.const 0
❾ local.set $i
...
```

Listing 8-14: Loop to move each object

The code in Listing 8-14 loops through all of our objects, changing the x- and y-coordinates based on the x and y velocities. The first few lines of the loop ❶ call $get_obj_attr for the x position, y position, x velocity, and y velocity attributes, passing in the loop index and the offset of the attribute to be set. Doing this pushes the value of the attribute onto the stack. The expression local.set is then used to set a local variable we'll use in the loop.

The loop will add the velocity variables ($xv and $yv) to the position variables ($x1 and $y1) with a call to i32.add ❷. Before $x1 is set to the new position, an i32.and ❸ is used to mask the last nine bits of the x position. This holds the value of the x-coordinate between 0 and 511, wrapping the value back around to 0 if it exceeds 511. The same is then done for $y1 ❹ to set the y position. Once the new values of $x1 and $y1 are set, the $set_obj_attr ❺ function is called for those values to set them in linear memory. The loop counter $i ❻ is incremented with a call to i32.and and local.tee ❼. If the value in $i is less than the object count ($obj_count ❽), the code branches back to the top of the loop. Otherwise, local.set ❾ is called to set $i to 0.

The squares in Listing 8-14 wrap around on the canvas so when one goes offscreen on the right, it loops back around and appears on the left side of the screen, as in the old-school arcade games. Games like Atari's *Asteroids* and Namco's *Pac-Man* didn't need any extra code to have this effect; instead, their screens were 256 pixels wide and used an 8-bit number to store the x-coordinate. So if a game object had an x-coordinate of 255 and moved one pixel to the right, the single byte value would roll back over to 0, and the game object would reappear on the left side of the screen, as shown in Figure 8-6.

Figure 8-6: Player's character goes off the screen to the right and appears on the left.

We can accomplish this effect using i32.and to mask all but the bottom nine bits. The code calls $get_obj_attr to get the attributes for $x1, $y1, $xv, and $yv ❶. The new $x1 value is calculated by adding $xv ❷ and then using the i32.and ❸ against the constant 0x1ff. In binary, 0x1ff has the lowest nine bits all set to 1, and all the higher bits are set to 0. Chapter 4 explained how to use an i32.and to set specific bits to 0, as illustrated in Figure 8-7.

Figure 8-7: The 0s in our mask turn any values in the initial value to 0.

When we call i32.and ❸ on $x1 and 0x1ff (binary 000000000000000000 00000111111111), the resulting value has the top 23 bits set to 0. That limits the $x1 value to nine bits, so if the number goes above what a 9-bit number can hold, the $x1 value rolls back over, similar to an odometer. That creates an old-school arcade effect where objects that move offscreen to the left reappear on the right, and objects that move offscreen on the top reappear on the bottom of the screen.

After making changes to the x- and y-coordinates, the $i index is incremented ❽, and if $i is less than $obj_count, the code branches back to the top of the $move_loop. When the loop is complete, the $i ❾ index variable is reset to 0.

Beginning of the Outer Loop

Now we need to define our double loop, which compares every object against every other object to see whether any collisions have occurred. The next part of the $main function defines the outer loop of our double loop, which will determine the first object of our collision test. The loop begins by initializing $j to 0. The $i local variable is the increment variable for the outer loop. The inner loop will use $j to loop through all the objects to check each one against $i until it finds a collision or makes its way through every object. The outer loop starts with the first object, and then the inner loop checks that object for a collision with every other object. This continues until the outer loop has checked every object. Add the code in Listing 8-15 to the $main function.

collide.wat
(part 10 of 12)

```
...
  (loop $outer_loop (block $outer_break
    i32.const 0
❶  local.tee $j          ;; setting j to 0

    ;; $i_hit is a boolean value.  0 for false, 1 for true
❷  local.set $i_hit      ;; setting i_hit to 0

    ;; get x attribute for object $i
    (call $get_obj_attr (local.get $i) (global.get $x_offset))
❸  local.set $x1

    ;; get y attribute for object $i
    (call $get_obj_attr (local.get $i) (global.get $y_offset))
❹  local.set $y1
...
```

Listing 8-15: The outer loop of a collision detection double loop

The beginning of the loop resets $j ❶ and $i_hit ❷ to 0. The code then calls the $get_obj_attr function to find the values for $x1 ❸ and $y1 ❹.

The Inner Loop

The next section of the $main function is the inner loop, whose function is to detect a collision between two squares. Square collision detection is very simple: you compare the x-coordinates and size to see whether the objects overlap on the x-axis. If the x-axis doesn't overlap but the y-axis does, it looks like Figure 8-8 and has no collision.

If the x-axis overlaps but the y-axis doesn't, there is no collision between the objects, as in Figure 8-9.

Figure 8-8: The x-axis doesn't overlap but the y-axis does.

Figure 8-9: The x-axis overlaps but the y-axis doesn't.

The only collision scenario is when the x-axis and y-axis overlap, as in Figure 8-10.

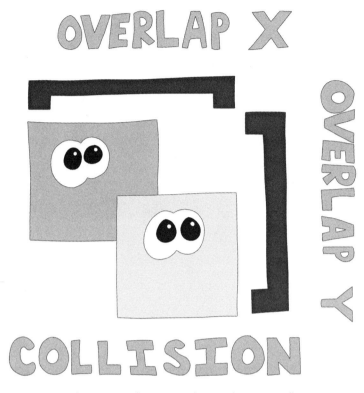

Figure 8-10: The x-axis and y-axis overlap, so there is a collision.

The inner loop performs this check against every object in linear memory. Listing 8-16 shows the code.

collide.wat
(part 11 of 12)

```
...
❶ (loop $inner_loop (block $inner_break
        local.get $i
        local.get $j
        i32.eq
    ❷ if                  ;; if $i == $j increment $j
        local.get $j
        i32.const 1
        i32.add
        local.set $j
      end

        local.get $j
        global.get $obj_cnt
        i32.ge_u
    ❸ if                  ;; if $j >= $obj_count break from inner loop
        br $inner_break
      end
```

```
     ;; get x attribute
❹ (call $get_obj_attr (local.get $j)(global.get $x_offset))
   local.set $x2   ;; set the x attribute for inner loop object

     ;; distance between $x1 and $x2
   (i32.sub (local.get $x1) (local.get $x2))

   call $abs   ;; distance is not negative so get the absolute value
❺ local.tee $xdist   ;; $xdist = the absolute value of ($x1 - $x2)

   global.get $obj_size
   i32.ge_u

❻ if   ;; if $xdist >= $obj_size object does not collide
     local.get $j
     i32.const 1
     i32.add
     local.set $j

     br $inner_loop   ;; increment $j and jump to beginning of inner loop
   end

     ;; get y attribute
   (call $get_obj_attr (local.get $j)(global.get $y_offset))
   local.set $y2

   (i32.sub (local.get $y1) (local.get $y2))
   call $abs
❼ local.tee $ydist

   global.get $obj_size
   i32.ge_u

❽ if
     local.get $j
     i32.const 1
     i32.add
     local.set $j

     br $inner_loop
   end

   i32.const 1
❾ local.set $i_hit
     ;; exit the loop if there is a collision
)) ;; end of inner loop
...
```

Listing 8-16: The inner loop of a collision detection double loop

The inner loop ❶ compares the current object of the outer loop against
every other object that hasn't already been checked against it. First, it needs
to make sure it's not checking an object against itself. An object always completely collides with itself, so if $i is equal to $j ❷, we ignore it and need to

increment $j. Then we compare $j with $obj_cnt ❸ to see whether the code has tested all the objects yet. If it has, the code exits the inner loop.

If the code hasn't tested all objects, the x attribute is loaded into the $x2 variable by calling $get_obj_attr ❹. We then get the distance between $x1 and $x2 by subtracting $x2 from $x1, taking the absolute value and setting the $xdist ❺ variable. We compare the x distance between the two objects to the object size to see whether the two objects overlap on the x-axis. If they don't overlap because $xdist is greater than $obj_size ❻, the code increments $j and jumps back to the top of the loop.

In the same way, the y distance is calculated and stored in the $ydist ❼ variable, and the code checks whether the $ydist variable is greater than $obj_size ❽. If so, these objects don't collide, so we increment $j and jump back to the top of the loop. If we haven't jumped to the top of the loop at this point, we know that the x- and y-axis of the objects overlap, indicating a collision, so we set $i_hit ❾ to 1 and exit the inner loop.

Redrawing the Objects

When the code has exited the inner loop, either a collision was found or it wasn't. The code checks the hit variable ($i_hit) and calls the $draw_obj function with the no collision color (green) if there wasn't a collision and with the $hit_color (red) if there was a collision. Then $i is incremented, and if $i is less than the number of objects, the code jumps back to the top of the outer loop. Listing 8-17 shows the last section of code to add to the WAT file.

collide.wat
(part 12 of 12)

```
...
    local.get $i_hit
    i32.const 0
    i32.eq
❶ if        ;; if $i_hit == 0 (no hit)
      (call $draw_obj
        (local.get $x1) (local.get $y1)  (global.get $no_hit_color))
❷ else      ;; if $i_hit == 1 (hit)
      (call $draw_obj
        (local.get $x1) (local.get $y1) (global.get $hit_color))
    end

    local.get $i
    i32.const 1
    i32.add
❸ local.tee $i          ;; increment $i

    global.get $obj_cnt
    i32.lt_u
❹ if                    ;; if $i < $obj_cnt jump to top of the outer loop
      br $outer_loop
    end
❺ )) ;; end of outer loop
) ;; end of function
) ;; end of module
```

Listing 8-17: Drawing the object inside the inner loop

Immediately after the inner loop ends, the outer loop checks whether the $i_hit variable was set to 0 ❶ , indicating no collision. If it was, $draw_obj is called, passing in the $no_hit_color global variable as the last parameter and drawing the square in green. If the $i_hit variable is set to 1 ❷ (true), $draw_obj is called with $hit_color (red). At this point, $i ❸ is incremented, and if it's less than $obj_cnt ❹, indicating we've not completed drawing our objects, the code jumps back to the top of the loop. If not ❺, the code exits the loop and this function is complete.

Compiling and Running the App

Before we run the collider application, we need to compile our WAT into a WebAssembly module. Use the following wat2wasm command to compile *collide.wat* into *collide.wasm*:

```
wat2wasm collide.wat
```

When you run a web server and open the *collide.html* file in a web browser from localhost, your screen should look similar to Figure 8-11.

Figure 8-11: The collider app

The boxes should move about the canvas, appearing on the left side of the canvas when they move off the right side and on the top when they move off the bottom. Boxes that collide with each other appear in red, and boxes that don't collide with other boxes appear in green.

Summary

In this chapter, we explored how WebAssembly and the HTML canvas can work together to create fantastic animations on a web page. You should now understand when it's best to use WebAssembly and when using JavaScript is a better option. Rendering to the canvas from WebAssembly can be done quickly and efficiently by modifying memory locations that represent bitmap data. The collider app we created used many JavaScript constants to define its details. That allowed us to tweak and play with the numbers in the app without recompiling the WebAssembly module. JavaScript can easily generate random numbers that we can use in the app. Generating random numbers from WebAssembly is much more challenging. Because the random numbers only need to be generated once, using JavaScript isn't a significant performance hit.

You learned about bitmap image data and how to use WebAssembly to generate that image data inside linear memory. We used the request AnimationFrame function from within JavaScript to call the WebAssembly module once per frame, using WebAssembly to generate the bitmap image data to be used in the canvas. This image data is moved into the HTML canvas using the putImageData function on the canvas context.

In the WAT module code, we set up and modified an area of memory dedicated to the image data, and created a canvas clearing function. We drew a specific pixel color to the canvas; then we drew objects larger than a single pixel and made those objects appear at the opposite side of the canvas when they moved out of the element's bounds. Lastly, we used box collision detection to detect and change the color of our objects if there were collisions between objects.

We didn't spend a lot of time or effort trying to make the collider application fast. In the next chapter, we'll make this application run as fast as possible with some performance tuning.

9

OPTIMIZING PERFORMANCE

This chapter is aimed squarely at developers who want lightning-fast applications and are willing to take the time to make that happen. We'll first discuss profiler tools to evaluate WebAssembly module performance and investigate how to compare the performance of WebAssembly with similar JavaScript code. We'll spend some time looking at strategies to improve the performance of our WebAssembly, including inlining functions, replacing multiplication and division with bit-shifts, combining constants, and removing code using Dead Code Elimination (DCE).

We'll also delve into other methods for determining a module's performance: we'll use `console.log` and `Date.now` to measure our application's performance and use the testing suite *benchmark.js* to gather detailed performance data for an application. Then, just for fun, we'll print the Chrome JavaScript V8 engine's Intermediate Representation (IR) bytecode for a JavaScript function. JavaScript IR bytecode can give you insight into the work a JavaScript function does, which is helpful for evaluating whether to write a function in WebAssembly or JavaScript.

Using a Profiler

Profilers are tools that analyze different aspects of an application's performance, including the app's memory usage and execution time. This can help you make decisions about where to optimize and what to optimize for. You'll often need to make trade-offs between different types of optimizations. For example, you'll need to decide whether to focus on improving your time to interactive (TTI) so users can begin using your application as soon as possible or focusing on peak performance once your application is up and running. If you're writing a game, it's worth having a long load time to ensure the game will run more smoothly once it finishes downloading. However, an online store might prefer to ensure the user can interact with the website as soon as possible. In most cases, you'll need to balance between the two, and using a profiler can help.

Profilers are also efficient at finding bottlenecks in your code, allowing you to focus your time and effort in those locations. We'll look at the Chrome and Firefox profilers, because they currently have the best support for WebAssembly. We'll be profiling the collision detection app from Chapter 8.

Chrome Profiler

You'll want to use a new incognito browser window with the Chrome profiler. Incognito windows don't load website caches, cookies, or Chrome plug-ins, which cause problems when profiling because they run additional JavaScript code and affect the performance of the site you want to profile. The caches and cookies are usually less problematic, but can clutter your environment with data unrelated to the code you're profiling. You can open an incognito window from the menu on the top right of your web browser by clicking **New incognito window**, as shown in Figure 9-1.

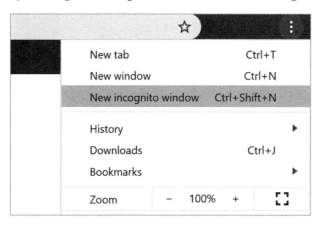

Figure 9-1: Open an incognito window in Chrome.

After opening an incognito browser window, make sure you're running a web server using the command node server.js from your command line and enter **localhost:8080/collide.html** into your web browser. Click **More Tools ▸ Developer tools** from the menu in the top right, as shown in Figure 9-2.

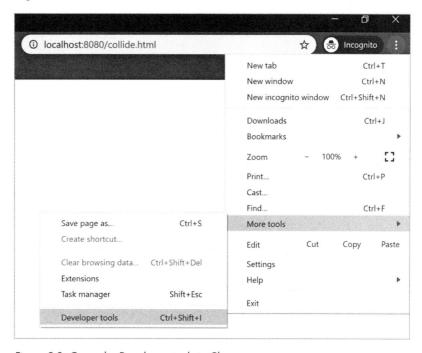

Figure 9-2: Open the Developer tools in Chrome.

You should see several tabs across the top of the Developer tools. To see the profiler, click **Performance**, as shown in Figure 9-3.

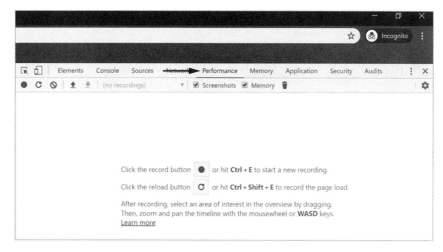

Figure 9-3: Open the Performance tab in Chrome.

The Performance tab offers two options when you initially open it: Record and Reload. The Record button begins recording a profile without reloading the application. This kind of profiling is most important when you're less concerned about the startup time of your application and more concerned with peak performance. Before we profile, make sure the Memory checkbox at the top of the Performance tab is selected. If it isn't, the memory heap won't be profiled. If you want to profile your application from initialization, you would click the Reload button. Click **Record** to continue. Once you've recorded for about five seconds, click **Stop** as shown in Figure 9-4.

Figure 9-4: Recording a profile in Chrome

When recording stops, the profiler will open and show a recording of every frame rendered by your application. A Summary tab in the bottom half shows that the vast majority of this application's execution time is tied up in Scripting (Figure 9-5), which includes JavaScript and WebAssembly time.

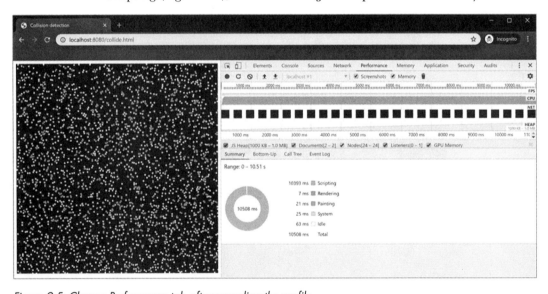

Figure 9-5: Chrome Performance tab after recording the profile

On this main Performance page, a pie chart shows the processing time spent Scripting, Rendering, Painting, System, and Idle. Above the pie chart is a series of tabs, including Summary, Bottom-Up, Call Tree, and Event Log, all of which we'll explore in this chapter. The section above these tabs shows the JS Heap memory allocated, and above that, the rendered frames,

CPU, and FPS information. Let's take a quick look at the JavaScript heap memory in the next section.

JavaScript Heap Memory

The profile in Figure 9-5 shows that there's been a growth in heap memory. We'll spend a little time investigating why this is happening. First, we'll check how much memory is allocated before it's garbage collected. Some developers believe that because JavaScript is a garbage collected language, they don't need to be concerned about memory. Unfortunately, that's not the case; it's still possible for your code to create objects faster than they can be garbage collected. It's also possible to hold on to references to objects longer than they're needed, leaving JavaScript unable to know if it should delete them. If an application is growing in memory size as quickly as this one is, it makes sense to watch how much memory is allocated before garbage collection. Then try to understand where the application allocates memory. Right now, the heap size is about 1MB.

After some additional profiling, we can see that the JS Heap grows to 2.2MB, and after the garbage collector runs, the heap size drops back down to 1.2MB. It might take several minutes before the garbage collector runs, so please be patient. Figure 9-6 shows the profile of the JS Heap during garbage collection. As you can see, on the right side of the graph, the size of the heap takes a sudden significant drop in size of 1MB.

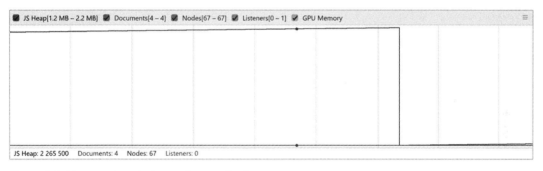

Figure 9-6: Memory drop during garbage collection

It's best to determine precisely where this memory allocation is happening, because if we could slow the growth of the heap, it would potentially reduce the burden on the garbage collector.

Following the Memory Allocation

Because the growth of the heap is consistent, we can deduce that memory allocation is likely happening every frame render. The majority of the work this application does is in the WebAssembly module, so we first comment out the WebAssembly call to see whether the memory continues to show the same JS Heap growth profile. Open *collide.html* and comment out the call to `animation_wasm()` inside the `animate` function, as shown in Listing 9-1.

collide.html   ...

```
function animate() {
//      animation_wasm();
  ctx.putImageData(image_data, 0, 0); // render pixel data
  requestAnimationFrame(animate);
}
```
...

Listing 9-1: Commenting out the animation_wasm function call

Now reload the page and record a new profile. Figure 9-7 shows the new JS Heap profile without the animation_wasm function call.

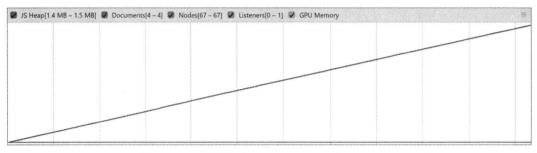

Figure 9-7: Heap memory allocation graph after the animation_wasm function is removed

Without the call to the WebAssembly module, the app no longer functions properly. However, you can still see the same JS Heap growth profile, so the growth in memory doesn't appear to be coming from the WebAssembly module. Let's uncomment the call to the WebAssembly module; then comment out the call to `ctx.putImageData` and create another profile, as shown in Listing 9-2.

collide.html

```
function animate() {
  animation_wasm();
//    ctx.putImageData(image_data, 0, 0); // render pixel data
  requestAnimationFrame(animate);
}
```

Listing 9-2: The animation_wasm function is back in; putImageData is removed.

With the call to `ctx.putImageData` commented out, we can now create a new profile to check the memory growth (Figure 9-8).

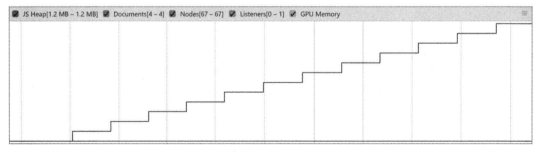

Figure 9-8: Memory growth is slower when the putImageData call is removed.

Without the call to `ctx.putImageData`, the memory growth slowed tremendously. Growth is still occurring, but it has a slower stair step growth pattern rather than an almost straight vertical line up. It appears that the call to `ctx.putImageData` is internally creating large objects that the garbage collector will eventually need to remove. Now we know how that memory is being allocated. Because `ctx.putImageData` is a built-in function, there isn't anything we can do to optimize it. If memory allocation had been the problem, we would need to look into an alternative means to render to the canvas.

Frames

In the Profiler window is an area above the heap memory that provides more performance information, including the frames per second (fps) rendered. It also shows a graph that displays CPU usage. And there are small thumbnails of each frame rendered. When you move your mouse over these frames, you can watch how your application rendered its animation (Figure 9-9), which can be very helpful if your application isn't working as expected.

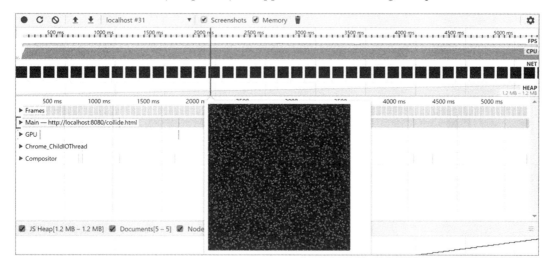

Figure 9-9: Viewing the individual frame render in the profiler

You can hover your mouse over the green *Frames* boxes to see the fps at any point in the profile (Figure 9-10).

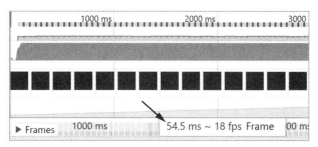

Figure 9-10: Viewing fps in the profiler

As you can see, the frame rate at this point in the application's execution is 18 fps. When we scrub over the frames, the number hovers between 17 and 20. Frames per second is the primary measure of performance for the collision detection app, so we'll need to remember the profile showing us roughly 18 fps to compare it with later results. Keep in mind that running the profiler appears to harm the app's performance, so although the results are useful relative to each other, they might not be totally accurate on how the app runs in the wild.

Bottom-Up

The Bottom-Up tab shows the functions called within the application, the total time they ran, and the Self Time, which is the amount of time the function ran excluding the time spent in the functions they call. Self Time is very useful because functions that call other functions that take a long time to run will always show a longer Total Time, as you can see in Figure 9-11.

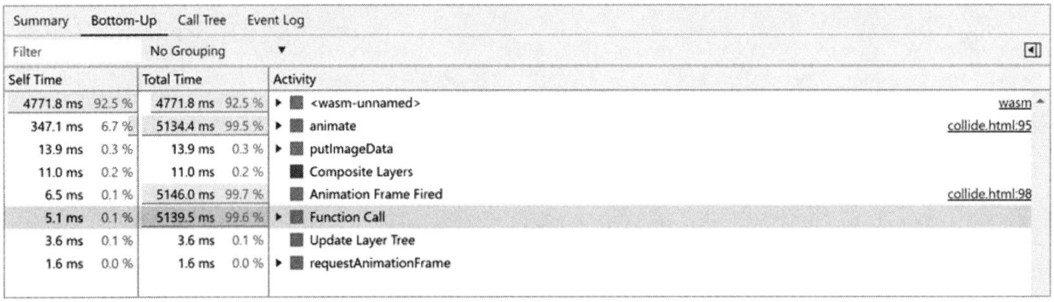

Summary	Bottom-Up	Call Tree	Event Log		
Filter		No Grouping ▼			◄|
Self Time		**Total Time**		**Activity**	
4771.8 ms	92.5 %	4771.8 ms	92.5 %	▶ ■ <wasm-unnamed>	wasm ▲
347.1 ms	6.7 %	5134.4 ms	99.5 %	▶ ■ animate	collide.html:95
13.9 ms	0.3 %	13.9 ms	0.3 %	▶ ■ putImageData	
11.0 ms	0.2 %	11.0 ms	0.2 %	■ Composite Layers	
6.5 ms	0.1 %	5146.0 ms	99.7 %	■ Animation Frame Fired	collide.html:98
5.1 ms	0.1 %	5139.5 ms	99.6 %	▶ ■ Function Call	
3.6 ms	0.1 %	3.6 ms	0.1 %	■ Update Layer Tree	
1.6 ms	0.0 %	1.6 ms	0.0 %	▶ ■ requestAnimationFrame	

Figure 9-11: Chrome's Bottom-Up tab window

The Self Time for <wasm-unnamed> is by far the longest. The Total Time is longer in several functions, such as animate, because the animate function calls the WebAssembly module. It's a bit disappointing that Chrome doesn't indicate which function it calls inside the WebAssembly module, but we can determine at a glance that the application spends more than 90 percent of its processing time executing WebAssembly.

Firefox Profiler

Using the Firefox profiler is another excellent way to gather performance data on your application. I recommend opening a private window when you run the Firefox profiler. Do this by opening the menu in the top right of the browser and clicking **New Private Window** (Figure 9-12).

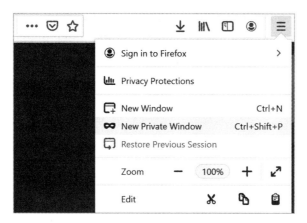

Figure 9-12: Open a New Private Window in Firefox.

Open the profiler by clicking **Web Developer ▶ Performance** (Figure 9-13).

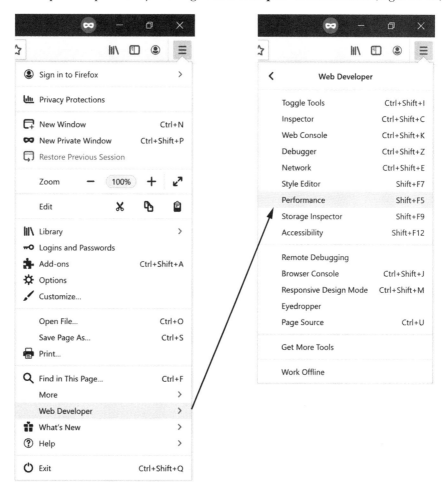

*Figure 9-13: Click **Web Developer ▶ Performance** in the Firefox menu.*

In the Performance menu, click the **Start Recording Performance** button to record performance data. After a few seconds, stop recording. Figure 9-14 shows something similar to what you should see in the Performance tab. The Waterfall tab (which is the default view after recording) shows the top-level function calls and how long they take to execute.

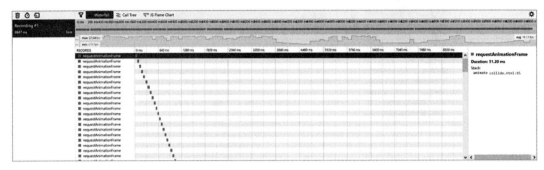

Figure 9-14: Firefox Performance window Waterfall tab

Scroll down to see where the garbage collection takes place and how long it takes to run. This report is a bit boring for our application, which primarily executes requestAnimationFrame. The three tabs across the top of the window provide more information. The Waterfall tab gives you a general idea of where tasks are running long. We won't go into detail about the Waterfall tab, because it's more of a *runtime at a glance* summary. Instead we'll look at the Call Tree and JS Flame Chart tabs.

Call Tree

The Call Tree tab shows the function calls in which the application spends most of its time. The interface allows you to drill down into each of the functions and see the calls they make. Figure 9-15 shows a screenshot of the Call Tree tab.

Total Time	Total Cost	Self Time	Self Cost	Samples	Function
11.23 ms	42.86%	11.23 ms	42.86%	6	▼ wasm-function[5] collide.wasm:426 localhost:8080
11.23 ms	42.86%	0 ms	0%	0	▼ wasm-function[6] collide.wasm:444 localhost:8080
11.23 ms	42.86%	0 ms	0%	0	animate collide.html:95:20 localhost:8080
9.36 ms	35.71%	9.36 ms	35.71%	5	▶ wasm-function[6] collide.wasm:444 localhost:8080
3.74 ms	14.29%	3.74 ms	14.29%	2	▶ wasm-function[1] collide.wasm:283 localhost:8080
1.87 ms	7.14%	1.87 ms	7.14%	1	Idle

Figure 9-15: Firefox Call Tree tab

One nice feature is that you can click the name of your WebAssembly file, and the link will take you to the proper function in your WebAssembly code. The function names are lost, but an index showing the function number in WAT follows the wasm-function label. That makes it a little easier to determine what the function calls.

JS Flame Chart

The JS Flame Chart tab is pretty much the same information you see in the Call Tree tab, but it's organized along a timeline instead of as a summary. You can zoom in on a specific portion of the chart to see which functions are running at that point in the profile (Figure 9-16).

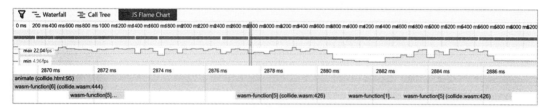

Figure 9-16: Firefox JS Flame Chart tab

Here is the call to the JavaScript animate function. The animate function spends most of its time running wasm-function[6], which is the seventh function in our WAT code, called $main. The $main function calls wasm-function[5], which is the sixth function ($get_obj_attr) and wasm-function[1] ($abs).

Each one of these tabs shows the minimum and maximum fps on the left side and the average fps on the right side. The left side of the profiler looks something like Figure 9-17.

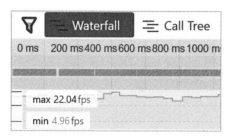

Figure 9-17: Firefox max and min fps

As you can see, the maximum fps is a bit more than 22, and the minimum is a little less than 5 fps. As mentioned earlier, running the profiler might impact the fps. The average fps is on the right side of the profiler (Figure 9-18).

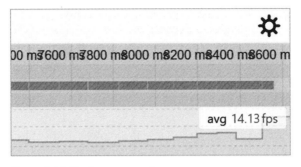

Figure 9-18: Firefox average fps

The average fps for this profile was approximately 14 fps. In the next section, we'll look at how to improve the app's performance using wasm-opt.

wasm-opt

We use the wasm-opt command line tool to run performance optimizations on a WebAssembly file. It comes with wat-wasm and *Binaryen.js*. If you've installed wat-wasm to use for the wat2wasm tool, you should already have a version and can skip the next section. If not, install *Binaryen.js*, which is a JavaScript version of the Binaryen WebAssembly tool for converting an Intermediate Representation (IR) into WebAssembly code. It has some helpful options for optimizing WebAssembly code.

Installing Binaryen

There are several options for installing Binaryen. I recommend using *Binaryen.js*, which you can install using npm with the following command:

```
npm install binaryen -g
```

For those interested in building it from the source, it's available on GitHub at *https://github.com/WebAssembly/binaryen*. There is also an npm package called wasm-opt that will install the platform-specific binaries for *Binaryen*, but I would recommend installing wat-wasm or *binaryen.js* using npm instead.

Running wasm-opt

The wasm-opt tool has a number of flags you can use to minimize the download size and optimize the execution of your WebAssembly module. You use these flags to tell the optimizer whether to focus on performance or download size. If a change can be made to reduce the file size without affecting performance, that change will be made in either case. The same is true if a change can be made to improve the performance without affecting download size. These flags tell the compiler which optimization to prefer when there is a trade-off to consider.

We'll run `wasm-opt` against our *collide.wasm* file with both types of flags, starting with the size optimization preference and then compiling it again with a performance preference. These flags will be the same with any toolchain that uses Binaryen, such as Emscripten or AssemblyScript. The first two flags we'll look at will optimize the WAT file for size.

Optimizing for Download Size

The `wasm-opt` command has two flags that optimize your WebAssembly file for download size: -Oz and -Os. The O is a capital letter O, not a zero. The -Oz flag creates a smaller WebAssembly file but takes longer to reduce the size of the file. The -Os file creates a slightly larger WebAssembly file but takes less time to execute. Our application is small, so the time it takes to run either optimization will also be minimal. You might use -Os if you're creating a sizeable Emscripten project that takes a long time to compile. For our purposes, we don't need to use -Os. Listing 9-3 shows how to optimize our *collide.wasm* file to reduce its size using the -Oz flag.

```
wasm-opt collide.wasm -Oz -o collide-z.wasm
```

Listing 9-3: Running wasm-opt to optimize the collide.wasm *file for download size*

When you run this optimization, the size of the WebAssembly file shrinks from 709 bytes to 666 bytes. That's only about a 6 percent reduction, but we didn't have to do any work to get there. Typically, you'll get better size reductions when you use this flag with a toolchain.

Optimizing for Execution Time

When you're writing a game, you'll be more interested in improving the fps than the download time. There are three optimization flags: -O1, -O2, and -O3. Again, the O is a letter o, not a zero. The -O3 flag provides the highest level of optimization but takes the longest to execute. The -O1 flag executes in the shortest time but provides the least optimization. The -O2 flag is somewhere in between the two. Because our app is so small there isn't a significant difference between the time it takes to run -O1 and -O3. In Listing 9-4, we use the -O3 flag to get the most from our optimization of the *collide.wasm* file.

```
wasm-opt collide.wasm -O3 -o collide-3.wasm
```

Listing 9-4: Using wasm-opt to optimize performance of the collide.wasm *file*

Once you have the new version of the *collide.wasm* file, modify the *collide.html* file to run the optimized version. Now when we run it through a profiler, we can get an idea of the performance improvement. Profiling with Chrome shows the app now running at 35 fps (Figure 9-19).

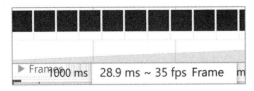

Figure 9-19: New fps in Chrome for the optimized collide-3.wasm file

Figure 9-10 showed that the original frame rate was 18 fps. Just running wasm-opt can double the frame rate of your application in Chrome. Let's see what happens when we run our profiler in Firefox (Figure 9-20).

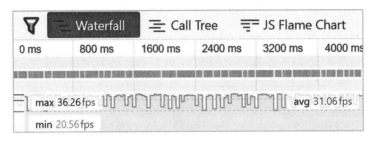

Figure 9-20: New fps in Firefox for the optimized collide-3.wasm file

Looking back at Figure 9-18, we were only running at an average of 14 fps in our initial run, so the frame rate more than doubled in Firefox. In the next section, we'll look at the disassembled optimized WAT code to see the kinds of optimizations wasm-opt made.

Looking at Optimized WAT Code

You should have the WebAssembly extension for VS Code installed (we did this in Chapter 1). In Visual Studio, you can right-click a WebAssembly file and select Show WebAssembly to view the WAT for a given WebAssembly file. In Listing 9-5, we use wasm2wat at the command line to convert the optimized *collide-3.wasm* file into a WAT file.

```
wasm2wat collide-3.wasm -f -o collide-3.wat
```

Listing 9-5: Run wasm2wat to disassemble collide-3.wasm to WAT.

Open *collide.wat* next to *collide-3.wat* in VS Code, and look at the updates wasm-opt made to the WebAssembly file, as shown in Figure 9-21.

In the optimized code, all the function and variable names are gone. I've added a few comments to help you follow along. You can quickly see that the optimization has reduced the number of functions from seven to three. The optimization achieved this by expanding many of the small functions into inline code. In one of the remaining functions, the optimization removed a variable. You might create two different variables when, technically, you need only one because it makes the code more straightforward to read. The optimizer can detect this and reduce the number of variables. Also notice that the optimizer replaces multiplication by powers of 2 with left shifts. For example, in the code in Figure 9-21, the optimizer has replaced a multiplication by 4 with a left shift of 2. In the next section, we'll take a closer look at how some of these strategies improve performance.

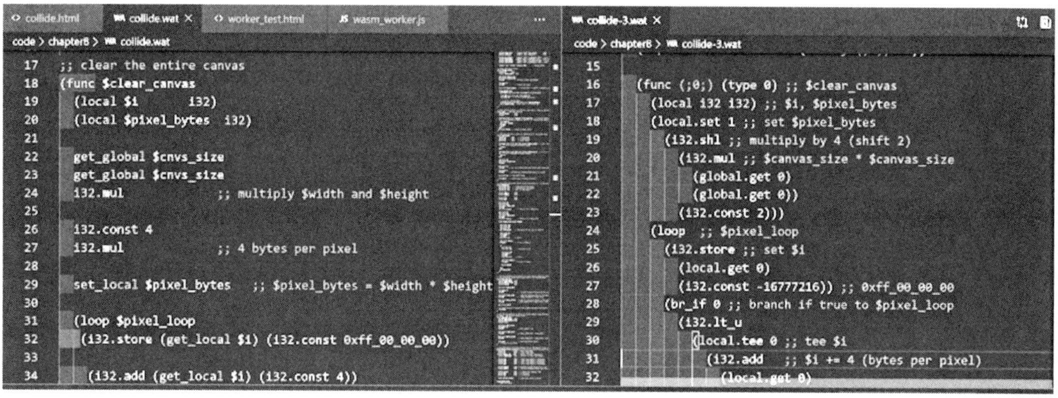

Figure 9-21: Comparing an optimized and an unoptimized version of collide.wat

Strategies for Improving Performance

Now we'll look into some of the strategies you can use to improve your WebAssembly application's performance. The optimizer uses some of these techniques, and you can code your application in such a way that you make the optimizer's job easier. Sometimes you might want to look at the WAT code generated by the optimizer to obtain tips on ways you can improve code. Let's look at a few common optimization techniques you can use with WAT.

Inlining Functions

Calling a function has a tiny bit of overhead. That overhead is not typically a big problem unless the function is called thousands or millions of times a second. Inlining a function is the process of replacing a function call with an inline copy of the same code. Doing this removes the additional processing overhead required to make the function call but increases the size of the WebAssembly module, because it duplicates the code wherever the function was called. When we ran the optimizer on the *collide.wasm* module, it inlined four of the seven functions. Let's look at a quick example of inlining a function. The following WAT code isn't a part of an application; it's just a demonstration. In Listing 9-6, we create a function that adds three numbers together and then create another function to call $add_three a few times.

```
(func $add_three ;; function adds three numbers together
  (param $a i32)
  (param $b i32)
  (param $c i32)
  (result i32)
```

```
    local.get $a
    local.get $b
    local.get $c
    i32.add
    i32.add
  )
  (func (export "inline_test")  ;; I will inline functions in inline_test
    (param $p1 i32)
    (param $p2 i32)
    (param $p3 i32)
    (result i32)
    (call $add_three (local.get $p1) (i32.const 2) (local.get $p2))
    (call $add_three (local.get $p3) (local.get $p1) (i32.const 13))
    ;; add the results together and return
    i32.add
  )
```

Listing 9-6: Demonstration code for us to inline

We'll focus on inlining as the optimization for this section. To inline these functions, we cut and paste the contents of the function in every place where it's called. In Listing 9-7, the grayed-out code is the original function call, and the code that follows is the inlined function.

```
  (func (export "inline_test");; I will inline the functions in inline_test
    (param $p1 i32)
    (param $p2 i32)
    (param $p3 i32)
    (result i32)
;;  (call $add_three (local.get $p1) (i32.const 2) (local.get $p2))
;;  the function above is inlined into the code below
    local.get $p1
    i32.const 2
    local.get $p2
    i32.add
    i32.add
;;  (call $add_three (local.get $p3) (local.get $p1) (i32.const 13))
;;  the function above is inlined into the code below
    local.get $p3
    local.get $p1
    i32.const 13
    i32.add
    i32.add

    i32.add
  )
```

Listing 9-7: Example of hand-inlined code

Inlining the function calls might expose other optimization opportunities. For example, you can see that we're adding 2 and later adding 13. Because both of these values are constants, the code would perform better if we just added 15.

Let's write a little module that could potentially be inlined, compile and optimize it, and then look at the code generated by wasm-opt. We'll create a module with three functions: $add_three, $square, and $inline_test. Create a WAT file named *inline.wat* and add the code in Listing 9-8.

inline.wat
```
(module
  (func $add_three
    (param $a i32)
    (param $b i32)
    (param $c i32)
    (result i32)
    local.get $a
    local.get $b
    local.get $c
    i32.add
    i32.add
  )
  (func $square
    (param $a i32)
    (result i32)
    local.get $a
    local.get $a
    i32.mul
  )
  (func $inline_test (export "inline_test")
    (param $p1 i32)
    (param $p2 i32)
    (param $p3 i32)
    (result i32)
    (call $add_three (local.get $p1) (i32.const 2) (local.get $p2))
    (call $add_three (local.get $p3) (local.get $p1) (i32.const 13))
    call $square
    i32.add
    call $square
  )
)
```

Listing 9-8: We'll use wasm-opt to inline this code

The $add_three function is the same function we inlined by hand in Listing 9-7. The $square function multiplies the value on the top of the stack against itself, and the $inline_test function is the calling function. Let's compile the $inline_test function using wat2wasm:

```
wat2wasm inline.wat
```

Now we can optimize it using wasm-opt:

```
wasm-opt inline.wasm -O3 -o inline-opt.wasm
```

Finally, let's convert it back to WAT using wasm2wat:

```
wasm2wat inline-opt.wasm
```

Now we can open *inline-opt.wat* and see what our optimized code looks like (Listing 9-9).

inline-opt.wat
```
(module
  (type (;0;) (func (param i32 i32 i32) (result i32)))
  (func (;0;) (type 0) (param i32 i32 i32)
    (result i32) ;; $inline_test function
    local.get 0
    local.get 1
    i32.const 2
    i32.add
    i32.add
    local.get 2
    local.get 0
    i32.const 13
    i32.add
    i32.add
    local.tee 0
    local.get 0
    i32.mul
    i32.add
    local.tee 0
    local.get 0
    i32.mul)
  (export "inline_test" (func 0)))
```

Listing 9-9: The optimized version of inline.wat, inline-opt.wat, inlines both functions.

The optimizer removed the two functions $add_three and $square, and placed that code inline in the inline_test function.

Multiply and Divide vs. Shift

Chapter 8 showed how to shift integer bits to the right as a faster way to multiply by powers of 2. For example, a shift left of 3 is the same as multiplying by 2^3, which is 8. Similarly, shifting an integer to the right is the same as dividing by that power of 2. For example, a right shift of 4 is the same as dividing by 2^4, which is 16. Let's see how wasm-opt deals with power-of-2 multiplication and division. Create a new WAT file named *pow2_mul.wat* and add the code in Listing 9-10, which creates a module to multiply and divide by powers of 2.

pow2_mul.wat
```
(module
  (func (export "pow2_mul")
    (param $p1 i32)
    (param $p2 i32)
    (result i32)
    local.get $p1
    i32.const 16
    i32.mul ;; multiply by 16, which is 24
    local.get $p2
    i32.const 8
    i32.div_u ;; divide by 8, which is 23
```

```
      i32.add
    )
)
```

Listing 9-10: A function to multiply and divide by powers of 2

Compile this code using wat2wasm, use wasm-opt to optimize the WebAssembly file, and then disassemble the WebAssembly file back into a WAT file using wasm2wat. Then open the optimized version of *pow2_mul.wat* in VS Code, as shown in Listing 9-11.

pow2_mul
_optimized.wat
```
(module
  (type (;0;) (func (param i32 i32) (result i32)))
  (func (;0;) (type 0) (param i32 i32) (result i32)
    local.get 1
    i32.const 8
    i32.div_u
    local.get 0
    i32.const 4
    i32.shl
    i32.add)
  (export "pow2_mul" (func 0)))
```

Listing 9-11: Optimized version of the pow2_mul function from Listing 9-10

Notice that the optimized code performs the division on the second parameter before performing the multiplication on the first parameter. When you multiply by a power-of-2 constant, wasm-opt will convert this into a left shift. However, wasm-opt doesn't always replace a power-of-2 division with a right shift. Later in this chapter, we'll spend some time running different versions of this code through *benchmark.js* to see how they perform. We'll compare the optimized code generated by wasm-opt to code we optimize by hand to see if we can do better.

NOTE *This code was generated with wat-wasm version 1.0.11. If you're using a later version of wat-wasm, the optimizations performed by wat2wasm will be different.*

Combining Constants

Often, optimizations will combine constants to improve performance. For example, say you have two constant offsets you need to add together. Your original code has $x = 3 + 8$, but this code would perform better if you just set $x = 11$ at the start. Cases like this aren't always obvious to the human eye, but wasm-opt is efficient at hunting down these situations for you. As an example, create a WAT file named *combine_constants.wat* and add the code in Listing 9-12, which simply combines three constants.

combine
_constants.wat
```
(module
  (func $combine_constants (export "combine_constants")
    (result i32)
    i32.const 10
    i32.const 20
    i32.add
```

```
      i32.const 55
      i32.add
    )
)
```

Listing 9-12: A function that adds three constants together

Notice that the value returned by $combine_constants will always be 85. The wasm-opt tool is smart enough to figure that out. When you run the code through wat2wasm, wasm-opt, and then wasm2wat, you'll see the code in Listing 9-13.

combine
_constants
_optimized.wat
```
(module
  (type (;0;) (func (result i32)))
  (func (;0;) (type 0) (result i32)
❶ i32.const 85)
  (export "combine_constants" (func 0)))
```

Listing 9-13: The addition of three constants is combined into a single constant.

The function in Listing 9-13 returns 85 ❶ and doesn't bother to perform the two additions.

DCE

Dead Code Elimination (DCE) is an optimization technique that removes any code not being called or exported by your module. This is a straightforward optimization that doesn't improve the execution time but does reduce the size of the download. DCE happens no matter which optimization flag you use. Let's look at a quick example. Open a new file named *dce_test.wat* and add the code in Listing 9-14, which creates a module with two functions that are never used.

dce_test.wat
```
(module
❶ (func $dead_code_1
    (param $a i32)
    (param $b i32)
    (param $c i32)
    (result i32)
    local.get $a
    local.get $b
    local.get $c
    i32.add
    i32.add
  )
❷ (func $dead_code_2
    (param $a i32)
    (result i32)
    local.get $a
    local.get $a
    i32.mul
  )
  (func $dce_test (export "dce_test")
    (param $p1 i32)
```

```
      (param $p2 i32)
      (result i32)
      local.get $p1
      local.get $p2
      i32.add
    )
  )
)
```

Listing 9-14: This module has two unused functions.

The first two functions, $dead_code_1 ❶ and $dead_code_2 ❷, aren't called and aren't exported. Any optimization we run will remove these functions. Run wat2wasm to generate the code, wasm-opt with the -O3 flag to optimize it, and wasm2wat to convert it back into a WAT file. Open that new file to view the code after the optimization has run, as shown in Listing 9-15.

dce_test
_optimized.wat
```
(module
  (type (;0;) (func (param i32 i32) (result i32)))
  (func (;0;) (type 0) (param i32 i32) (result i32)
    local.get 0
    local.get 1
    i32.add)
  (export "dce_test" (func 0)))
```

Listing 9-15: Two functions are removed by DCE.

The only function that remains is "dce_test". Using DCE has reduced the size of the module from 79 bytes to 46 bytes.

Comparing the Collision Detection App with JavaScript

We've seen how our WebAssembly collision detection app performs. Let's write that code in JavaScript relatively quickly and compare how it performs to the WebAssembly version. Create a new web page named *collidejs.html*. Begin by adding a header and a canvas element to the *collide.html* page and resaving it as *collidejs.html*, as shown in Listing 9-16.

collidejs.html
(part 1 of 2)
```
<!DOCTYPE html>
<html lang="en">
<head>
    <meta charset="UTF-8">
    <meta name="viewport" content="width=device-width, initial-scale=1.0">
    <title>Collide JS</title>
</head>
<body>
    <canvas id="canvas" width="1024" height="1024"></canvas>
...
```

Listing 9-16: HTML header and canvas element in collidejs.html

This code is similar to the WebAssembly version of the app. The main difference will be in the script tag, shown in Listing 9-17. Add the following JavaScript in the script tag.

```
<script type="text/javascript">
    // javascript version
    var animate_callback;
    const out_tag = document.getElementById('out');
    const cnvs_size = 1024 | 0;

    const noh_color = 0xff00ff00 | 0;
    const hit_color = 0xff0000ff | 0;

    const obj_start = cnvs_size * cnvs_size * 4;
    const obj_size = 8 | 0;
    const obj_cnt = 3000 | 0;

    const canvas = document.getElementById("canvas");
    const ctx = canvas.getContext("2d");

    class Collider {
        constructor() {
            this.x = Math.random() * cnvs_size;
            this.y = Math.random() * cnvs_size;
            this.xv = (Math.round(Math.random() * 4) - 2);
            this.yv = (Math.round(Math.random() * 4) - 2);
            this.color = "green";
        }

        move = () => {
            this.x += this.xv;
            this.y += this.yv;
            this.x %= 1024;
            this.y %= 1024;
        }
        draw = () => {
            ctx.beginPath();
            ctx.fillStyle = this.color;
            ctx.fillRect(this.x, this.y, obj_size, obj_size);
            ctx.stroke();
        }
        hitTest = (c2) => {
            let x_dist = this.x - c2.x;
            let y_dist = this.y - c2.y;

            if (Math.abs(x_dist) <= obj_size &&
                Math.abs(y_dist) <= obj_size) {
                this.color = "red";
                return true;
            }
            else {
                this.color = "green";
            }
            return false;
        }
    }
```

```
let collider_array = new Array();
for (let i = 0; i < obj_cnt; i++) {
    collider_array.push(new Collider());
}

let animate_count = 0;

function animate() {
    // clear
    ctx.clearRect(0, 0, canvas.width, canvas.height);
    for (let i = 0; i < collider_array.length; i++) {
        collider_array[i].move();
    }

    // loop and render
    for (i = 0; i < collider_array.length; i++) {
        for (let j = 0; j < collider_array.length; j++) {
            if (i === j) {
                continue;
            }
            if (collider_array[i].hitTest(collider_array[j]))
            {
                break;
            }
        }
        collider_array[i].draw();
    }
    requestAnimationFrame(animate);
}
requestAnimationFrame(animate);
</script>
</body>
</html>
```

Listing 9-17: JavaScript version of our collision detection application

I won't go into detail about the code in Listing 9-17 because its purpose is just to provide a comparison with the WebAssembly code in Chapter 8. Now we can run *collidejs.html* in the Chrome and Firefox profilers to see how they perform. Figure 9-22 shows the frame rate for *collidejs.html* inside the Chrome profiler.

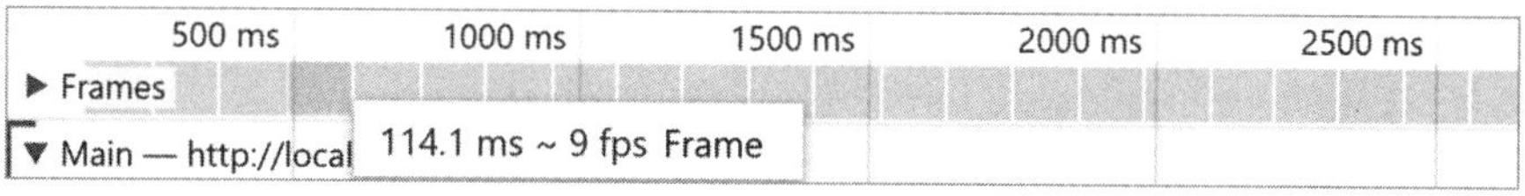

Figure 9-22: The frame rate of our JavaScript app running in the Chrome profiler

Chrome ran the JavaScript version of the app at about 9 fps, slower than both the unoptimized WebAssembly version, which ran at about 18 fps in Chrome, and the optimized version, which ran at 35 fps. The optimized version of the WebAssembly code was almost four times as fast in Chrome.

Now let's look at how our JavaScript performed in Firefox (Figure 9-23).

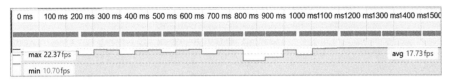

Figure 9-23: The frame rate of our JavaScript app running in the Firefox profiler

Firefox performed quite a bit better than Chrome for this application (almost twice as fast). It even managed to outperform the unoptimized version of the WebAssembly app on Firefox, which ran at around 14 fps. This was only a little more than half as fast as the optimized version of the WebAssembly app on Firefox, which ran at about 31 fps.

In this section, you learned how to compare your WebAssembly code with similar JavaScript code using the Firefox and Chrome profilers. You should now be able to use this knowledge to compare different versions of your application on different browsers to get a feel for the kind of code that is best done in WebAssembly and what is best to do in JavaScript.

Hand Optimizing WAT

I spent some time hand optimizing my WebAssembly collider app and was able to improve my fps number even more. There were more changes than I can describe in this book. However, I want to point out the kinds of performance gains you might achieve if you want to take the time to optimize by hand. I was able to get the collider app to perform up to 36 fps in the Chrome profiler (Figure 9-24).

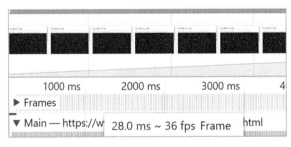

Figure 9-24: Hand optimized collider app running in Chrome

Firefox had an even higher frame rate of 52 fps (Figure 9-25).

Figure 9-25: Hand optimized collider app running in Firefox

You can see the product of my hand optimization efforts at *https://wasmbook.com/collide.html* and the WAT code at *https://wasmbook.com/collide .wat*. I ran the Binaryen optimizer on my finely tuned code, and it actually slowed it down by a few fps. Binaryen is constantly improving their optimized output. Results may be different by the time you read this.

Logging Performance

One of the simplest ways to log performance from a JavaScript app is by using the Date class and the console.log function. WebAssembly can't write to the console without using JavaScript. For this reason, we'll need to use JavaScript to log the performance of our WebAssembly and JavaScript code to the console.

Let's look at the overhead involved in making many calls from our JavaScript into the WebAssembly module. We'll create a WebAssembly module with a few small functions that we can call repeatedly from JavaScript. Create a file named *mod_and.wat* file and add the code in Listing 9-18.

mod_and.wat
```
(module
  (func $mod (export "mod")
    (param $p0 i32)
    (result i32)
    local.get $p0
    i32.const 1000
    i32.rem_u
  )

  (func $and (export "and")
    (param $p0 i32)
    (result i32)
    local.get $p0
    i32.const 0x3ff
    i32.and
  )
)
```

Listing 9-18: Compare performance of remainder versus bitwise AND

There are two functions in this module, a $mod function that finds the remainder of a division by 1000 and a $and function that uses a bitwise AND mask. Compile the *mod_and.wat* file using wat2wasm, and optimize it using wasm-opt.

Next, we need to create a JavaScript function to run this WAT module and test it against the equivalent JavaScript code. Create a new file named *mod_and.js* and add the code in Listing 9-19.

mod_and.js
```
const fs = require('fs');
const bytes = fs.readFileSync('./mod_and.wasm');

(async () => {
  const obj =
    await WebAssembly.instantiate(new Uint8Array(bytes));
  let mod = obj.instance.exports.mod;
  let and = obj.instance.exports.and;
```

```
      let start_time = Date.now(); // reset start_time
      // The '| 0' syntax is a hint to the JavaScript engine to tell it
      // to use integers instead of floats, which can improve performance in
      // some circumstances
      for (let i = 0 | 0; i < 4_000_000; i++) {
        mod(i);  // call the mod function 4 million times
      }
  // calculate the time it took to run 4 million mod calls
      console.log(`mod: ${Date.now() - start_time}`);
      start_time = Date.now(); // reset start_time

      for (let i = 0 | 0; i < 4_000_000; i++) {
        and(i); // call the and function 4 million times
      }
  // calculate the time it took to run 4 million and calls
      console.log(`and: ${Date.now() - start_time}`);
      start_time = Date.now(); // reset start_time
      for (let i = 0 | 0; i < 4_000_000; i++) {
        Math.floor(i % 1000);
      }
  // calculate the time it took to run 4 million modulo calls
      console.log(`js mod: ${Date.now() - start_time}`);
  })();
```

Listing 9-19: Recording the runtime with `Date.now` *and* `console.log`

Before running each block of code, we set a variable `start_time` to `Date.now()`. Doing so sets the `start_time` variable to the current time in milliseconds. When we complete the code, we log `Date.now()` - `start_time`, which gives us the runtime of our test in milliseconds. We'll do this for our WebAssembly module and our JavaScript code to compare the two.

NOTE *The* `| 0` *syntax is a hint to the JavaScript engine to tell it to use integers instead of floats. That can improve performance in some circumstances.*

Now that we have our *mod_and.js* function, we can run it using the following node command:

```
node mod_and.js
```

Listing 9-20 shows the output after running *mod_and.js*.

```
mod: 29
and: 23
js mod: 4
```

Listing 9-20: Output from mod_and.js

The `mod` function took 29 milliseconds to run four million times. The `and` function took 23 milliseconds to run four million times. The JavaScript version only took 4 milliseconds to run four million times. So if WebAssembly is so fast, why did it take between five and seven times as long to run those functions? The problem is that calls between JavaScript and WebAssembly have some overhead. Calling a small function four million times also incurs the cost of that overhead four million times. Let's rewrite our code to execute our functions a few million times from within the WebAssembly rather than from a loop in the JavaScript.

First, we'll rewrite our WebAssembly module to include the loop inside the module instead of inside the JavaScript. Create a new WAT file named *mod_and_loop.wat* and add the code in Listing 9-21.

mod_and_loop.wat

```
(module
  (func (export "mod_loop")
    (result i32)
    (local $i i32)
    (local $total i32)
    i32.const 100_000_000 ;; loop 100 million times
    local.set $i

    (loop $loop
      local.get $i
      i32.const 0x3ff
      i32.rem_u
      local.set $total

      local.get $i
      i32.const 1
      i32.sub
      local.tee $i   ;; i--

      br_if $loop
    )
    local.get $total
  )

  (func (export "and_loop")
    (result i32)
    (local $total i32)
    (local $i i32)
    i32.const 100_000_000 ;; loop 100 million times
    local.set $i

    (loop $loop
      local.get $i
      i32.const 0x3ff
      i32.and
      local.set $total

      local.get $i
      i32.const 1
      i32.sub
      local.tee $i ;; i--

      br_if $loop
    )
```

```
        local.get $total
    )
)
```

Listing 9-21: Looping version of the bitwise AND/modulo functions

These functions do the same tasks as the functions in the original, but the program runs them 100 million times. We'll need to change the JavaScript file to call these functions once and to run the JavaScript 100 million times. That way, we can compare the performance with the WebAssembly module, which we earlier changed to execute our function 100 million times. Create a new function named *mod_and_loop.js* and add the code in Listing 9-22.

mod_and_loop.js
```
const fs = require('fs');
const bytes = fs.readFileSync('./mod_and_loop.wasm');

(async () => {
  const obj =
    await WebAssembly.instantiate(new Uint8Array(bytes));
  let mod_loop = obj.instance.exports.mod_loop;
  let and_loop = obj.instance.exports.and_loop;

  let start_time = Date.now(); // set start_time
  and_loop();
  console.log(`and_loop: ${Date.now() - start_time}`);

  start_time = Date.now(); // reset start_time
  mod_loop();
  console.log(`mod_loop: ${Date.now() - start_time}`);
  start_time = Date.now(); // reset start_time
  let x = 0;
  for (let i = 0; i < 100_000_000; i++) {
    x = i % 1000;
  }
  console.log(`js mod: ${Date.now() - start_time}`);
})();
```

Listing 9-22: JavaScript that runs the and_loop, mod_loop, and comparable JavaScript

We call the mod_loop and the and_loop functions, recording the time each loop took to execute. Next, we run our loop where we perform a modulo 100 million times and record how long that took. If we compile and optimize our WebAssembly module and then run *mod_and_loop.js* using node, we should see something like the output in Listing 9-23.

```
and_loop: 31
mod_loop: 32
js mod: 52
```

Listing 9-23: Output from mod_and_loop.js

Now the WebAssembly is 67 percent faster than the same JavaScript code. It was somewhat disappointing that the bitwise AND didn't perform much better than a modulo, as I had hoped it would. However, we now know how to do the simplest performance test using `console.log` in conjunction with `Date.now()`.

More Sophisticated Testing with benchmark.js

If you want to make your testing a bit more sophisticated than just using logs and `Date.now`, you can install a performance testing module, such as *benchmark.js*. Earlier in Listing 9-10, we created a WebAssembly function that multiplied by 16 and then divided by 8, and ran it through `wasm-opt` to see how Binaryen would optimize the code for us. The optimizer swapped the multiplication actions with a shift but didn't swap in a shift for the divide. It also rearranged the division and the multiplication.

Let's test several versions of this WebAssembly module, including the original and the version generated by the optimizer, to see whether it's possible to outdo the optimizer with a bit of effort. We'll use *benchmark.js* to test the performance of all of these functions. Create a new WAT file named *pow2_test.wat* and add the code in Listing 9-24.

pow2_test.wat
(part 1 of 5)

```
(module
  ;; this is the original function we wrote
  (func (export "pow2")
    (param $p1 i32)
    (param $p2 i32)
    (result i32)
    local.get $p1
    i32.const 16
    i32.mul
    local.get $p2
    i32.const 8
    i32.div_u
    i32.add
  )
...
```

Listing 9-24: The beginning of the module with the original function

Listing 9-24 shows the original version of our power-of-2 test, where we multiplied by 16 and divided by 8.

The next function, in Listing 9-25, runs the division before the multiplication. I wanted to test this because `wasm-opt` swapped the multiplication and division functions, and I was curious to know whether that had a positive effect on the function's performance.

pow2_test.wat
(part 2 of 5)

```
...
  ;; wasm-opt placed the div before mul, so let's see if that helps
  (func (export "pow2_reverse")
    (param $p1 i32)
    (param $p2 i32)
    (result i32)
    local.get $p2
```

```
      i32.const 8
      i32.div_u
      local.get $p1
      i32.const 16
      i32.mul
      i32.add
    )
...
```

Listing 9-25: Swap the division and multiplication

The next function, in Listing 9-26, uses a shift for both power-of-2 multiplication and division. We also use the order inserted by the optimizer, where the division happens before the multiplication.

```
...
;; change multiply and divide to shifts
(func (export "pow2_mul_div_shift")
  (param $p1 i32)
  (param $p2 i32)
  (result i32)
  local.get $p2
  i32.const 3
  i32.shr_u
  local.get $p1
  i32.const 4
  i32.shl
  i32.add
)
...
```

Listing 9-26: Change the multiply and divide expressions to binary shifts

Next, in Listing 9-27, we use a shift for both division and multiplication, but this time we don't change the order of the division and multiplication from the original code.

```
...
;; back to original order of multiply and divide
(func (export "pow2_mul_div_nor")
  (param $p1 i32)
  (param $p2 i32)
  (result i32)
  local.get $p1
  i32.const 4
  i32.shl
  local.get $p2
  i32.const 3
  i32.shr_u
  i32.add
)
...
```

Listing 9-27: The original order with multiply before divide

This next function, in Listing 9-28, is the version of the code produced by wasm-opt with the -O3 flag.

```
...
;; this was what was generated by wasm-opt
  (func (export "pow2_opt") (param i32 i32) (result i32)
    local.get 1
    i32.const 8
    i32.div_u
    local.get 0
    i32.const 4
    i32.shl
    i32.add
  )
)
```

Listing 9-28: The wasm-opt optimized version of the function

Now we can compile this module with wat2wasm, but we should *not* optimize it, because we're trying to test the WAT code as it is without modifications from the optimizer. Next, we need to create our *benchmark.js* code. First, we'll need to install the *benchmark.js* module using npm:

```
npm i --save-dev benchmark
```

Now we can write a JavaScript program to test the WebAssembly functions using *benchmark.js*. Let's break this program into several chunks and walk through them a piece at a time. Add the code in Listing 9-29 to *benchmark_test.js*.

```
// import benchmark.js
❶ var Benchmark = require('benchmark');
❷ var suite = new Benchmark.Suite();

// use fs to read the pow2_test.wasm module into a byte array
❸ const fs = require('fs');
const bytes = fs.readFileSync('./pow2_test.wasm');
const colors = require('colors'); // allow console logs with color

// Variables for the WebAssembly functions
var pow2;
var pow2_reverse;
var pow2_mul_shift;
var pow2_mul_div_shift;
var pow2_mul_div_nor;

console.log(`
================= RUNNING BENCHMARK =================
`.rainbow ❹);
...
```

Listing 9-29: The first part of the benchmark_test.js *JavaScript file*

First, we require ❶ the benchmark module, and then create a new suite ❷ object from that module. We require the fs ❸ module and use that to load the WebAssembly module into a byte array. We then define a series of variables to hold the functions in the WebAssembly module. We log out a rainbow ❹ color separator that displays RUNNING BENCHMARK to make it easier to spot where the benchmark begins as we scroll back up through our stats. If you're like me, you might change the module as you benchmark it, in which case, it can be helpful to have a conspicuous place where the benchmarking begins.

In Listing 9-30, we'll add a function we can call to initialize and run the benchmark suite. Add the following function to *benchmark_test.js*.

benchmark   ...
_test.js ❶ function init_benchmark() {

```
    // adds the callbacks for the benchmarks
❷ suite.add('#1 '.yellow + 'Original Function', pow2);
    suite.add('#2 '.yellow + 'Reversed Div/Mult order', pow2_reverse);
    suite.add('#3 '.yellow + 'Replace mult with shift',
                pow2_mul_shift);
    suite.add('#4 '.yellow + 'Replace mult & div with shift',
                pow2_mul_div_shift);
    suite.add('#5 '.yellow + 'wasm-opt optimized version', pow2_opt);
    suite.add('#6 '.yellow + 'Use shifts with OG order',
                pow2_mul_div_nor);
    // add listeners
❸ suite.on('cycle', function (event) {
        console.log(String(event.target));
    });

❹ suite.on('complete', function () {
        // when the benchmark has finished, log the fastest and slowest functions
        let fast_string = ('Fastest is ' +
          ❺ this.filter('fastest').map('name'));
        let slow_string = ('Slowest is ' +
            this.filter('slowest').map('name'));
❻ console.log(`
        -----------------------------------------------------------
        ${fast_string.green}
        ${slow_string.red}
        -----------------------------------------------------------
        `);

        // create an array of all successful runs and sort fast to slow
❼ var arr = this.filter('successful');
❽ arr.sort(function (a, b) {
        return a.stats.mean - b.stats.mean;
        });

        console.log(`

        `);
        console.log("============ FASTEST ============".green);
❾ while (obj = arr.shift()) {
```

```
      let extension = '';
      let count = Math.ceil(1 / obj.stats.mean);

    if (count > 1000) {
      count /= 1000;
      extension = 'K'.green.bold;
    }

    if (count > 1000) {
      count /= 1000;
      extension = 'M'.green.bold;
    }

    count = Math.ceil(count);
    let count_string = count.toString().yellow + extension;
    console.log(
      `${obj.name.padEnd(45, ' ')} ${count_string} exec/sec`
      );
    }
    console.log("============ SLOWEST ============".red);
  });
  // run async
❿ suite.run({ 'async': false });
}
...
```

Listing 9-30: The `init_benchmark` function

We define the init_benchmark() ❶ function, which calls suite.add ❷ from the benchmark module for each of the functions in our WebAssembly module. Using suite.add tells the benchmark suite to test that function and log the results with the string passed as the second parameter. The suite.on function sets an event callback for different events that occur during a benchmark test. The first call to suite.on ❸ sets the callback for each cycle, which will output the function we tested and the stats for that test. The next call to suite.on ❹ sets the callback for the completion of the benchmark test, which will use the filter ❺ method to log ❻ the fastest and slowest functions. We then filter on 'successful' ❼ to get an array of all the functions that ran successfully. We sort ❽ that array by the mean (average) runtime for that cycle. That sorts the cycles from the fastest to the slowest runtime. We can then loop ❾ through each of those cycles, printing them from fastest to slowest. At the end of this function, we run ❿ the suite.

With the init_benchmark function defined, in Listing 9-31 we create the asynchronous IIFE to instantiate our WebAssembly module and call init_benchmark.

benchmark
_test.js
```
...
(async () => {
❶ const obj = await WebAssembly.instantiate(new Uint8Array(bytes));
❷ pow2 = obj.instance.exports.pow2;
  pow2_reverse = obj.instance.exports.pow2_reverse;
  pow2_mul_shift = obj.instance.exports.pow2_mul_shift;
  pow2_mul_div_shift = obj.instance.exports.pow2_mul_div_shift;
```

```
    pow2_opt = obj.instance.exports.pow2_opt;
    pow2_mul_div_nor = obj.instance.exports.pow2_mul_div_nor;
❸ init_benchmark();
})();
```

Listing 9-31: Asynchronous IIFE instantiates WebAssembly and runs benchmark.js.

Here we instantiate ❶ our WebAssembly module and set all of the functions ❷ we'll be calling from *benchmark.js*. We then run *benchmark.js* by calling init_benchmark() ❸. Now we can run our application using node with the following command:

```
node benchmark_test.js
```

Figure 9-26 shows the output.

```
$ node benchmark_test.js

================= RUNNING BENCHMARK =================

#1 Original Function x 44,641,095 ops/sec ±0.69% (91 runs sampled)
#2 Reversed Div/Mult order x 45,393,937 ops/sec ±0.52% (95 runs sampled)
#3 Replace mult with shift x 45,304,429 ops/sec ±0.39% (94 runs sampled)
#4 Replace mult & div with shift x 50,317,467 ops/sec ±0.47% (97 runs sampled)
#5 wasm-opt optimized version x 44,139,754 ops/sec ±0.48% (92 runs sampled)
#6 Use shifts with OG order x 50,117,233 ops/sec ±0.48% (93 runs sampled)

    -------------------------------------------------------------
    Fastest is #4 Replace mult & div with shift,#6 Use shifts with OG order
    Slowest is #5 wasm-opt optimized version
    -------------------------------------------------------------



============ FASTEST ============
#4 Replace mult & div with shift    51M execs/sec
#6 Use shifts with OG order         51M execs/sec
#2 Reversed Div/Mult order          46M execs/sec
#3 Replace mult with shift          46M execs/sec
#1 Original Function                45M execs/sec
#5 wasm-opt optimized version       45M execs/sec
============ SLOWEST ============
```

Figure 9-26: Output from benchmark_test.js

Interestingly, the slowest of these functions was the wasm-opt optimized version: the original version and the wasm-opt optimized version executed in about the same time. The fastest run was the code where we replaced the i32.mul and i32.div_u operations with shifts, and reordered the calls in the way that the wasm-opt tool rearranged them. This illustrates that you can't assume that wasm-opt (or any programmatic optimizer) will always give you the highest-performing code. Running performance tests on your application is always advisable.

NOTE *These tests were done with wat-wasm version 1.0.11. Later versions might improve wasm-opt optimization.*

Comparing WebAssembly and JavaScript with --print-bytecode

In this section, we'll geek out on low-level bytecode. It's fun and interesting to look at what the JavaScript JIT generates. It's also fascinating to compare with WebAssembly and intriguing to think about how to improve performance. If this topic doesn't interest you, feel free to skip ahead to the next section.

Let's briefly look at how to make a better comparison between WebAssembly code and JavaScript. V8 compiles JavaScript into an IR bytecode, which looks a lot like an assembly language or WAT. IR uses registers and an accumulator but isn't machine specific. We can use IR to compare the JavaScript code after it runs through the JIT compiler with our WebAssembly code. Because they're both low-level bytecodes, it gives us a better *apples to apples* comparison to look at. But keep in mind that the JavaScript code will need to be parsed and compiled into this bytecode at runtime, whereas WebAssembly is compiled ahead of time.

Let's create a small JavaScript program and use the node --print-byte code flag to look at the bytecode generated from that JavaScript. Create a JavaScript file named *print_bytecode.js* and add the code in Listing 9-32.

print_bytecode.js
```
❶ function bytecode_test() {
    let x = 0;
❷ for (let i = 0; i < 100_000_000; i++) {
    ❸ x = i % 1000;
    }
❹ return 99;
  }

  // if we don't call this, the function is removed in dce check
❺ bytecode_test();
```

Listing 9-32: The bytecode_test function that we'll execute with the --print-bytecode flag

This bytecode_test function is similar to the code that we performance tested in Listing 9-22. It's a simple for loop that takes the modulo of the i counter, stores it in x, and then returns 99. It doesn't really do anything useful, but I wanted to work with a function that is easy to understand, so we can compile it into bytecode.

We then call the function in addition to defining it; otherwise, V8 will remove it as a part of DCE. We can then run the node command in Listing 9-33 to print the bytecode.

```
node --print-bytecode --print-bytecode-filter=bytecode_test print_bytecode.js
```

Listing 9-33: Run node with the --print-bytecode flag

We pass the --print-bytecode flag to node to instruct it to print the bytecode. We also pass in the --print-bytecode-filter flag, setting it to the name of our function to print that function's bytecode. If we don't include the filter flag, the output will be way more bytecode than we want to look at. Finally, we pass node the name of the JavaScript file. Run *print_bytecode.js* with the flags from Listing 9-33, and you should get the output in Listing 9-34.

```
[generated bytecode for function: bytecode_test]
Parameter count 1
Register count 2
Frame size 16
 22 E> 0000009536F965F6 @    0 : a5                StackCheck
 38 S> 0000009536F965F7 @    1 : 0b                LdaZero
       0000009536F965F8 @    2 : 26 fb             Star r0
 57 S> 0000009536F965FA @    4 : 0b                LdaZero
       0000009536F965FB @    5 : 26 fa             Star r1
 62 S> 0000009536F965FD @    7 : 01 0c 00 e1 f5 05 LdaSmi.ExtraWide [100000000]
 62 E> 0000009536F96603 @   13 : 69 fa 00          TestLessThan r1, [0]
       0000009536F96606 @   16 : 99 16             JumpIfFalse [22]
(0000009536F9661C @ 38)
 44 E> 0000009536F96608 @   18 : a5                StackCheck
 89 S> 0000009536F96609 @   19 : 25 fa             Ldar r1
 95 E> 0000009536F9660B @   21 : 00 44 e8 03 01 00 ModSmi.Wide [1000], [1]
       0000009536F96611 @   27 : 26 fb             Star r0
 78 S> 0000009536F96613 @   29 : 25 fa             Ldar r1
       0000009536F96615 @   31 : 4c 02             Inc [2]
       0000009536F96617 @   33 : 26 fa             Star r1
       0000009536F96619 @   35 : 8a 1c 00          JumpLoop [28], [0]
(0000009536F965FD @ 7)
111 S> 0000009536F9661C @   38 : 0c 63             LdaSmi [99]
121 S> 0000009536F9661E @   40 : a9                Return
Constant pool (size = 0)
Handler Table (size = 0)
```

Listing 9-34: Bytecode output from print_bytecode.js

The right side of the output in Listing 9-34 has the opcodes for the IR. Here I've listed those opcodes and added WAT-style comments on the right side. Instead of a stack machine, the bytecode that the V8 engine generated is for a virtual register machine with an accumulator register. The *accumulator* is where this virtual machine performs its calculations. Take a quick look at the code in Listing 9-35, which V8 generated.

```
;; A = Accumulator R0 = Register 0, R1 = Register 1
StackCheck
LdaZero                                  ;; A = 0
Star r0                                  ;; R0 = A
LdaZero                                  ;; A = 0
Star r1                                  ;; R1 = A
;; THIS IS THE TOP OF THE LOOP
LdaSmi.ExtraWide [100000000]             ;; A=100_000_000
TestLessThan r1, [0]                     ;; R1 < A
JumpIfFalse [22] (0000006847C9661C @ 38) ;; IF R1 >= A GO 22 BYTES
                                         ;;   AHEAD [END OF LOOP]
StackCheck
Ldar r1                                  ;; A = R1
```

```
ModSmi.Wide [1000], [1]                          ;; A %= 1_000
Star r0                                           ;; R0 = A
Ldar r1                                           ;; A = R1
Inc [2]                                           ;; A++
Star r1                                           ;; R1 = A
JumpLoop [28], [0] (0000006847C965FD @ 7)         ;; 28 BYTES BACK [LOOP TOP]
LdaSmi [99]                                       ;; A = 99 | END OF LOOP
Return                                            ;; RETURN A
```

Listing 9-35: Opcodes with an explanation after the ;; characters

The IR for V8 uses an accumulator. Accumulator machines have one general-purpose register where the accumulator does all of the math instead of doing it in the other registers. The opcodes with the letter a in them usually refer to the accumulator, and r usually refers to a register. For example, the first opcode after StackCheck is LdaZero, which loads (Ld) the accumulator (a) with 0 (Zero). Then the line Star r0 stores (St) the value in the accumulator (a) into a register (r) and then passes in r0 to define that register. It does this because the IR can't set Register0 to a value of 0 directly; instead, it needs to load that value into the accumulator and then move the value in the accumulator into Register0. Later in the code, you see LdaSmi.ExtraWide. This loads (Ld) the accumulator (a) with a small integer (Smi) that uses all 32 bits (ExtraWide). If you loaded a number that used 16 bits, it would have displayed Wide instead of ExtraWide, and 8 bits wouldn't have anything following LdaSmi. The TestLessThan opcode compares the value in the register specified (r1) with the value in the accumulator. The line JumpIfFalse [22] checks whether the TestLessThan resulted in false, and if so, jumps 22 bytes forward.

The --print-bytecode flag can be a useful tool to help performance tune your JavaScript. If you're familiar with WAT or assembly, it's not difficult to understand. It can also be useful in comparing your WAT code with JavaScript for performance tuning reasons in both parts of your WebAssembly application.

Summary

In this chapter, we discussed several tools for evaluating the performance of our WAT code. We also compared our code to the performance of equivalent JavaScript. Then we explored several strategies for improving the performance of our WebAssembly module.

We looked at the profiler in the Chrome web browser and discussed the Summary page and the JS Heap Memory section, which provided information about memory spikes and garbage collection. We also looked at the fps in our profile, which is an excellent way to determine the performance of a game or UI heavy application.

We used the Firefox profiler to investigate our collision detection application. The Firefox profiler offers a few extra tools, including the Call Tree and the JS Flame Chart. We tracked down the WAT function that was called by using the wasm-function[index] listed in the profiler.

Next, we installed *Binaryen.js* and used the `wasm-opt` tool to optimize our WebAssembly module for either download size or peak performance. We also disassembled it back into WAT code, so we could view the changes the optimizer made.

We then looked into a variety of strategies for improving the peak performance of our application, including inlining functions, replacing multiplication and division with bit-shifts, and combining constants. We discussed DCE, which the optimizer performs to remove any unused functions from our module.

We created a JavaScript version of our application to compare the performance of JavaScript against that of the WebAssembly module.

After using the profiler throughout most of this chapter, we looked at other methods for determining our module's performance. Using `console .log` and `Date.now` is the simplest method of measuring performance in an application, and the testing suite *benchmark.js* provides more detailed information for evaluating the performance of different functions. Just for fun, we printed the V8 IR bytecode to evaluate JavaScript code further and compared it with WebAssembly. In the next chapter, you'll learn about debugging the WebAssembly modules.

10

DEBUGGING WEBASSEMBLY

In this chapter, you'll learn several techniques to debug your WAT code. We'll discuss logging to the console and using alerts, as well as how to log stack traces to the console. We'll cover using the debugger in Firefox and Chrome, the differences between them, and the limitations of each debugger.

A *source map* maps code running in the browser to the original precompiled source code. It allows a developer writing in languages like TypeScript or frameworks, such as React, to step through their original code to debug it. WebAssembly toolchains, such as Emscripten, map the generated WebAssembly binary back to the original C++ source code. At the time of this writing, *wat2wasm* doesn't generate source maps for WAT code converted to the WebAssembly binary format. This doesn't render debugging WAT code useless, but it does mean that any names for local or global variables are lost when it is converted to binary. Therefore, the code you write in WAT doesn't look exactly like what you see in your debugger.

You have to manually map the specific names you give variables to the generic names assigned by your browser debugger. Later in this chapter, you'll learn how to understand this mapping. Once you've learned to debug your WebAssembly code, you'll have the tools to step through any WebAssembly code you find on the web, even when you don't have the source code.

Debugging from the Console

The simplest way to start debugging your WebAssembly code is by logging statements to the browser console. As you learned earlier, WebAssembly must rely on JavaScript to do this. In this chapter, we'll use a JavaScript function to create debugging logs. Let's create a simple WebAssembly function to calculate the distance between two points using the Pythagorean theorem. We'll introduce an error in the code and use it as code to debug. Create a new file named *pythagoras.wat* and add the code in Listing 10-1.

pythagoras.wat
```
(module
  (import "js" "log_f64" (func $log_f64(param i32 f64)))

  (func $distance (export "distance")
    (param $x1 f64) (param $y1 f64) (param $x2 f64) (param $y2 f64)
    (result f64)
    (local $x_dist f64)
    (local $y_dist f64)

    local.get $x1
    local.get $x2
    f64.sub              ;; $x1 - $x2
    local.tee $x_dist    ;; $x_dist = $x1 - $x2
    local.get $x_dist
    f64.mul              ;; $x_dist * $x_dist on stack

    local.get $y1
    local.get $y2
❶ f64.add              ;; should be $y1 - $y2
    local.tee $y_dist    ;; $y_dist = $y1 - $y2
    local.get $y_dist
    f64.mul              ;; $y_dist * $y_dist on stack
    f64.add              ;; $x_dist * $x_dist + $y_dist * $y_dist on stack

    f64.sqrt             ;; take the square root of x squared plus y squared
  )
)
```

Listing 10-1: Using the Pythagorean theorem to find the distance between two points

To use the Pythagorean theorem, we make a right triangle on the x-axis and y-axis between the two points. The length on the x-axis is the distance between the two x values. We can find the distance on the y-axis the same way. We can find the distance between the two points by squaring these two values, adding them, and then taking the square root (Figure 10-1).

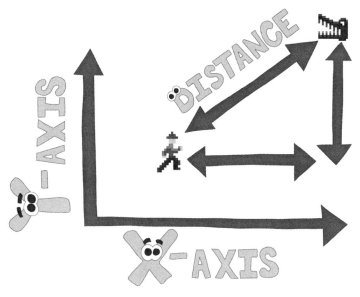

Figure 10-1: Calculating the distance between game objects using the Pythagorean theorem

The math in this example isn't terribly important. The important detail is that we've introduced a bug into this code by adding the values of $y1 and $y2 instead of subtracting them ❶ to get the distance between the two y-coordinates. Compile *pythagoras.wat* into *pythagoras.wasm* and create a new file named *pythagoras.html*. Then add the code in Listing 10-2 to *pythagoras.html*.

pythagoras.html

```html
<!DOCTYPE html>
<html lang="en">
<body>
❶ X1: <input type="number" id="x1" value="0">
❷ Y1: <input type="number" id="y1" value="0">
❸ X2: <input type="number" id="x2" value="4">
❹ Y2: <input type="number" id="y2" value="3">
  <br><br>
❺ DISTANCE: <span id="dist_out">??</span>
  <script>
    var distance = null;
    let importObject = {
      js: {
      ❻ log_f64: function(message_index, value) {
          console.log(`message #${message_index} value=${value}`);
        }
      }
    };

    ( async () => {
    let obj = await WebAssembly.instantiateStreaming(
                    fetch('pythagoras.wasm'), importObject );
    distance = obj.instance.exports.distance;
```

```
        })();
    ❼ function set_distance() {
        ❽ let dist_out = document.getElementById('dist_out');
            let x1 = document.getElementById('x1');
            let x2 = document.getElementById('x2');
            let y1 = document.getElementById('y1');
            let y2 = document.getElementById('y2');

        ❾ let dist = distance(x1.value, y1.value, x2.value, y2.value);
            dist_out.innerHTML = dist;
        }
    </script>
    <br>
    <br>
  ❿ <button onmousedown="set_distance()">Find Distance</button>
</body>
</html>
```

Listing 10-2: A web application that calls the WebAssembly distance function

Inside the body tag, we set up the user interface by adding number type input tags for x1 ❶, y1 ❷, x2 ❸, and y2 ❹ coordinates. We add a span tag that will hold the distance ❺ between the two points after the WebAssembly function runs.

Inside the script tag, the importObject contains a log_f64 ❻ function that takes as its parameters a message index and a value. This function logs these two values to the browser console. WebAssembly cannot directly pass strings back and forth to JavaScript (it must pass an index into linear memory), so it's frequently easier to use a message code and define the strings you want to log from within JavaScript. This function uses the template string `message #${message_index} value=${value}` to log the message_index and value to the console. Alternatively, you could choose from other template strings based on the message_index variable. The function set_distance ❼ executes when the user clicks the Find Distance button ❿. This function will get the element ids for the dist_out ❽ span tag, as well as the x1, x2, y1, and y2 input fields. It then executes the WebAssembly distance ❾ function using the values in those input fields.

Run a web server and load the *pythagoras.html* page into a browser; you should see something like Figure 10-2.

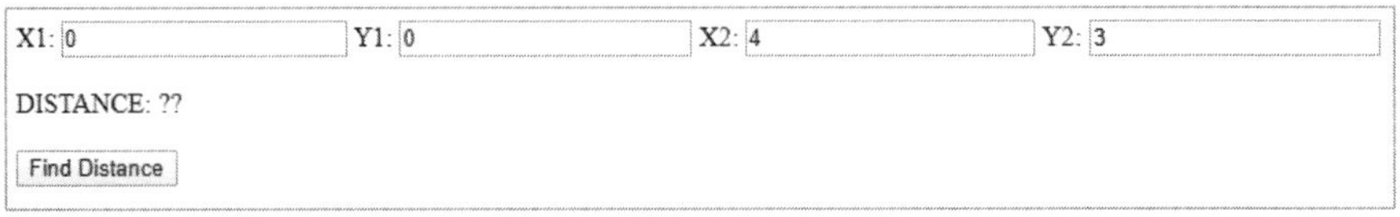

X1: 0   Y1: 0   X2: 4   Y2: 3

DISTANCE: ??

Find Distance

Figure 10-2: The pythagoras.html web page screenshot

The values you see in Figure 10-2 are the default values populated in the form. The distance is listed as "??" below where the user can enter the coordinates. When we click **Find Distance**, the distance should be 5. We're using a 3-4-5 triangle to test this distance calculator. As long as the distance on the x-axis is 3 and the distance on the y-axis is 4, the distance between the two points will be 5 because $3^2 + 4^2 = 5^2$, as shown in Figure 10-3.

Figure 10-3: Using a 3-4-5 triangle

When you click the **Find Distance** button on the app, you will see the DISTANCE field populated with the value 5 as in Figure 10-4.

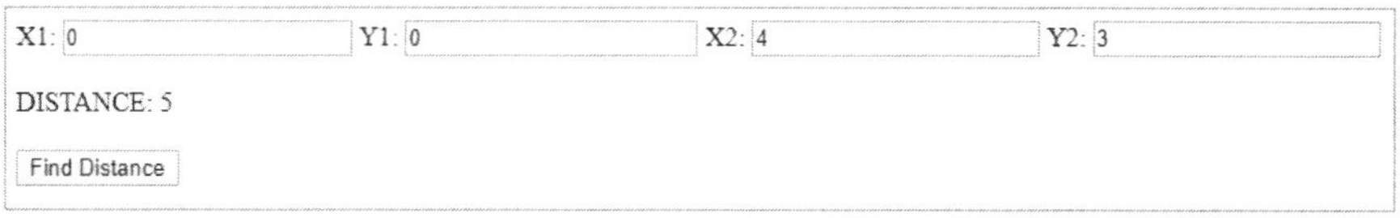

| X1: 0 | Y1: 0 | X2: 4 | Y2: 3 |

DISTANCE: 5

Find Distance

Figure 10-4: Distance calculated for a 3-4-5 triangle

When we change both X and Y values by the same amount, the distance between the two points should remain the same. However, because of a bug we introduced intentionally, adding 1 to both Y1 and Y2 results in the wrong value displayed in the DISTANCE field (Figure 10-5).

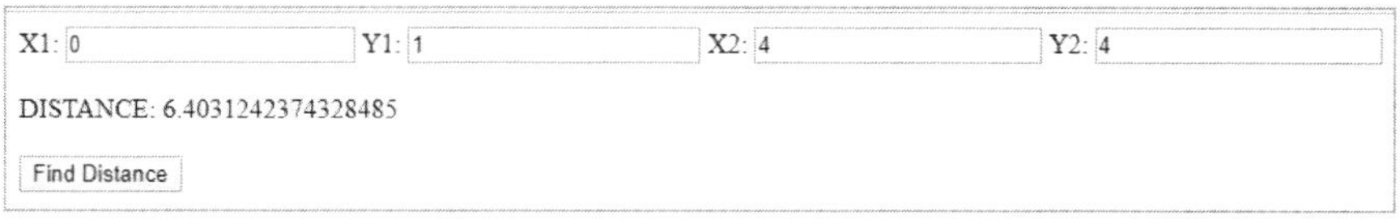

| X1: 0 | Y1: 1 | X2: 4 | Y2: 4 |

DISTANCE: 6.4031242374328485

Find Distance

Figure 10-5: A bug in the calculated distance

We should still see 5 in the DISTANCE field, but it's a different number entirely. We need to track down what went wrong; the first step is to add log statements at several points in our distance function.

As we know, dealing with strings directly in WAT isn't a simple task. Therefore, to step through and debug this code, we use a message id along with a value passed to the JavaScript from the WebAssembly module. Using Listing 10-3, modify the *pythagoras.wat* file to call $log_f64 from within the $distance function.

```
...
(func $distance (export "distance")
  (param $x1 f64) (param $y1 f64) (param $x2 f64) (param $y2 f64) (result f64)
  (local $x_dist f64)
  (local $y_dist f64)
  (local $temp_f64 f64)

  local.get $x1
  local.get $x2
  f64.sub             ;; $x1 - $x2

  local.tee $x_dist   ;; $x_dist = $x1 - $x2

❶ (call $log_f64 (i32.const 1) (local.get $x_dist))

  local.get $x_dist
  f64.mul             ;; $x_dist * $x_dist on stack

❷ local.tee $temp_f64 ;; used to hold top of the stack without changing it
❸ (call $log_f64 (i32.const 2) (local.get $temp_f64))

  local.get $y1
  local.get $y2
  f64.add             ;; should be $y1 - $y2
  local.tee $y_dist   ;; $y_dist = $y1 - $y2

❹ (call $log_f64 (i32.const 3) (local.get $y_dist))

  local.get $y_dist
  f64.mul             ;; $y_dist * $y_dist on stack

❺ local.tee $temp_f64 ;; used to hold top of the stack without changing it
❻ (call $log_f64 (i32.const 4) (local.get $temp_f64))

  f64.add             ;; $x_dist * $x_dist + $y_dist * $y_dist on stack

❼ local.tee $temp_f64 ;; used to hold top of the stack without changing it
❽ (call $log_f64 (i32.const 5) (local.get $temp_f64))

  f64.sqrt            ;; take the square root of x squared plus y squared

❾ local.tee $temp_f64 ;; used to hold top of the stack without changing it
❿ (call $log_f64 (i32.const 6) (local.get $temp_f64))
)
...
```

Listing 10-3: The pythagoras.wat *file updated with JavaScript function calls to log f64 variables*

We've added calls to the log_f64 function in several places here (❶❸ ❹❻❽❿). The first parameter in log_f64 is the message id, which will be an integer we'll use as the unique id for this message. Later we use this id to output a specific message from the JavaScript.

The second parameter is a 64-bit floating-point value, which can show us the value at several different stages of our distance calculation. In a number of these calls, we want to log the value on the top of the stack but *not* take it off, so we use local.tee (❷❺❼❾) to set the value of $temp\_f64$, which will set the value but not remove it from the stack. We then use the value in $temp\_f64$ in the call to log_f64 (❸❻❽❿).

Logging Messages to the Console

As mentioned earlier, WebAssembly modules cannot directly log messages to the browser's console, and WAT has no native string manipulation libraries. The log_f64 function we've used so far is imported from JavaScript by the WebAssembly module. So, in Listing 10-4, we'll implement this function in the JavaScript.

pythagoras.html

```
log_f64: function(message_index, value) {
    console.log(`message #${message_index} value=${value}`);
}
```

Listing 10-4: The JavaScript function called by pythagoras.wat

This is a pretty straightforward version that logs the message index and the value but doesn't customize the message for any of the message_index values. To see the console in Chrome, we'll open Developer tools. Go to the browser menu and click **More tools** (Figure 10-6).

NOTE *Updates to the Chrome or Firefox debugger might mean that what you see in your browser is slightly different than the screenshots shown in this chapter.*

Figure 10-6: Opening the Chrome Developer tools

Click **Developer tools**, and then click the **Console** tab to see the console, as shown in Figure 10-7.

Figure 10-7: Opening the Chrome console

To open the console inside Firefox, click the **Web Developer** submenu from within the Firefox browser menu, as shown in Figure 10-8.

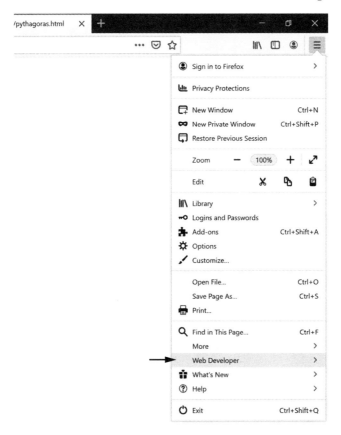

Figure 10-8: Opening the Firefox Web Developer menu

Click **Web Console**, as shown in Figure 10-9.

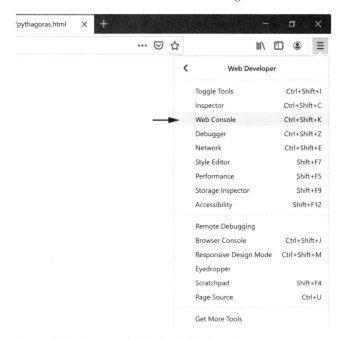

Figure 10-9: Opening the Firefox Web Console

Your Firefox screen should look similar to Figure 10-10.

Figure 10-10: Displaying messages in the Web Console

All messages begin with `message #` followed by the message id.

This sort of messaging is frequently all you need, but we'll make a modification to the function to log more specific messages. For example, you might want the messages to be more specific to the issue if you're having trouble keeping track of what each message means. You could do it this way, as in Listing 10-5, or you could have a series of different log functions for different circumstances.

pythagoras.html

```
log_f64: function(message_index, value) {
    switch( message_index ) {
        case 1:
            console.log(`$x_dist=${value}`);
            break;
```

```
      case 2:
        console.log(`$x_dist*$x_dist=${value}`);
        break;
      case 3:
        console.log(`$y_dist=${value}`);
        break;
      case 4:
        console.log(`$y_dist*$y_dist=${value}`);
        break;
      case 5:
        console.log(`$y_dist*$y_dist + $x_dist*$x_dist=${value}`);
        break;
      case 6:
        console.log(`dist=${value}`);
        break;
      default:
        console.log(`message #${message_index} value=${value}`);
    }
  }
```

Listing 10-5: Updated pythagoras.html *to have a more detailed message*

There are six messages, so we create a switch on the message_index parameter, which prints a different message to the console for each value of message_index. The switch has a default that displays the original message in case an unexpected value for message_index is logged. With these messages changed, the console output should look similar to Figure 10-11.

Figure 10-11: Descriptive messages logged to the console

Using Alerts

Next, we'll use JavaScript alerts to pause code execution to give you time to look at the logged messages. For this task, we'll use the alert function, which opens a dialog with the error text. Know that overusing alerts can make checking the logs time-consuming, so it's best to use them sparingly.

In the earlier log_f64 example, you might want to alert the user immediately if a certain case executes. An alert stops code execution and creates a pop-up window to notify the user. You only want to use a call to alert for unusual circumstances that require immediate attention when you're debugging. In Listing 10-6, we change the `case 1:` code to output an alert in a pop-up window instead of to the console. Change the beginning of the `log_f64` function to look like Listing 10-6.

pythagoras.html
```
log_f64: function(message_index, value) {
  switch( message_index ) {
    case 1:
    ❶ alert(`$x_dist=${value}`);
    break;
```

Listing 10-6: Update the pythagoras.html *file to call an alert from* `log_f64`.

We changed the `console.log` function call to `alert` ❶ to display the alert box when the `message_index` is 1. The result, shown in Figure 10-12, should display in the browser.

Figure 10-12: Displaying the alert box

Stack Trace

A *stack trace* displays a list of the functions that have been called to get to the current point in the code. For example, if function A calls function B, which calls function C, which then executes a stack trace, the stack trace will show the functions C, B, and A as well as the lines that called those functions. WebAssembly doesn't offer this feature directly, so as with logging to the console, we call the stack trace from JavaScript. The trail of the functions called should look similar to Figure 10-13.

We display the stack trace with a call to the JavaScript `console.trace` function. Firefox and Chrome currently offer stack traces that look quite different from each other. Using `console.trace` in Firefox currently gives you more useful information about the WAT file than you get using the Chrome browser. The Firefox browser converts the WebAssembly binary into a WAT file and provides you with a stack trace that references the line in that disassembled WAT file. Chrome, on the other hand, gives you a reference to a function index, which can appear quite cryptic if you're not familiar with it.

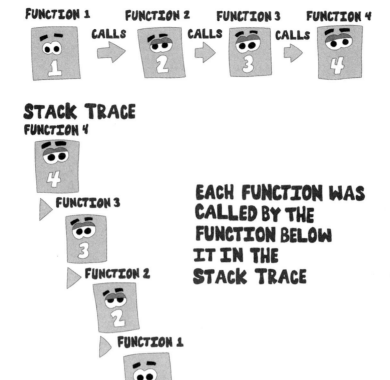

FUNCTION 1 FUNCTION 2 FUNCTION 3 FUNCTION 4

CALLS   CALLS   CALLS

STACK TRACE
FUNCTION 4

FUNCTION 3

FUNCTION 2

FUNCTION 1

EACH FUNCTION WAS
CALLED BY THE
FUNCTION BELOW
IT IN THE
STACK TRACE

Figure 10-13: Function 1 calls function 2, which calls function 3, which calls
function 4 in stack trace

Create a file named *stack_trace.wat* and add the code in Listing 10-7 to it.

stack_trace.wat

```
(module
❶ (import "js" "log_stack_trace" (func $log_stack_trace (param i32)))

❷ (func $call_level_1 (param $level i32)
    local.get $level
    call $log_stack_trace
  )

❸ (func $call_level_2 (param $level i32)
    local.get $level
    call $call_level_1
  )

❹ (func $call_level_3 (param $level i32)
    local.get $level
    call $call_level_2
  )

❺ (func $call_stack_trace (export "call_stack_trace")
```

```
❻ (call $log_stack_trace (i32.const 0))
    (call $call_level_1 (i32.const 1))
    (call $call_level_2 (i32.const 2))
    (call $call_level_3 (i32.const 3))
  )
)
```

Listing 10-7: WebAssembly module demonstrating calls to stack trace

This WebAssembly module imports the log_stack_trace ❶ function from JavaScript that will call console.trace from the embedding JavaScript. We define four more functions that demonstrate how each browser logs the WebAssembly call stack. The imported function $log_stack_trace is called by $call_stack_trace and $call_level_1 ❷. The function $call_level_1 is called by $call_stack_trace and $call_level_2 ❸. The function $call_level_2 is called by $call_stack_trace and $call_level_3 ❹. Finally, $call_level_3 is called by $call_stack_trace. We nest these function calls to demonstrate how stack traces look when called from different function levels.

Notice that $call_stack_trace ❺ calls each of the other functions. First, it calls $log_stack_trace directly, passing in a constant 0. Next, it calls $call_level_1, which calls $log_stack_trace, passing it a constant value of 1. When the stack trace is logged, it should show $call_level_1, $log_stack_trace ❻, and $call_stack_trace in the call stack. The $call_level_2 and $call_level_3 functions each add additional layers that will display in the stack trace.

Now create a new file named *stack_trace.html* and add the code in Listing 10-8.

stack_trace.html
```
<!DOCTYPE html>
<html lang="en">
<body>
    <h1>Stack Trace</h1>
    <script>
      let importObject = {
        js: {
❶        log_stack_trace: function( level ) {
              console.trace(`level=${level}`);
          }
        }
      };

      ( async () => {
        let obj =
          await WebAssembly.instantiateStreaming( fetch('stack_trace.wasm'),
                                                  importObject );
        obj.instance.exports.call_stack_trace();

      })();
    </script>
</body>
</html>
```

Listing 10-8: HTML file with JavaScript calls to stack trace

This is a very basic HTML file, similar to *pythagoras.html*. The primary code is the `log_stack_trace` function ❶ defined inside `importObject`, which calls the JavaScript function `console.trace`, passing in a string that prints to the console before the stack trace. Once you've saved this HTML file, open it in the Firefox browser; you should see similar console logs to Figure 10-14.

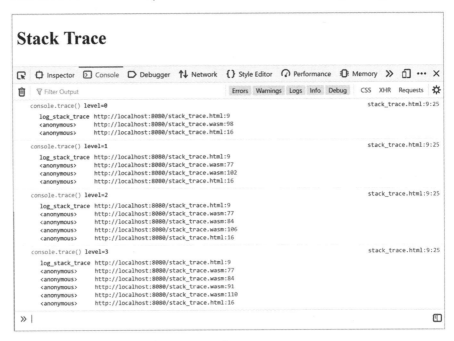

Figure 10-14: Displaying stack traces in Firefox

As you can see, the first stack trace was logged with `level=0` because we had passed a value of `0` directly into the first call to `$log_stack_trace` in the WAT code. That was a direct call from the WebAssembly function `$call_stack_trace` to the imported JavaScript function. Because that first call was direct to `$log_stack_trace`, there is only one stack frame logged for the *stack_trace.wasm* file in this first stack trace. This log indicates that the stack trace was executed from line 98 of *stack_trace.wasm*. This isn't necessarily line 98 in your WAT file; you'll need to look at the WAT inside the browser to see which line it's referring to. Each trace adds an additional function call in the WebAssembly file because we added an additional function layer to each call to `$log_stack_trace` in the WAT. Notice that in each stack trace an additional line is inside *stack_trace.wasm* that appears in the trace.

Click one of these lines; Firefox opens the *stack_trace.wasm* file to the location in the code where the function call occurred.

If you haven't yet opened *stack_trace.wasm* in the Firefox debugger, you might be prompted to refresh your browser page to view the contents as disassembled WAT. When *stack_trace.wasm* opens to byte 98, you should see something like Figure 10-15 in your Firefox debugger console.

Figure 10-15: Clicking a location in stack_trace.wasm displays the WAT code

The line that makes the call is temporarily highlighted in gray. Notice that the byte number on the left (62) is in hexadecimal, unlike the console log, where the byte is the decimal number 98.

Chrome doesn't display the byte number inside the WAT file for each stack trace; rather, it looks like Figure 10-16.

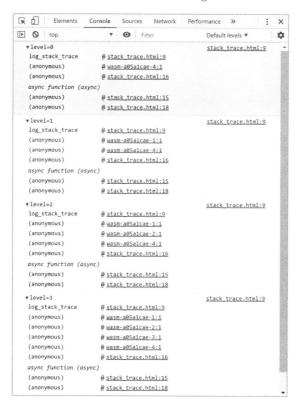

Figure 10-16: Displaying stack traces in Chrome

In the Chrome browser, the line number is always 1. However, when you click the link in the console, Chrome opens a disassembled version of that specific function. All WebAssembly functions begin with the wasm- prefix and end with an index for the function followed by :1. Figure 10-17 shows what it should look like when you click the first WebAssembly function that appears in a stack trace.

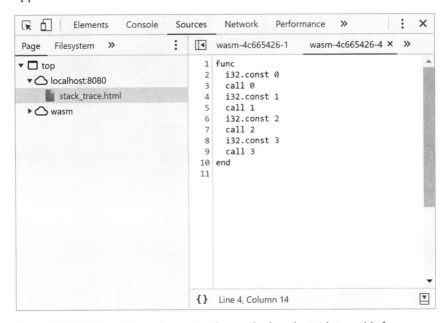

Figure 10-17: Clicking the stack trace in Chrome displays the WebAssembly function.

The disassembled function is different in Chrome than in Firefox. We'll cover these differences in more detail beginning in the next section. For now, notice that Chrome uses variable and function indexes rather than labels for disassembly, which are more challenging to read.

Stack traces can be beneficial when you're trying to figure out how certain functions execute. When you're unsure of how a function is called, stack traces can be a lifesaver. Now let's look at the code in the debuggers for Firefox and Chrome.

The Firefox Debugger

In this section, we'll write some code we can step through in our debugger. First, take a moment to review the *pythagoras.html* and *pythagoras.wat* files. We intentionally introduced a bug so we could track it in the debugger. We'll modify *pythagoras.wat* by removing calls to log output to JavaScript so we can step through it using the debugger. Create a file named *debugger.wat* and add the code in Listing 10-9, or simply remove the log calls from *pythagoras.wat* and resave the file.

debugger.wat

```
(module
  (func $distance (export "distance")
    (param $x1 f64) (param $y1 f64) (param $x2 f64) (param $y2 f64)
    (result f64)
    (local $x_dist f64)
    (local $y_dist f64)

    local.get $x1
    local.get $x2
    f64.sub             ;; $x1 - $x2

    local.tee $x_dist   ;; $x_dist = $x1 - $x2
    local.get $x_dist
    f64.mul             ;; $x_dist * $x_dist on stack

    local.get $y1
    local.get $y2
    f64.add             ;; Should be $y1 - $y2
    local.tee $y_dist   ;; $y_dist = $y1 - $y2

    local.get $y_dist
    f64.mul             ;; $y_dist * $y_dist on stack

    f64.add             ;; $x_dist * $x_dist + $y_dist * $y_dist on stack

    f64.sqrt            ;; take the square root of x squared plus y squared
  )
)
```

Listing 10-9: We modify pythagoras.wat *by removing the log calls.*

Earlier, we introduced a bug to sometimes give an incorrect result by adding $y1 to $y2 instead of subtracting them. Copy *pythagoras.html* to a new file named *debugger.html*, and change the JavaScript code inside the <script> tags to instead fetch *debugger.wasm*. Then remove the importObject to make it look like the code in Listing 10-10.

pythagoras.html

```
...
<script>
  var distance = null;

  ( async () => {
    let obj = await WebAssembly.instantiateStreaming( fetch('debugger.wasm')
);

    distance = obj.instance.exports.distance;

  })();
  function set_distance() {
    let dist_out = document.getElementById('dist_out');
    let x1 = document.getElementById('x1');
    let x2 = document.getElementById('x2');
    let y1 = document.getElementById('y1');
```

```
    let y2 = document.getElementById('y2');

    let dist = distance(x1.value, y1.value, x2.value, y2.value);
    dist_out.innerHTML = dist;
  }
</script>
...
```

Listing 10-10: HTML file to test debugger.wasm

Load *debugger.html* into Firefox and open the console; then click the
Debugger tab to access the Firefox debugger. From the **Sources** tab on the
left, select *debugger.wasm* to see the disassembled version of your WAT code,
which should look like Figure 10-18.

Figure 10-18: WAT code in the Firefox debugger

This code is a disassembly of the WebAssembly binary, so now the
names of functions and variables are no longer available. This result is
similar to what you'd see if you disassembled a binary you found on the
web. Because source maps aren't yet available in *wat2wasm*, we can't step
through the original source code in the debugger. Instead, you need to do
a side-by-side comparison of the original code and the disassembled code.
Listing 10-11 shows what that disassembled code looks like.

```
(module

  (type $type0 (func (param f64 f64 f64 f64) (result f64)))
  (export "distance" (func $func0))
❶ (func $func0
    (param ❷$var0 f64)(param ❸$var1 f64)(param ❹$var2 f64)(param ❺$var3 f64)
    (result f64)
    (local ❻$var4 f64) (local ❼$var5 f64)
    local.get $var0
```

```
    local.get $var2
    f64.sub
    local.tee $var4
    local.get $var4
    f64.mul
    local.get $var1
    local.get $var3
    f64.add
    local.tee $var5
    local.get $var5
    f64.mul
    f64.add
    f64.sqrt
  )
)
```

Listing 10-11: WAT code generated by Firefox disassembly

This code was disassembled from the WebAssembly binary file and has
no awareness of the labels we've given variables or functions. It's also unaware
of any comments in the code. If you look back at the original WAT code
(Listing 10-9), you can see that the function $distance has become $func0 ❶.
The parameter variables $x1, $y1, $x2, and $y2 have become $var0 ❷, $var1 ❸,
$var2 ❹, and $var3 ❺, respectively. The local variables $x_dist and $y_dist have
become $var4 ❻ and $var5 ❼. Once you know which of the original variables
corresponds to which of the disassembly variables, you can step through the
code knowing the variable used. To watch the values in these variables, you
can enter them into the Watch expressions window on the right without the $.
In the Watch window you can watch the $var0 variable by entering **var0**. I use
a simple trick to keep track of which variable is which. I add a JavaScript comment along with my watch expression, labeling the variable with its original
name. For example, I might enter $var0 into Watch expressions as var0 // $x1.
Figure 10-19 shows what that looks like in Watch expressions.

*Figure 10-19: Watch expressions in Firefox
using comments*

To step through the WAT code, make sure the WebAssembly file is
selected. We need to create a breakpoint, which is the point at which the
debugger stops executing the code to allow you to step through one line

at a time. To set a breakpoint, click the byte number on the left side of the WAT code. You can watch how the variables change in your Watch expressions window on the right. With the breakpoint set, execute the WebAssembly code by clicking **Find Distance** (Figure 10-20).

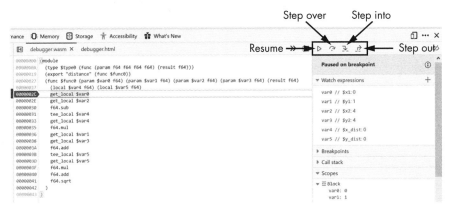

Figure 10-20: Setting a breakpoint in the Firefox debugger

When execution reaches the breakpoint, click the **Step over** button ↷ located above Watch expressions. That allows you to step through your code one line at a time. To step into a function instead of executing it, click the **Step into** button ↓ located next to the Step over button. To the right of the Step into button, click the **Step out** button ↗ if you want to step out of the current function you're in. Click the **Resume** button ▷, which looks like a play button, to tell the debugger to execute until it reaches another breakpoint.

To locate the error in the code, click the **Step over** button until you reach line 3D. At this point, var5 is set, and we can see the value inside the Watch expressions window, as shown in Figure 10-21.

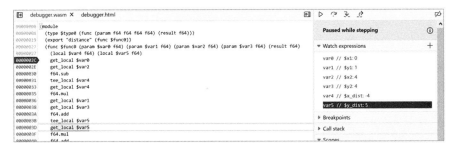

Figure 10-21: Stepping through the code in the Firefox debugger

Notice that $y_dist is set to a value of 5 when Y1 was set to 1 and Y2 was set to 4. That means that $y_dist should have been 3. Earlier, we changed the line numbered 3A from f64.sub to f64.add to introduce this error. Stepping through our code a line at a time in the debugger helped us track down the problem.

The Chrome Debugger

Debugging WebAssembly in Chrome is somewhat different from debugging the same code in Firefox. The WAT code isn't broken down by the WebAssembly file; rather, Chrome groups the WAT code by functions. The number at the end of the WebAssembly function is an index number based on where you defined the function in your code.

To get to the debugger, open the Chrome **Developer tools** and click the **Sources** tab. Located in a section labeled Page, you should see a cloud icon labeled wasm. Expand this branch to see a page for each function defined in your WebAssembly module. Because we've only defined one function in this module, only one function exists. Click that function to bring up the function's code in the window on the right. In that window, set a breakpoint on line 3 that contains the code local.get 0 (Figure 10-22).

Figure 10-22: Setting a breakpoint in the Chrome debugger

Notice that `local.get` is getting a number instead of a variable name. The reason is that following `local.get` with a number gets the local variable based on an index instead of a name. Using `local.get` 0 is the equivalent to `local.get` $var0 in the Firefox browser. As in Firefox, you can look at the code and match it with the code in your function. Listing 10-12 shows the code as it appears in the Chrome debugger.

```
❶ func (param f64 f64 f64 f64) (result f64)
❷ (local f64 f64)
   local.get 0
   local.get 2
   f64.sub
   local.tee 4
   local.get 4
   f64.mul
   local.get 1
   local.get 3
   f64.add
   local.tee 5
   local.get 5
   f64.mul
   f64.add
   f64.sqrt
end
```

Listing 10-12: Chrome WAT disassembly in the debugger

Notice that Chrome uses indexes for local variables, parameters, and functions. The function ❶ doesn't have a name associated with it, nor do any of its parameters or local variables ❷. The same is true for globals and types. If we were using global variables, we would use `global.get` and `global.set`, passing in an index number that corresponds to the order in which the variables were defined.

NOTE *As of Chrome v86, the debugger shows function names.*

One nice feature of the Chrome debugging functionality is that you have access to the stack in the Scope window. As you step through the code, you can watch values get pushed onto and popped off the stack. One of the downsides is that the Watch window is much less useful than it is in Firefox, because Chrome doesn't make variables available as if they were JavaScript variables.

As in Firefox, Chrome has a Resume button ▮▶, a Step over button ⤾, a Step into button ⬇, and a Step out button ⬆, as highlighted in Figure 10-23.

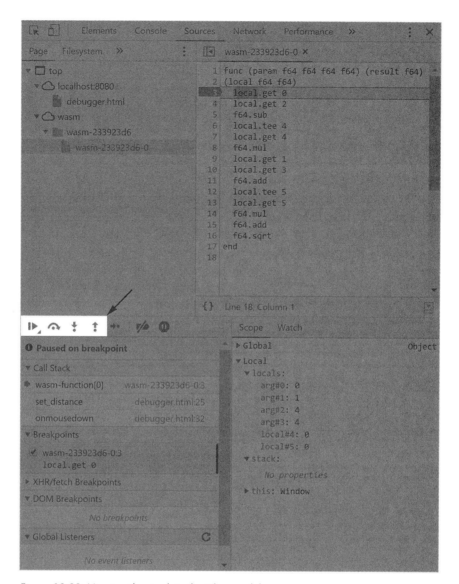

Figure 10-23: Viewing the stack in the Chrome debugger

Summary

In this chapter, we debugged WAT code using a variety of different techniques in Chrome and in Firefox. We looked at logging to the console in more depth than we had in earlier chapters. We then used the JavaScript alert function to stop execution and wait for user instruction. We also explored using *console.trace* to log a stack trace and discussed the differences between the way the stack trace works in Chrome and Firefox. Finally, we used the built-in debuggers in Chrome and Firefox.

Many options are available for debugging WebAssembly. Some of the options, such as using the Chrome or Firefox debuggers, are still being developed. Which tools you decide to use will depend on the code and your goal when debugging. In the next chapter, we'll use WebAssembly to build Node.js modules.

11

ASSEMBLYSCRIPT

AssemblyScript is a high-level language explicitly designed to compile to WebAssembly or WAT. AssemblyScript is more expressive than WAT but can compile to it. When you use AssemblyScript, you lose some of the fine optimization control that you have with WAT, but it's much faster to write.

We'll begin this chapter by creating a simple `AddInts` function, like the `AddInt` one we created in Chapter 1. We'll write an AssemblyScript hello world app and compile it into WAT to see the WebAssembly that the AssemblyScript compiler generates. We'll examine AssemblyScript's use of length-prefixed strings, and then install the AssemblyScript loader to see how it can make it easier to transfer strings between AssemblyScript and JavaScript. We'll pass strings into AssemblyScript by writing a string concatenation app. We'll also explore OOP in AssemblyScript. We'll create a couple of classes to demonstrate class inheritance and discuss `private` attributes that prevent AssemblyScript from exporting attributes to the embedding environment. Next, we'll write JavaScript that allows us to create public, private, and protected members directly, as well as use the AssemblyScript loader. Then we'll compare the performance of direct and loader function calls.

The AssemblyScript team designed it to be similar to TypeScript and JavaScript. Unlike WAT, AssemblyScript is a high-level language with features such as classes, strings, and arrays. Along with high-level features, AssemblyScript allows users to code with low-level WAT-like memory commands. AssemblyScript has a *Command Line Interface (CLI)* that can compile AssemblyScript into a WebAssembly module for use from within JavaScript applications.

For JavaScript developers interested in using WebAssembly to improve the performance of their JavaScript applications, AssemblyScript is a great tool. Unfortunately, as with everything in WebAssembly, merely tweaking your TypeScript until it compiles with the AssemblyScript compiler might not result in a considerable performance boost. Understanding what AssemblyScript does under the hood allows you to write code in a language that looks like JavaScript but runs like C++. To gain this understanding, we'll compile AssemblyScript code to WAT to explore the AssemblyScript compiler's output.

AssemblyScript CLI

Install AssemblyScript using the following command:

```
npm install assemblyscript -g
```

The npm command installs AssemblyScript globally, which allows you to use the AssemblyScript compiler asc command from the command line. Running asc -h provides a list of compiler command examples and options.

I won't explain all the command line arguments but will mention a few that are useful. The -O option optimizes in the same way as wasm-opt in Chapter 9. You follow -O with a number 0 to 3, s, or z, instructing the compiler to optimize for size or performance and how much optimization to apply. The -o flag when followed by the name of a *.wat* file will generate WAT code from the AssemblyScript, and when followed by the name of a *.wasm* file will generate a binary WebAssembly module. The --sourceMap flag creates a source map file to help you debug your AssemblyScript from the browser.

We'll first create a simple AssemblyScript module. Create the file *as_add.ts* and add the code in Listing 11-1. This is a much simpler version of the AddInt function in Chapter 1.

```
as_add.ts ❶ export function AddInts(❷a: i32, ❸b: i32 ): i32 {
             ❹ return a + b;
           }
```

Listing 11-1: Adding two integers

We make the function available to the embedding JavaScript using the export ❶ keyword. It takes two i32 parameters a ❷ and b ❸, and returns a + b ❹ as an i32. Compile *as_add.ts* using the command in Listing 11-2.

```
asc as_add.ts -Oz -o as_add.wat
```

Listing 11-2: Compiling AddInts to WAT

The -Oz flag makes the size of the output binary as small as possible. The final flag, -o as_add.wat, tells the compiler to output WAT. Alternatively, we could have compiled a *.wasm* file, such as *as_add.wasm*, which would output a WebAssembly binary. When we look at the *as_add.wat* file that is output, we see the WAT code in Listing 11-3.

as_add.wat
```
(module
  (type $i32_i32_=>_i32 (func (param i32 i32) (result i32)))
  (memory $0 0)
❶ (export "AddInts" (func $as_add/AddInts))
  (export "memory" (memory $0))
❷ (func $as_add/AddInts (param $0 i32) (param $1 i32) (result i32)
  ❸ local.get $0
  ❹ local.get $1
  ❺ i32.add
  )
)
```

Listing 11-3: AssemblyScript AddInts function compiled to WAT

Writing code in AssemblyScript is much easier than writing code directly in WAT. This code produces the AddInts ❶ function that exports a function ❷ that takes two i32 parameters and returns an i32. The output function uses a local.get to retrieve the first ❸ and second ❹ parameters, and uses an i32.add ❺ to add those two values.

AssemblyScript is a beautiful little language that is relatively easy to learn for anyone familiar with TypeScript or JavaScript. Understanding WAT is a great way to get the most from your AssemblyScript or whichever high-level language you choose for WebAssembly development.

Hello World AssemblyScript

Next, we'll build an AssemblyScript version of the WAT hello world application from Chapter 2. Create a new AssemblyScript file named *as_hello.ts* and add the code in Listing 11-4.

as_hello.ts
```
❶ declare function console_log( msg: string ):void;

❷ export function HelloWorld():void {
❸ console_log("hello world!");
}
```

Listing 11-4: A hello world AssemblyScript app

The function declaration in AssemblyScript must correspond with a JavaScript function passed into the WebAssembly module. So we'll need to pass in a function through the importObject that logs our string to the console. The declare function ❶ imports the console_log function from the JavaScript. This function will pass a string from the AssemblyScript back to the calling JavaScript app. We create an export function called HelloWorld ❷ that calls the imported console_log ❸ function, passing in the string "hello world!". Before we compile this into a WebAssembly module, we'll use asc to compile a WAT file so we can look at the WebAssembly created (Listing 11-5).

```
asc as_hello.ts -Oz -o as_hello.wat
```

Listing 11-5: Compile the as_hello.ts AssemblyScript file into as_hello.wat.

Then we can open *as_hello.wat* in Listing 11-6 to see the WebAssembly that AssemblyScript generated.

```
;; The comments were added by the author and not generated by asc ❶
(module
  (type $none_=>_none (func))
  (type $i32_=>_none (func (param i32)))
  ;; the declare command at the top of the AssemblyScript created an import
  ;; that imports the console_log function inside of the outer as_hello
  ;; object.  AssemblyScript requires its imports in the AssemblyScript file name
  ;; not including the .ts extension
  (import "as_hello" "console_log" (func $as_hello/console_log (param i32))) ❷
  ;; using a string automatically creates the memory expression
  (memory $0 1) ❸
  ;; the data line below wraps because the line is too long
  ;; The "hello world!" string is preceded by a header and has a hex 00 byte in
  ;; between every letter in the string.  This is because AssemblyScript uses
  ;; the UTF-16 character set instead of ASCII as we did when we were manipulating
  ;; string data in WAT.
  (data (i32.const 16) ❹
    "\18\00\00\00\01\00\00\00\01\00\00\00\18\00\00\00h\00e\00l\00l\00o\00
\00w\00o\00r\00l\00d\00!")
  (export "memory" (memory $0))
  ;; The module exports our function with the AssemblyScript name we gave it.
  (export "HelloWorld" (func $as_hello/HelloWorld)) ❺
  ;; the function name we gave AssemblyScript is prefixed by the name of our file
  ;; without the .ts extension
  (func $as_hello/HelloWorld (; 1 ;) ❻
  ;; 32 is the location in linear memory of the 'h' byte in "hello world"
  i32.const 32 ❼
  ;; the console_log function is called passing in the location of "hello world"
  ;; in linear memory
  call $as_hello/console_log ❽
  )
)
```

Listing 11-6: The as_hello.wat file generated from the as_hello.ts AssemblyScript

I've added comments to clarify the code ❶. This module imports console_log ❷ wrapped in the object as_hello, the name of our AssemblyScript file without the *.ts* extension. This is the naming convention AssemblyScript uses for its importObject; when you write your JavaScript, you must name your object inside the imported object accordingly.

AssemblyScript creates a memory ❸ expression to hold the string data. The string has a prefixed header that includes the length of the string, which AssemblyScript uses to manipulate the data from within WebAssembly. The string data ❹ uses two bytes per character, and because AssemblyScript uses UTF-16, every character in this example is separated by a null byte \00. UTF-16 is the 16-bit version of the Unicode character set that allows for many additional characters not available in ASCII.

After the data expression, the WAT exports ❺ the function with the name we gave it in the AssemblyScript, prefixed with the $ character and excluding the *.ts* extension. The HelloWorld ❻ function calls console_log ❽, passing in the location of the first character in our hello world! string in linear memory, which is 32 ❼.

With our WAT file compiled, we can use the asc command in Listing 11-7 to compile our WebAssembly module.

```
asc as_hello.ts -Oz -o as_hello.wasm
```

Listing 11-7: Compiling our AssemblyScript to WebAssembly binary

Next, we create our JavaScript.

JavaScript for Our Hello World App

Currently, we have a WebAssembly module named *as_hello.wasm*. Next, we'll write a Node.js app that will load and run this module. In this section, we'll decode the string data the way we did in Chapter 5 to understand how AssemblyScript transfers strings to JavaScript. Then we'll use the AssemblyScript loader tool to do much of this work for us.

First, we'll write a function to pull the string out of linear memory using the index passed from the WebAssembly module. AssemblyScript places the length of the string in the four bytes immediately preceding the string data. We can use Uint32Array to obtain the string length integer and use that length to create our string in JavaScript. Create a file named *as_hello.js* and add the code in Listing 11-8.

as_hello.js
```
const fs = require('fs');
const bytes = fs.readFileSync(__dirname + '/as_hello.wasm');

// The memory object is exported from AssemblyScript
❶ var memory = null;

let importObject = {
  // module's file name without extension is used as the outer object name
❷ as_hello: {
    // AssemblyScript passes a length prefixed string with a simple index
```

```
❸ console_log: function (index) {
    // in case this is called before memory is set
    if (memory == null) {
      console.log('memory buffer is null');
      return;
    }

  ❹ const len_index = index - 4;

    // must divide by 2 to get from bytes to 16-bit unicode characters
  ❺ const len = new Uint32Array(memory.buffer, len_index, 4)[0];
  ❻ const str_bytes = new Uint16Array(memory.buffer,
      index, len);

    // decode the utf-16 byte array into a JS string
  ❼ const log_string = new TextDecoder('utf-16').decode(str_bytes);
    console.log(log_string);
    }
  },
  env: {
    abort: () => { }
  }
};

(async () => {
  let obj = await WebAssembly.instantiate(new Uint8Array(bytes),
    importObject);

  // memory object exported from AssemblyScript
❽ memory = obj.instance.exports.memory;
  // call the HelloWorld function
❾ obj.instance.exports.HelloWorld();
})();
```

Listing 11-8: Calling the AssemblyScript HelloWorld from JavaScript

WebAssembly modules that AssemblyScript generates always create
and export their own memory unless they're compiled with the --import-
Memory flag. By default, AssemblyScript creates its own linear memory in the
WebAssembly module. Therefore, in the JavaScript, we don't create a linear
memory object. Instead, we create a var called memory ❶, which we'll later set
to the linear memory object that the WebAssembly module exports.

Inside importObject, the object that holds the data for import must
have the same name as the AssemblyScript file importing it: as_hello ❷ for
our AssemblyScript file *as_hello.ts*. Inside as_hello is console_log ❸, which
is passed a string parameter when called from the AssemblyScript. When
the WebAssembly module calls as_hello, the JavaScript function receives
just a single numeric index into WebAssembly linear memory, which is
the location of the string data portion of the length prefixed string that
AssemblyScript uses to define its string type.

The length is a 32-bit integer in the four bytes that precede the index.
To get the index of the length integer, we subtract four from the string
index. We use the value for the length located in linear memory by creating

a new Uint32Array, passing in the memory.buffer, the len_index ❹, and a value of 4 for the number of bytes. Because Uint32Array ❺ is an array of 32-bit integers, we need to get the first and only item in the array using [0].

We retrieve the string byte data from linear memory using new Uint16 Array ❻ and convert that byte array into a JavaScript string by using a new TextDecoder that decodes for utf-16 text data. The code calls the TextDecoder ❼ decode function, passing in the string data, which returns a JavaScript string we then log to the console. We use an IIFE to instantiate the AssemblyScript WebAssembly module. Note that we must set the memory ❽ object to the memory object exported from the WebAssembly module before calling the HelloWorld ❾ function. The console_log function uses the memory object, and if it isn't set, calling HelloWorld will do nothing.

Fortunately, there is an easier way to move string data between AssemblyScript and JavaScript, which is by using the AssemblyScript loader. This code is provided by the AssemblyScript team. In the "Performance of Loader vs. Direct WebAssembly Calls" section, we'll see whether we can improve the performance of the AssemblyScript loader with code we've written.

Hello World with the AssemblyScript Loader

The AssemblyScript loader is a set of helper functions from the AssemblyScript team designed to make it easier to make calls to AssemblyScript from JavaScript. We'll compare the code we wrote earlier with code written using the AssemblyScript loader. Initially, we'll consider ease of use and later look into the performance implications of using or not using the loader.

We use the AssemblyScript loader to send a string back to the JavaScript from the AssemblyScript. The loader helper function converts the index coming from WebAssembly into a JavaScript string. Now we will install the loader using npm:

```
npm install @assemblyscript/loader --save
```

NOTE *You might need to upgrade Node.js to use the loader. At the time of this writing, the newest version of the AssemblyScript loader requires Node.js version 14.*

Now we'll create a JavaScript file to load and run our WebAssembly module. Create a file named *as_hello_loader.js* and add the code in Listing 11-9.

```
as_hello   ❶ const loader = require("@assemblyscript/loader");
_loader.js    const fs = require('fs');
           ❷ var module;

             const importObject = {
           ❸ as_hello: {
           ❹   console_log: (str_index) => {
           ❺     console.log(module.exports.__getString(str_index));
                 }
               }
```

```
};

(async () => {
  let wasm = fs.readFileSync('as_hello.wasm');
❻ module = await loader.instantiate(wasm, importObject);
❼ module.exports.HelloWorld();
})();
```

Listing 11-9: Using the AssemblyScript loader to call the WebAssembly module

This JavaScript function first requires ❶ the AssemblyScript loader. We use this loader object to load the `module` ❷ object, which we declare globally. The `module` object is an AssemblyScript loader module that includes additional AssemblyScript loader helper functions. Inside the `importObject` is a child object with the `as_hello` ❸ name of our AssemblyScript module. That is where the AssemblyScript code expects to locate the imported functions. Inside the `as_hello` object is `console_log` ❹, which takes the string index `str_index` as its only parameter. This function uses the `__getString` ❺ function on the `module` object created by the loader. When given the string index, the `__getString` function retrieves a JavaScript string from linear memory. This string is printed to the console with `console.log`. The IIFE function loads an AssemblyScript module using the AssemblyScript `loader` ❻ object. Finally, the IIFE calls the `HelloWorld` ❼ function. When you run this JavaScript file using `node`, you'll see the output in Listing 11-10.

```
hello world!
```

Listing 11-10: Output from the AssemblyScript hello world app

Using the AssemblyScript loader makes the JavaScript code significantly simpler. Later, in the "Performance of Loader vs. Direct WebAssembly Calls" section, we'll explore the performance implications.

AssemblyScript String Concatenation

Now that we know how to receive strings from AssemblyScript, we'll send a string to an AssemblyScript module. This next function concatenates two strings separated by a pipe character (|). We'll use the loader to make it easier to write the code on the JavaScript side. String concatenation is the kind of functionality that is challenging to implement directly in WAT but is very simple in AssemblyScript. Create a new file named *as_concat.ts* and add the code in Listing 11-11.

as_concat.ts ❶ `export function cat( str1: string, str2: string ): string {`
             ❷ `return str1 + "|" + str2;`
               `}`

Listing 11-11: Concatenating strings using AssemblyScript

We export ❶ `cat`, which takes two string parameters and returns a string. This function concatenates ❷ the string with a pipe character (|) separating them.

Now we can compile *as_concat.ts* using the asc command in Listing 11-12.

```
asc as_concat.ts --exportRuntime -Oz -o as_concat.wasm
```

Listing 11-12: Compiling the as_concat.ts *file using* asc

We pass the --exportRuntime flag, which is necessary for passing strings into the WebAssembly module. Compiling with --exportRuntime adds code that allows you to call the __allocString function from JavaScript. If we fail to export the runtime, the following error occurs when the application executes:

```
TypeError: alloc is not a function
```

When you compile *as_concat.ts* into WAT, notice that the WAT file is much larger than our *as_hello.ts* file. The reason is that the runtime adds several string functions that perform necessary tasks, such as copy memory, concatenate strings, and get/set string length methods.

Now we can write our JavaScript app. The code in Listing 11-13 creates two strings in linear memory and calls the WebAssembly function cat. Create a new JavaScript file named *as_concat.js* and add the code in Listing 11-13.

as_concat.js
```
const fs = require('fs');
const loader = require("@assemblyscript/loader");

(async () => {
  let module = await loader.instantiate(fs.readFileSync('as_concat.wasm'));

  //__newString, __getString functions require
  //compile with --exportRuntime flag
❶ let first_str_index = module.exports.__newString("first string");
❷ let second_str_index = module.exports.__newString("second string");
❸ let cat_str_index = module.exports.cat(first_str_index,second_str_index);
❹ let cat_string = module.exports.__getString(cat_str_index);
❺ console.log(cat_string);
})();
```

Listing 11-13: JavaScript uses the AssemblyScript loader to call the cat AssemblyScript function.

The cat function we defined in the WebAssembly module doesn't take a string as a parameter directly, so it needs an index into linear memory for the string location. The module.exports.__newString loader helper function takes a JavaScript string, copies it into linear memory, and returns an index to pass into module.cat. We call module.exports.__newString twice, passing "first string" ❶ and then passing "second string" ❷. Each of these calls returns an index that we store in first_str_index and second_str_index. Next, we call module.exports.cat, passing in these indexes, from which we receive a JavaScript string index that we store in cat_str_index ❸. Then we call module.exports.__getString ❹, passing in cat_str_index, and storing that string in cat_string ❺, which we log to the console.

Now that we have our JavaScript and WebAssembly, we can run our application using node:

```
node as_concat.js
```

And here's the output to your console:

```
first string|second string
```

There is a lot more to AssemblyScript to explore. As you can see, it's much simpler to write code that works with strings in AssemblyScript than it is in WAT. That doesn't necessarily tell you when you should work with string data in WebAssembly, but it exposes it as an option. AssemblyScript, like WebAssembly more broadly, is a quickly developing project. Taking the time to learn more about it from the project home page at *assemblyscript.org* is worth the time spent.

Object Oriented Programming in AssemblyScript

OOP is almost impossible to use in WAT format, but because AssemblyScript is modeled on TypeScript, it offers significantly more options for OOP. In this section, we'll cover some of the basics of OOP in AssemblyScript, as well as some of its limitations, which might no longer apply in future releases.

Let's begin by creating a new AssemblyScript file named *vector.ts*. Right now, AssemblyScript is piggybacking on top of TypeScript file formatting, which works in most cases.

Saule Cabrera has created an AssemblyScript language server plug-in for VS Code, which is available at *https://marketplace.visualstudio.com/items?itemName=saulecabrera.asls*.

Next, we'll write an AssemblyScript Vector2D class to hold the coordinates of the collider objects that are similar to what we wrote for the collision detection app in Chapter 8. We'll compile the code to WAT so we can explore the output of the AssemblyScript compiler. Gaining a better understanding of the compiler and its output can be extremely beneficial when optimizing WebAssembly code. Add Listing 11-14 to your file to create the class Vector2D.

```
vector.ts  ❶ export class Vector2D {
           ❷ x: f32;
           ❸ y: f32;

           ❹ constructor(x: f32, y: f32) {
                this.x = x;
                this.y = y;
              }

           ❺ Magnitude(): f32 {
                return Mathf.sqrt(this.x * this.x + this.y * this.y);
              }
            }
```

Listing 11-14: Creating a vector class in AssemblyScript

We export a class called Vector2D ❶ that has two attributes, x ❷ and y ❸. It also has a constructor ❹ that creates a new Vector2D object from the x and y parameters. The Magnitude ❺ method calculates the magnitude of the vector by summing the squares of x and y and taking the square root of that sum.

If you're familiar with TypeScript, you'll notice that this code looks just like the class structures in TypeScript. However, rather than using the TypeScript number type, we're using f32 types for 32-bit floating-point numbers. If you use the number type in your AssemblyScript, it's the same as using an f64 64-bit floating-point, which has the poorest performance of the WebAssembly types in most circumstances.

The following command compiles *vector.ts* into a WAT file using asc:

```
asc vector.ts -o vector.wat
```

This creates a WAT file we can examine in VS Code. To asc we pass the name of the AssemblyScript file and then we pass the -o flag with the filename for the output file, vector.wat. The extension determines whether the output will be WAT or the WebAssembly binary file. Open *vector.wat* and scroll down a bit until you get to the exports shown in Listing 11-15.

vector.wat
```
    ...
      (export "memory" (memory $0))
      (export "Vector2D" (global $vector/Vector2D))
    ❶ (export "Vector2D#get:x" (func $vector/Vector2D#get:x))
    ❷ (export "Vector2D#set:x" (func $vector/Vector2D#set:x))
    ❸ (export "Vector2D#get:y" (func $vector/Vector2D#get:y))
      (export "Vector2D#set:y" (func $vector/Vector2D#set:y))
    ❹ (export "Vector2D#constructor" (func $vector/Vector2D#constructor))
    ❺ (export "Vector2D#Magnitude" (func $vector/Vector2D#Magnitude))
    ...
```

Listing 11-15: The exported functions in our WAT file

Notice how the compiler generated get ❶ and set ❷ accessor functions for the x ❷ and y ❸ attributes, and exported them so you can access them from the embedding environment. This indicates that when the user sets an object attribute using the loader, it calls a function in the WebAssembly module. One implication of this is that if you're setting several attributes at once, you might want to consider creating a function to do this all at once for performance reasons. That way, you're not making multiple function calls to the WebAssembly module. You can also see that the WebAssembly module exported the constructor ❹ and Magnitude ❺ functions.

The naming conventions are important to understand if you want to call functions in the WebAssembly module from JavaScript. The methods are all prefixed with the name of the class and a hash mark (#) character (Vector2D#). The set and get methods have a suffix that indicates which attribute they're setting and getting, such as :x or :y. To access these functions and attributes from our JavaScript without using the AssemblyScript loader, we need to use this naming convention.

Using Private Attributes

If you don't want to export all the attributes to the embedding environ-
ment, you need to use the `private` keyword before the x and y attributes.
Do that now in your AssemblyScript and recompile with the `asc` command.
Listing 11-16 shows the new version.

```
vector.ts    export class Vector2D {
          ❶ private x: f32;
          ❷ private y: f32;

             constructor(x: f32, y: f32) {
               this.x = x;
               this.y = y;
             }

             Magnitude(): f32 {
               return Mathf.sqrt(this.x * this.x + this.y * this.y);
             }

           }
```

Listing 11-16: Creating private functions in AssemblyScript

The private ❶ modifier before x ❶ and y ❷ tells the AssemblyScript
compiler that these attributes shouldn't be publicly accessible. Recompile
the WebAssembly module, which no longer exports the accessor methods
that set and get the x and y variables to the embedding environment, as
shown in Listing 11-17.

```
vector.wat   ...
           (export "memory" (memory $0))
           (export "Vector2D" (global $vector/Vector2D))
           (export "Vector2D#constructor" (func $vector/Vector2D#constructor))
           (export "Vector2D#Magnitude" (func $vector/Vector2D#Magnitude))
           ...
```

Listing 11-17: Exports in the WAT file

TypeScript has three modifiers, `public`, `private`, and `protected`, to define
how attributes can be accessed. These modifiers behave a little differently
in AssemblyScript than in other languages, such as TypeScript. In most
languages, protected attributes are available to classes that extend the class
but cannot be accessed outside the parent or child class. The `protected`
method in AssemblyScript isn't implemented fully and behaves the same as
the `public` modifier. For now, you should avoid using it to prevent confusion.
The keywords may eventually work as they do in TypeScript, but be aware
that these limitations still exist in AssemblyScript version 0.17.7.

The private modifier prevents AssemblyScript from exporting the get
and set methods when it compiles the module.

Unlike in other OOP languages, the private modifier in AssemblyScript doesn't prevent classes that extend the original from accessing that attribute.

Let's use the following command to compile our AssemblyScript into a WebAssembly module so we can call it from our JavaScript:

```
asc vector.ts -o vector.wasm
```

When we change the -o flag to *vector.wasm*, we tell the asc compiler to output a WebAssembly binary file. That will allow us to load and run the module from a JavaScript embedding environment. Next, let's look at how to load and call WebAssembly functions using Node.js.

JavaScript Embedding Environment

We'll use Node.js to load and execute the WebAssembly module. If we instead use a browser, the JavaScript would use WebAssembly.instantiateStreaming and fetch instead of using fs to load the WebAssembly module from the filesystem and calling WebAssembly.instantiate.

Create the file *vector.js* and add the code in Listing 11-18.

```
vector.js  ❶ const fs = require('fs');

❷ (async () => {
❸   let wasm = fs.readFileSync('vector.wasm');
❹   let obj = await WebAssembly.instantiate(wasm,{env:{abort:()=>{}}});

❺   let Vector2D = {
❻     init: function (x, y) {
         return obj.instance.exports["Vector2D#constructor"](0, x, y)
       },
❼     Magnitude: obj.instance.exports["Vector2D#Magnitude"],
     }

❽   let vec1_id = Vector2D.init(3, 4);
     let vec2_id = Vector2D.init(4, 5);

     console.log(`
❾   vec1.magnitude=${Vector2D.Magnitude(vec1_id)}
     vec2.magnitude=${Vector2D.Magnitude(vec2_id)}
       `);
})();
```

Listing 11-18: Calling functions on the Vector2D AssemblyScript class

We use the fs ❶ Node.js module to load ❸ the binary WebAssembly data from a file inside an asynchronous IIFE ❷. Once we have the binary data, we pass it to WebAssembly.instantiate ❹, which returns a WebAssembly module object. We then create the JavaScript object Vector2D ❺, which mirrors the functions inside the WebAssembly module.

We create an init ❻ function that calls the WebAssembly module's Vector2D constructor, passing in 0 as the first parameter. Passing this value to the `constructor` function allows some degree of choice of object placement in linear memory. We are passing 0, which makes the constructor create a new object at the next available memory location. The function will then return the location in linear memory where it created this object. The `Magnitude` ❼ attribute in `Vector2D` takes its value from `obj.instance.exports["Vector2D#Magnitude"]`, which is a function in our WebAssembly module.

After defining the JavaScript `Vector2D` object, we call `Vector2D.init` ❽ twice to create two `Vector2D` WebAssembly objects in linear memory, as well as return the linear memory address of these objects, which we use for method calls. We then call `Vector2D.Magnitude` twice inside a `console.log` template string. We pass in the vector ids (`vec1_id` and `vec2_id`) we saved in Listing 11-18, which tell the WebAssembly module which object it's using. The `Magnitude` ❾ function passes back the magnitude of the given vector, which the app logs to the console. Run this app using `node`:

```
node vector.js
```

Here's the result:

```
vec1.magnitude=5
vec2.magnitude=6.4031243324279785
```

The two values are the magnitude of our first vector where x = 3 and y = 4, and the magnitude of the second vector where x = 4 and y = 5.

Now that we know how to make calls into our AssemblyScript app directly, let's look at how to use the AssemblyScript loader to make coding the JavaScript a little easier.

AssemblyScript Loader

Now we'll modify our AssemblyScript code to use the AssemblyScript loader library. This will allow us to compare the methods of interfacing with an AssemblyScript module in terms of ease of use and performance. As mentioned previously, it's important to understand when it's possible to improve your application's performance and how much effort that requires. This information helps you make decisions concerning the trade-off between development time and application performance.

Open *vector_loader.ts* and add the code in Listing 11-19 to use the AssemblyScript loader.

vector_loader.ts
```
export class Vector2D {
❶ x: f32;
❷ y: f32;

  constructor(x: f32, y: f32) {
    this.x = x;
    this.y = y;
  }
```

```
  Magnitude(): f32 {
    return Mathf.sqrt(this.x * this.x + this.y * this.y);
  }

❸ add(vec2: Vector2D): Vector2D {
    this.x += vec2.x;
    this.y += vec2.y;
    return this;
  }
}
```

Listing 11-19: Remove the private modifier from the x and y attributes

There are two changes to *vector.ts* that we will add into *vector_loader.ts*. First, we remove the private modifiers from the x ❶ and y ❷ attributes so we can access x and y from JavaScript. Second, we create an add ❸ function that adds a second vector. This function allows us to add two vectors together. In Listing 11-20, we compile *vector_loader.ts* using asc.

```
asc vector_loader.ts -o vector_loader.wasm
```

Listing 11-20: Compiling vector.ts to a WebAssembly file using asc

Next, we'll create a new JavaScript file named *vector_loader.js* so we can run the new WebAssembly module. Add the code in Listing 11-21 to *vector_loader.js*.

vector_loader.js
```
  const fs = require('fs');
❶ const loader = require('@assemblyscript/loader');

  (async () => {
    let wasm = fs.readFileSync('vector_loader.wasm');
    // instantiate the module using the loader
❷  let module = await loader.instantiate(wasm);

    // module.exports.Vector2D mirrors the AssemblyScript class.
❸  let Vector2D = module.exports.Vector2D;

❹  let vector1 = new Vector2D(3, 4);
    let vector2 = new Vector2D(4, 5);

❺  vector2.y += 10;
❻  vector2.add(vector1);

    console.log(`
❼  vector1=(${vector1.x}, ${vector1.y})
    vector2=(${vector2.x}, ${vector2.y})

    vector1.magnitude=${vector1.Magnitude()}
    vector2.magnitude=${vector2.Magnitude()}
    `);
  })();
```

Listing 11-21: Using the AssemblyScript loader in JavaScript

When using the loader, you can interact with AssemblyScript classes almost as if they're JavaScript classes. There is a slight difference in that you call the demangled constructor function without using the JavaScript new operator, as you would do if these classes were created in JavaScript. However, once you've instantiated the object, you can interact with it as if it were written in JavaScript.

We first require the AssemblyScript loader ❶. Rather than using the WebAssembly.instantiate function from the IIFE, we call the loader .instantiate ❷ function, which returns a loader module. This module works a little differently than the WebAssembly module object returned by the WebAssembly.instantiate call. The AssemblyScript loader adds functionality that allows the JavaScript to work with high-level AssemblyScript objects, such as classes and strings.

We then call loader.demangle, passing it the module returned by loader .instantiate. The demangle function returns an object structure that provides us with functions we can use to instantiate objects from our WebAssembly module. We pull the Vector2D ❸ function out of the object structure so we can use it as a constructor function for creating Vector2D objects in JavaScript. Note that we didn't use the new operator when instantiating Vector2D ❹. However, the current loader version supports use of the new operator.

We use the Vector2D function to create a vector1 and vector2 object, passing in the x and y values for those vectors. We can now use these objects as regular JavaScript objects. The loader wires everything up for us. For example, we call vector2.y += 10 ❺ to increase the value of vector2.y by 10, and vector2.add(vector1) ❻ calls the add function on the vector2 object, passing in vector1. In our console.log ❼ call, we can use values like vector1.x and vector1.y.

Run the JavaScript using node:

```
node vector_loader.js
```

You should see the following output:

```
vector1=(3, 4)
vector2=(7, 19)

vector1.magnitude=5
vector2.magnitude=20.248456954956055
```

The AssemblyScript loader interface allows you to work with WebAssembly modules created in AssemblyScript almost as if they were classes, objects, and functions created in JavaScript. This creates an ergonomic experience that you might not have when you write your own interface with the WebAssembly module. If you have specific performance targets, you'll need to perform additional testing to see whether the loader meets all your needs. In the next section, we'll extend our AssemblyScript class through inheritance.

Extending Classes in AssemblyScript

OOP allows developers to extend a class by adding additional attributes or functionality to a base class. The syntax for extending classes in AssemblyScript is the same as it is in TypeScript. In Listing 11-22, we'll extend the Vector2D class with a Vector3D class that will add an additional attribute z, which will represent a third dimension for our vector.

Open the *vector_loader.ts* file and add the code in Listing 11-22 after the Vector2D definition.

vector_loader.ts

```
...
❶ export class Vector3D extends Vector2D {
❷ z: f32;

  constructor(x: f32, y: f32, z: f32) {
  ❸ super(x, y);
    this.z = z;
  }

❹ Magnitude(): f32 {
    return Mathf.sqrt(this.x * this.x + this.y * this.y + this.z * this.z);
  }

  add(vec3: Vector3D): Vector3D {
  ❺ super.add(vec3);
  ❻ this.z += vec3.z;
    return this;
  }
}
```

Listing 11-22: Extending the Vector2D class using the Vector3D class

The new Vector3D ❶ class keeps the original x and y attributes, and adds a third z ❷ attribute for the third dimension. Its constructor calls super ❸, which runs the constructor from the Vector2D class. It then sets the value of this.z to the z parameter passed into the constructor. We override the Magnitude ❹ method from Vector2D so it takes the third dimension into account when calculating the magnitude of the vector. Then the add function calls the Vector2D class's add function using super.add ❺ and increases the value of this.z ❻ using the vec3 parameter's z attribute value.

Now we can recompile our WebAssembly module using asc:

```
asc vector_loader.ts -o vector_loader.wasm
```

Next, in Listing 11-23, we modify the *vector_loader.js* file to pull in the Vector3D class.

vector_loader.js

```
const fs = require('fs');
const loader = require("@assemblyscript/loader");

(async () => {
  let wasm = fs.readFileSync('vector_loader.wasm');
  let module = await loader.instantiate(wasm);
```

```
❶ let { Vector2D, Vector3D } = await loader.demangle(module).exports;

  let vector1 = Vector2D(3, 4);
  let vector2 = Vector2D(4, 5);
❷ let vector3 = Vector3D(5, 6, 7);

  vector2.y += 10;
  vector2.add(vector1);
❸ vector3.z++;

  console.log(`
  vector1=(${vector1.x}, ${vector1.y})
  vector2=(${vector2.x}, ${vector2.y})
❹ vector3=(${vector3.x}, ${vector3.y}, ${vector3.z})

  vector1.magnitude=${vector1.Magnitude()}
  vector2.magnitude=${vector2.Magnitude()}
❺ vector3.magnitude=${vector3.Magnitude()}
  `);
})();
```

Listing 11-23: JavaScript using the AssemblyScript loader to load Vector2D and Vector3D classes

We modify the line that took the Vector2D function from the call to demangle, and change it to destructure ❶ the result, creating a Vector2D and Vector3D function variable. We create an object vector3 ❷, using the function Vector3D, to which we pass x, y, and z values. We increment vector3.z ❸ for no particular reason other than to show that we can do it. Inside the template string passed to console.log, we add a line that displays the x, y, and z ❹ values in vector3, as well as the magnitude of vector3 ❺.

When you run this JavaScript from the command line using node, you get the output in Listing 11-24.

```
vector1=(3, 4)
vector2=(7, 19)
vector3=(5, 6, 8)

vector1.magnitude=5
vector2.magnitude=20.248456954956055
vector3.magnitude=11.180339813232422
```

Listing 11-24: Output from vector_loader.js

Now let's look at how the performance of the loader compares to direct calls into the WebAssembly module.

Performance of Loader vs. Direct WebAssembly Calls

The AssemblyScript loader provides a more intuitive structure for interaction between the AssemblyScript module and our JavaScript. The final section of this chapter compares the loader with direct calls into the

WebAssembly modules. To run this test, we don't need to write any additional AssemblyScript. We'll use the WebAssembly modules created earlier in this chapter, so we only need to create a new JavaScript file to call the existing modules. Create a new file named *vector_perform.js* and add the code in Listing 11-25.

<table>
<tr><td>vector_perform.js</td><td>

```javascript
const fs = require('fs');
const loader = require("@assemblyscript/loader");

(async () => {
  let importObject = {
    env: {
      abort: () => { }
    }
  };
  let wasm = fs.readFileSync('vector_loader.wasm');
  let module = await loader.instantiate(wasm);
  let obj = await WebAssembly.instantiate(wasm, importObject);

  // This JavaScript class will have all the functions
  // exported from AssemblyScript
❶ let dVector2D = {
    // the init function will call the constructor on Vector2D
    init: function (x, y) {
      return obj.instance.exports["Vector2D#constructor"](0, x, y)
    },
    getX: obj.instance.exports["Vector2D#get:x"],
    setX: obj.instance.exports["Vector2D#set:x"],
    getY: obj.instance.exports["Vector2D#get:y"],
    setY: obj.instance.exports["Vector2D#set:y"],
    Magnitude: obj.instance.exports["Vector2D#Magnitude"],
    add: obj.instance.exports["Vector2D#add"],
  }

  // This JavaScript class will have all the functions
  // exported from AssemblyScript
  let dVector3D = {
    // the init function will call the constructor on Vector3D
    init: function (x, y, z) {
      return obj.instance.exports["Vector3D#constructor"](0, x, y, z)
    },
    getX: obj.instance.exports["Vector3D#get:x"],
    setX: obj.instance.exports["Vector3D#set:x"],
    getY: obj.instance.exports["Vector3D#get:y"],
    setY: obj.instance.exports["Vector3D#set:y"],
    getZ: obj.instance.exports["Vector3D#get:z"],
    setZ: obj.instance.exports["Vector3D#set:z"],
    Magnitude: obj.instance.exports["Vector3D#Magnitude"],
    add: obj.instance.exports["Vector3D#add"],
  }
  // prepare to log the time it takes to run functions directly
❷ let start_time_direct = (new Date()).getTime();

❸ let vec1_id = dVector2D.init(1, 2);
```

</td></tr>
</table>

```
   let vec2_id = dVector2D.init(3, 4);
   let vec3_id = dVector3D.init(5, 6, 7);

❹ for (let i = 0; i < 1_000_000; i++) {
     dVector2D.add(vec1_id, vec2_id);
     dVector3D.setX(vec3_id, dVector3D.getX(vec3_id) + 10);
     dVector2D.setY(vec2_id, dVector2D.getY(vec2_id) + 1);
     dVector2D.Magnitude(vec2_id);
   }
❺ console.log("direct time=" + (new Date().getTime() - start_time_direct));

❻ let { Vector2D, Vector3D } = await loader.demangle(module).exports;

❼ let start_time_loader = (new Date()).getTime();

❽ let vector1 = Vector2D(1, 2);
   let vector2 = Vector2D(3, 4);
   let vector3 = Vector3D(5, 6, 7);

❾ for (i = 0; i < 1_000_000; i++) {
     vector1.add(vector2);
     vector3.x += 10;
     vector2.y++;
     vector2.Magnitude();
   }
❿ console.log("loader time=" + (new Date().getTime() - start_time_loader));
})();
```

Listing 11-25: Comparing loader function calls with direct function calls

Now we can see what it costs for us to use that pretty AssemblyScript loader syntax. This JavaScript creates an object to hold the direct calls to the Vector2D AssemblyScript class dVector2D ❶ and one for the Vector3D class called dVector3D. We then set the variable start_direct_time ❷ to the current time, which we'll use to track the performance, and initialize ❸ three vector objects. Two of the vector objects are Vector2D objects, and one is a Vector3D object.

After initializing the vectors, we loop one million times ❹, making calls to those objects. We didn't test every function, so this isn't a perfect performance test. The goal is simply to get some numbers and see how they compare. As long as we make the same calls to the direct and loader versions, we should be able to get a reasonable comparison. We then use console.log ❺ to log out the amount of time it took to initialize the vectors and run through the loop. This first loop tests the performance of the direct call to the WebAssembly module without using the AssemblyScript loader. Next, the code tests the performance of the module with the loader.

We use the loader.demangle ❻ function to create the Vector2D and Vector3D factory functions. We then initialize start_time_loader ❼ to the current time and call the Vector2D ❽ and Vector3D functions to create three objects mirroring the code in the first loop ❹ that tested the direct initialization calls. We loop one million times ❾, executing the same functions as earlier, except through the loader. Finally, we log ❿ the amount of time it took to execute the code using the loader.

Run *vector_perform.js* from the command line using `node`:

```
node vector_perform.js
```

This is the output I received when I executed the file:

```
direct time=74
loader time=153
```

As you can see, the version using the loader took roughly twice as long to execute. The difference is even starker when we include the initialization calls in a loop. If you're going to use the AssemblyScript loader, it's best to structure your code to make as few calls as possible between the JavaScript and AssemblyScript.

Summary

In this chapter, you learned about the AssemblyScript high-level language, the AssemblyScript CLI, and the `asc` command you can use to compile AssemblyScript apps.

We created an `AddInts` function and a hello world app to show how writing an app in AssemblyScript compares to writing the same app in WAT. We compiled it to WAT format, looked through the code that the AssemblyScript compiler generated, and wrote a JavaScript app that ran the hello world app directly. While doing this, you learned how to use WAT to understand what the WebAssembly, created by the AssemblyScript compiler, is doing under the hood.

We then installed the AssemblyScript loader and used the JavaScript functions written by the AssemblyScript team to help us write the JavaScript code.

We discussed using strings in AssemblyScript, wrote a string concatenation app, and looked at how we must use additional flags with the `asc` compiler to allow `asc` to include additional WebAssembly libraries when compiling.

In the latter half of the chapter, we explored OOP in AssemblyScript. We created a class and looked at the exports from the WAT file it generated. We looked at `private` attributes and how they prevent AssemblyScript from exporting those attributes so they can't be used by the embedding environment. We wrote JavaScript that allowed us to create the glue classes directly, and then used the AssemblyScript loader to create the glue code for us. We compared the performance of the direct and the loader methods. Finally, we extended our `Vector2D` class with a `Vector3D` class and discussed the differences between class inheritance in AssemblyScript and TypeScript.

FINAL THOUGHTS

Thank you for reading my book! I hope by now you understand how WebAssembly works at a low level and are ready to begin using it for high-level and low-level web development. WebAssembly is a young technology, but it's already available in every major browser. Using Node.js, you can also develop high-performance server code as WebAssembly modules. More languages for developing WebAssembly applications become available all the time. New features and platforms are being added. The future is a world where the web is safe, secure, and fast with WebAssembly.

For updates to the code in this book, and more WebAssembly tutorials, please visit *https://wasmbook.com*.

Please contact me if you need help or have questions.

On Twitter: *https://twitter.com/battagline* (@battagline)

On LinkedIn: *https://www.linkedin.com/in/battagline*

On AssemblyScript Public Discord: *https://discord.com/invite/assemblyscript*

On GitHub: *https://github.com/battlelinegames/ArtOfWasm*

INDEX

heap memory, 189

hexadecimal, 70, 79, 93, 101, 105, 108, 147, 148, 151, 152, 154, 155, 160, 165, 166

high-order bit, 78

HyperText Markup Language (HTML), 6, 14, 140, 141, 142, 144, 155, 163, 164, 184

  block, 145

  body, 145, 146, 149, 150

  button, 146, 149, 150

  canvas, 157, 158, 159, 160

  canvas.height, 158

  canvas.width, 158

  div, 150, 153

  H1, 151, 154

  H4, 151, 154

  id, 145, 146

  input, 146, 149, 150

  onclick, 146, 150

  onload, 146, 150

  script, 143, 145, 148, 149, 162, 205, 239

  span, 226

  title, 147, 148

  type, 150

  value, 150

I

i32 (AssemblyScript), 249

i32.add (WAT), 9, 10, 17, 29, 31, 176

i32.and (WAT), 35–37, 80, 100, 105, 108, 110, 112, 176, 177

i32.const (WAT), 21, 31, 47, 60, 89, 104, 109

i32.div_u (WAT), 218

i32.eq (WAT), 36, 48

i32.eqz (WAT), 37

i32.ge_s (WAT), 37

i32.ge_u (WAT), 37, 51

i32.gt_s (WAT), 35–36

i32.gt_u (WAT), 37

i32.le_s (WAT), 36

i32.le_u (WAT), 36, 57

i32.load (WAT), 120, 173

i32.load8_u (WAT), 96, 103

i32.lt_s (WAT), 35

i32.lt_u (WAT), 36

i32.mul (WAT), 29, 31, 218

i32.ne (WAT), 36

i32.or (WAT), 37, 80, 82, 83

i32.reinterpret/f32 (WAT), 33

i32.rem_u (WAT), 48

i32.rem_u (WAT), 49, 102, 171

i32.set (WAT), 176

i32.shr_u (WAT), 79, 108, 112

i32.store (WAT), 120, 168, 169

i32.store8 (WAT), 97, 103, 112

i32.sub (WAT), 31

i32.tee (WAT), 176

i32.trunc_s/f32 (WAT), 33

i32.trunc_s/f64 (WAT), 33

i32.trunc_u/f32 (WAT), 33

i32.trunc_u/f64 (WAT), 33

i32.wrap/i64 (WAT), 33

i32.xor (WAT), 37, 83, 84

i64.add (WAT), 17

i64.and (WAT), 37

i64.div_s (WAT), 73

i64.div_u (WAT), 73

i64.eq (WAT), 36

i64.eqz (WAT), 37

i64.extend_s/i32 (WAT), 33

i64.extend_u/i32 (WAT), 33

i64.ge_s (WAT), 37

i64.ge_u (WAT), 37

i64.gt_s (WAT), 37

i64.gt_u (WAT), 37

i64.le_s (WAT), 36

i64.le_u (WAT), 36

i64.load (WAT), 98

i64.lt_s (WAT), 36

i64.lt_u (WAT), 36

i64.mul (WAT), 73

i64.ne (WAT), 36

i64.or (WAT), 82, 83

i64.reinterpret/f64 (WAT), 33

i64.store (WAT), 98

i64.sub (WAT), 73

i64.trunc_s/f32 (WAT), 33

i64.trunc_s/f64 (WAT), 33

i64.trunc_u/f32 (WAT), 33

i64.trunc_u/f64 (WAT), 33

i64.xor (WAT), 37, 83

id (HTML), 145, 146

Idle (Chrome profiler), 188

loader.instantiate (JavaScript), 262
local.get (WAT), 26, 29, 32, 51, 243, 249
local.set (WAT), 29, 51, 53, 176
local.tee (WAT), 51, 136, 171
loop (WAT), 39–40, 52, 122, 136, 166,
  176, 181, 182
low-level programming, 69
low-order bit, 78

M

macOS, 11–13
malloc (C/C++), 116
mantissa, 73, 76
mean (benchmark.js), 217
memory (JavaScript), 161
memory (WAT), 21, 89, 117, 118, 251
memory.buffer (JavaScript), 54, 161
memory size, 189
Microsoft Edge, 11
Minimum Viable Product (MVP), 3
MIPS CPU, 9
module (WAT), 4, 6, 7, 10–16
More tools (Chrome), 229
most significant bit, 78
most significant digit, 78
Mozilla Foundation, 2, 11
mutable globals, 25, 56
MVP (Minimum Viable Product), 3

N

new (C/C++), 116
new (JavaScript), 262
__newString (AssemblyScript loader),
  255
nibble, 79, 105, 110
Node.js, 1, 5, 11–16
node package manager (npm), 1, 12,
  13, 14, 122, 196, 215
  benchmark.js, 213, 215
  binaryen.js, 196
  colors, 122
  connect, 140
  serve-static, 141
null byte, 92
null-terminated string, 91, 100

O

-0 (asc), 248

-o (asc), 257, 258
object-oriented programming (OOP),
  55, 59, 247, 256, 259, 263, 267
offset, 126, 129
offset (WAT), 127
onclick (HTML), 146, 150
onload (HTML), 146, 150
opcodes, 220
optimization, 3, 11, 185–222
Optimization flags
  -01, 197
  -02, 197
  -03, 197, 205, 215
  -0s, 197
  -0z, 197
OR masking, 82
-0z (asc), 249

P

padded stride, 126
Page tab (Chrome debugger), 243
pages, 116
Painting (Chrome profiler), 188
param (WAT), 47, 171
Performance menu (Firefox
  profiler), 194
Performance tab (Chrome profiler),
  188–194
Performance tab (Firefox
  profiler), 194
Portability, 4
PowerPC, 9
--print-bytecode, 219–220
private (AssemblyScript), 247, 248,
  258, 259, 261, 262, 267
Private Window (Firefox), 192
Processing time (Chrome
  profiler), 188
Profiler (Chrome), 186
profilers, 186-196
protected (AssemblyScript), 248, 258
public (AssemblyScript), 248, 258
putImageData (JavaScript), 162, 163

R

r0 (Chrome IR), 221
React, 223
Record button (Chrome profiler), 188

The Art of WebAssembly is set in New Baskerville, Futura, Dogma, and TheSansMono Condensed. The book was printed and bound by Sheridan Books, Inc. in Chelsea, Michigan. The paper is 60# Finch Offset, which is certified by the Forest Stewardship Council (FSC).

The book uses a layflat binding, in which the pages are bound together with a cold-set, flexible glue and the first and last pages of the resulting book block are attached to the cover. The cover is not actually glued to the book's spine, and when open, the book lies flat and the spine doesn't crack.